Studying Sexualities

Studying Sexualities
Theories, Representations, Cultures

Niall Richardson
Sussex University

Clarissa Smith
Sunderland University

Angela Werndly
Sunderland University

palgrave
macmillan

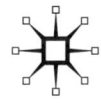

Niall Richardson, Clarissa Smith, Angela Werndly © 2013

All rights reserved. No reproduction, copy or transmission of this publication may be made without written permission.

No portion of this publication may be reproduced, copied or transmitted save with written permission or in accordance with the provisions of the Copyright, Designs and Patents Act 1988, or under the terms of any licence permitting limited copying issued by the Copyright Licensing Agency, Saffron House, 6–10 Kirby Street, London EC1N 8TS.

Any person who does any unauthorized act in relation to this publication may be liable to criminal prosecution and civil claims for damages.

The authors have asserted their rights to be identified as the authors of this work in accordance with the Copyright, Designs and Patents Act 1988.

First published 2013 by
PALGRAVE MACMILLAN

Palgrave Macmillan in the UK is an imprint of Macmillan Publishers Limited, registered in England, company number 785998, of Houndmills, Basingstoke, Hampshire RG21 6XS.

Palgrave Macmillan in the US is a division of St Martin's Press LLC, 175 Fifth Avenue, New York, NY 10010.

Palgrave Macmillan is the global academic imprint of the above companies and has companies and representatives throughout the world.

Palgrave® and Macmillan® are registered trademarks in the United States, the United Kingdom, Europe and other countries.

ISBN: 978-0-230-22042-3   hardback
ISBN: 978-0-230-22043-0   paperback

This book is printed on paper suitable for recycling and made from fully managed and sustained forest sources. Logging, pulping and manufacturing processes are expected to conform to the environmental regulations of the country of origin.

A catalogue record for this book is available from the British Library.

A catalog record for this book is available from the Library of Congress.

10 9 8 7 6 5 4 3 2 1
22 21 20 19 18 17 16 15 14 13

Printed in China

Contents

Introduction	1
Part I: Why Theory?	**15**
Introduction to Part I	17
1　Michel Foucault and the 'Invention' of Sexuality	21
2　Psychoanalysis and Sexuality	33
3　Queer Theory and Postmodern Sexualities	43
Part II: Representations	**55**
Introduction to Part II	57
4　Representations of Homosexuality 　　Case Study: *Will and Grace*	61
5　Representations of Lesbians on Television 　　Case Study: *The L Word*	72
6　Representations of Heterosexuality 1 　　Case Study: *Sex and the City*	83
7　Representations of Heterosexuality 2 　　Case Study: *Entourage*	94
8　Representations of Teenage Sexuality 　　Case Study: *Point Horror* and *Twilight*	110
Part III: Sexual Cultures	**123**
Introduction to Part III	125
9　Sexualization, Commodifying Sex and the Mainstreaming of Masturbation	129
10　Sadomasochism: Definitions and Legislation	141
11　Online Sexual Practices	154
Conclusion	169
Bibliography	171
Media and Fiction	183
Index	185

Introduction

Many commentators are agreed that Western culture is obsessed by sex, and that the media – television, cinema, magazines, music, books and the internet – are saturated with sexual content. It's hard not to agree when you hear Rihanna extolling the virtues of whips and chains, and see advertising which suggests that a particular brand of shampoo can induce multiple orgasms in a woman completing her morning ablutions. The old adage 'sex sells' has never seemed more appropriate. Yet there is something fundamentally worrying in the assertion that sex is everywhere, and always persuasive. There's a sense of something underhand being perpetrated by representations of sex, an implication that sex can only appeal to our baser natures, and a suggestion that sex is, at best, trivial and superficial. For some, we'd all be better off if sex weren't mentioned or referenced so frequently in popular culture. Yet, it is precisely this idea that sex is an entirely private matter that renders sex and sexuality so important to studies of contemporary culture and society.

Why should sex be so important? Well, read this comment from the *Daily Mail*'s self-styled right-wing columnist Richard Littlejohn.

> Take the latest episode of *Torchwood*, the *Doctor Who* spin-off. It began with a seven-minute gay sex scene, which outraged many viewers. Why? The BBC says: 'We aim to depict relationships, whether heterosexual or homosexual, in an honest and realistic way.' Fair enough. But what on earth has sex got to do with a science fiction show? Why does the lead character have to be a 'pansexual'? They'll be telling us next that the Daleks all wore bondage gear under their tinfoil armour.
>
> But this is what you get when you hire a proselytising homosexual like Russell T. Davies to write mainstream drama. Gifted writer he may be, but he comes with an agenda.
>
> There is a place for exploring gay themes on TV, but not at prime time on BBC1 in a programme watched by many children and their parents.
>
> (Littlejohn, 2011)

Look at the ways in which Littlejohn expresses himself: defining 'primetime BBC1' as *not* the place for gay themes and their exploration and *not* the place for pansexual heroes. Prime time is *family* time, family time is not a place for homosexuality or sex, nor is science fiction – Littlejohn clearly doesn't know his science fiction very well: sex has been a key component of SciFi television, opening up visions of future sex in, for example, *Star Trek* (NBC:

1966–69), *Farscape* (Nine Network: 1999–2003), *The Outer Limits* (Showtime: 1995–2002) and *Stargate Atlantis* (Sci-Fi Channel: 2004–09) (Garber and Paleo, 1990), themes which fans have eagerly taken up and worked into explicitly sexual 'slash fictions' (see Bacon-Smith, 1992; Jenkins, 1992). Yet here pansexuality supposedly contributes nothing to the characterizations of the protagonists. According to Littlejohn, to include any reference to homosexuality is to be *proselytising* – that is, attempting to persuade or convert others to your point of view. *Torchwood* didn't just have a gay sex scene, it had a '*seven-minute gay sex scene, which outraged many viewers*'. Littlejohn suggests that there is simply no *need* for showing or mentioning gay sex in a prime-time series watched by children and adults, and that therefore Russell T. Davis is doing more than providing entertainment – he's *preaching* homosexuality to that prime-time audience. 'Sex' is apparently unnecessary for a drama like *Torchwood*. But would Littlejohn express the same irritations if Captain Jack only flirted with, and seduced, young female sidekicks – like his friend Dr Who at an earlier time with an even larger audience of child viewers? What we could take to be a reasonable objection to 'gratuitous' sex on TV or in film could, on further inspection, turn out to be a political rejection of *any* expression of sexual interests, possibilities or imaginings that do not fit with a very narrow sense of 'proper' sexuality. The demand to keep your private life private can often be a demand to keep quiet about sexual interests and identities that don't fit with 'natural' heterosexuality.

How this book works

Given the media's increasing fascination with sexuality it is hardly surprising that university courses in media, film and cultural studies are now introducing students to debates in sexuality studies. While discussions about sexuality had previously been tagged on at the end of a 'feminism' or 'gender and representation' module, university courses have now devised full modules, at both undergraduate and postgraduate level, to introduce students to the critical study of sexuality. The problem, however, is that much critical writing in the area, especially the work often labelled 'queer theory', is written in dense academic jargon which can be off-putting to the new student. This book is intended to address this problem.

Studying Sexualities is an introduction to the critical study of sexuality in a media, film and cultural studies context. It does not claim to provide all the answers or summarize all the relevant debates, but instead aims to provide some groundwork on the key topics in sexuality studies, mapping out the field and providing examples of further reading for the student. We hope that all of the writing in this book is accessible and as jargon free as we can possibly make it. When, on occasions, we have used terms specific to the discipline, we have always tried to explain and contextualize them.

Studying Sexualities is divided into three parts. The first part, entitled 'Why Theory?', aims to summarize some of the main theoretical paradigms employed in sexuality studies. The grandfather of sexuality studies, Michel Foucault, is addressed in Chapter 1, and his thesis is developed and expanded in a discussion of contemporary queer theory in Chapter 3. The other theoretical paradigm that has much critical purchase within sexuality studies is psychoanalysis, and this is addressed in Chapter 2. Throughout the rest of the book we attempt to demonstrate the importance of these theories by applying them in the critical readings of popular cultural representations offered in the later chapters. It is important to stress, though, that we are introducing you to a set of complex arguments and we cannot reduce the entire works of these theorists into short chapters, and so we urge you to engage with the original writings. Some of the original texts cited are more difficult to read than others, but all are worth grappling with, and you will expand your knowledge and understanding if you do so.

Part II addresses representations of sexuality in a range of film, television and media texts. It commences, in Chapter 4, with a discussion of homosexuality, providing an overview of the traditions and codes employed in the representation of homosexuality in film and media. This chapter concludes with an analysis of the popular sitcom *Will and Grace* (NBC: 1998–2006). Chapter 5 considers the history of the representation of lesbians in the media and concludes with a discussion of the television drama *The L Word* (Showtime: 2004–09). Chapters 6 and 7 examine one of the most difficult areas in the critical study of representations of sexualities: heterosexuality. Discussing heterosexuality is rather like asking a fish to think critically about water given that it is something which simply appears to be there. Queer theory has, however, insisted on the reconsideration of the status of heterosexuality, and Chapter 6 concludes with an examination of one of the most controversial of recent television dramas – *Sex and the City* (HBO: 1998–2004) – while Chapter 7 examines the 'straight' male in *Entourage* (HBO: 2004–11). The final chapter in this part, Chapter 8, examines the representation of teenage sexuality in popular fiction. Given that adolescence is a relatively recent cultural construct (in previous eras children simply moved from childhood to being 'young adults') there has been, and continues to be, considerable anxiety about teenage sexuality. Indeed, in recent years a number of texts have addressed this issue directly and Chapter 8 considers two of the most popular: *Point Horror* (Scholastic: 1986–) and *Twilight* (Meyer, Little, Brown and Company: 2005; dir. Catherine Hardwicke: 2008).

In this part we have taken a case study approach, focusing on individual television series and young adult fictions. In each of these we try to offer a broader exploration of some relevant contextual issues and then zoom in to examine some of the central themes and patterns that underpin contemporary representations of sexualities. These are not intended to stand as the definitive view of each of these representations – you should be aware that there is considerable debate about the meanings, intentions and politics of each of the shows or novels we focus on – but the individual chapters should give you a sense of the possible ways of interrogating the representational framings of heterosexualities and culturally marginalized subjects such as gay males, lesbians and teenagers. These critical readings are intended to help you think about how you might develop your own research questions and analyses.

The final part is entitled 'Sexual Cultures' and addresses three areas which have raised particular concerns for a variety of commentators. Chapter 9 looks at the ways in which sex is no longer (if it ever was) something one just *does* but is also a part of the 'project of the self' (Giddens, 1991) thought to characterize life in late modernity. Through a focus on the mainstreaming of masturbation and the retailing of sex toys we show how sex, like home decoration and fashion, is also a focus of consumerist lifestyling and a way of demonstrating one's tastes and expressing individuality. This chapter explores concerns about the commodification of sex and the sexualization of culture.

Throughout this book we examine the cultural construction of sexual norms, and the ways in which sexuality is regulated through the dense transfer points of power. In Chapter 10 we turn to sadomasochism: a set of sexual practices that are increasingly visible, but also the subject of much debate and regulation. In this chapter we explore the various ways in which 'kinky sex' has been represented in the media and how questions of morality have pervaded attempts to regulate representations and behaviours considered unlawful and 'unnatural'. At the same time, we examine the ways in which sadomasochism has been discussed as an erotics of sensation, offering gender mobility and the possibility of a radical re-figuring of what *counts* as contributing to sexual pleasures.

Sexual self-presentations are also addressed in Chapter 11, which examines the rise of representations made possible via new technologies. Sexual representations are no longer confined to the products of the 'pornography industry'; instead, digital technologies have 'democratized' production, such that individuals are now able to produce their own pornography, filming and uploading images of themselves for others to search and catalogue. Furthermore, the virtual realm of the internet provides a space for connection across time and place between individuals which problematizes the idea that sex only takes place between co-present bodies and that community is dependent upon geography.

Our central interest here is illuminating the ways in which 'sexuality' is a hugely intriguing subject. Not only is it difficult to describe in exact detail, but it is also as varied as culture itself and, most importantly, linked to larger questions about the role of media in everyday life, democracy and freedoms. We hope that this short book will serve as an inspiring introduction to these exciting debates and will lead you to further study in this subject area. Before we move on, we need to introduce you to a few contextual issues.

What *is* sexuality and why study it?

The word 'sexuality' can itself have a variety of different meanings. Most people would suggest that sexuality is to do with sex. However, what *exactly* do we mean by sex in this respect? Sex can refer to the sexed body – a body's anatomical, chromosomal sex – male or female, but it can also refer to the idea of *having* sex, or what we could term sexual intercourse or interaction. Unfortunately, neither of these two concepts is quite as clear-cut or fixed as most people like to imagine.

First, the concept of having a sexed body: notwithstanding the fact that there are many bodies which are inter-sexed (that is, neither completely male nor female), what most people read as 'sex' – a male or female identity – is in fact 'gender' – masculine or feminine. 'Gender' refers to how the body performs his or her sex. Someone with a male body is expected to act out or perform traits deemed appropriate to male bodies. Likewise someone with a female body is taught how to perform or 'do' femininity. Therefore, what people usually see or acknowledge as 'sex' is, in fact, 'gender'. This has particular relevance to sexuality if we acknowledge that what we are attracted to in another body is its *performance* of gender – which may be a cross-dressed or drag performance (see Chapter 3 for more elaboration of this). If what we eroticize is, in fact, gender rather than sex, can we say that sexuality is fixed or clearly defined?

The second area is even harder to define. Sexuality has to do with sexual acts: having sex. Yet the problem here is what *exactly is* sexual activity or having sex? Many people understand sexual activity to mean penetrative sex, a penis entering a vagina or anus. However, many people, for different reasons, choose never to engage in such sexual activity. Indeed, for many people 'sex' may be oral-genital stimulation (oral sex) or manual-genital stimulation (masturbation) only. Moreover, for many others, 'sex' may have absolutely nothing to do with genital stimulation – for some, sex may be bondage activity (see Chapter 10 on sadomasochism) or for others it may be something totally removed from what many people consider to be specifically *sexual* activity, for example caressing pumped-up muscles (muscle-worship). The point is that genital sexuality, or penetrative sexual activity, may not stimulate some people at all who instead find erotic pleasure from alternate activities. Given the seemingly endless array of what could then be termed 'sexual', it is practically impossible to define sexuality in terms of a single sexual act. Therefore, we come up against a problem in definition right from the very start. If the concept of the sexed body is cloudy and the idea of the 'sexual act' is so varied, what exactly *is* sexuality?

Indeed, this is the key point which this book, *Studying Sexualities*, wants to stress: the sexual is *cultural* and *social*. Sexuality cannot be reduced to biological, anatomical imperatives and indeed this is what makes the study of human sexuality so fascinating. It could be argued that there are really only two cultural performances that distinguish humans from animals. The first is eating. For humans, food is never simply 'feed'. We do not eat, we dine. Humans do not get down on all fours and guzzle a bowl of 'feed' as dogs and cats do. Indeed, in the history of civilization, whenever dominant factions have wanted to dehumanize minority groups they have forced those groups to feed like animals. Slaves and prisoners in concentration camps have had to endure the ultimate degradation of being forced to feed like animals. Eating, for humans, is always implicated in cultural discourses and is almost always a social activity. Though cultures differ across the world, all societies observe specific times of the day when it is considered appropriate to eat and which foods should be eaten. For example, in Western cultures, ice cream is not eaten for breakfast – it is usually reserved as a dessert or a treat. Related to this, humans have established rules about *how* to eat: it is not, for example, considered appropriate in Western societies to eat a bowl of ice cream with our fingers; instead we use spoons (this is both practical – ice cream melts and needs to be scooped into the mouth – and social). However, eating sandwiches with our fingers is appropriate. Obviously, animals may enjoy their food as much as humans – they may have particular likes and dislikes, and they may well enjoy the sensations of having a full stomach – but dogs and cats do not have the broad range of cultural regulations or observations around food that humans do; they feed when hungry. The point here is that rules about *dining* are purely cultural. There is no biological reason why we should not eat ice cream for breakfast, or indeed why we should not lap it up from a bowl with our tongue as a cat might.

The other area that, arguably, distinguishes humans from animals is sex. Humans are not like dogs and cats, who can only have sex at certain times of the year when the female is in heat. This is not to say that animals never experience pleasure in their sexual interactions, but that in humans, even when our sexual desires may be very powerful at times (some of us might even employ the phrase 'I'm on heat' to describe periods of intense sexual feelings), the dictates of culture ensure that the majority of us don't give into our sexual impulses in the supermarket car park. Indeed, we have created specific cultures around sex in which our mating processes adhere to particular regimes. Of course, these mating processes differ widely across human cultures. The rituals of gay male coupling can differ markedly from those associated with heterosexual activity, for example. However, the key point is that sex for humans does not just happen at certain times of the year because of uncontrollable, biological impulses. Unlike the household cat, we don't suddenly go into heat and have to be confined indoors lest we start having sex with the first random human who strolls along the street.

Sex for humans is not related exclusively to procreation. Of course, there are innumerable couples at any time attempting to get pregnant, but many others are engaging in the same forms of sexual activity for pleasure rather than procreation. And, as we've already suggested, there are many others whose sexual pleasures are not centred on the genitals and instead are derived from, and experienced in, erogenous zones which are not directly connected with reproduction. Unless someone credits the idea that sex is solely for the purpose of creating babies, there is no one specific sexual act which is 'correct' or 'natural'. Sex can involve a wide array of activities that can be experienced individually and/or in partnership with another or others.

An important reason why sexuality has inspired so much academic interest lies in the conceptual linking, by philosophers and authors over many centuries, of sexual pleasure with life and death. The archaic French term for orgasm is *le petit mort* (the little death), which draws attention to the specifically *spiritual* release of orgasm – a kind of transcendence or overwhelming of the senses that follows from intense physical pleasure. The sensation of orgasm is considered by some to take us beyond the realm of physical pleasure, and the word 'ecstasy', or 'ex-stasis', literally means a move beyond the self. This transcendence of the self has been compared to a form of 'death' – that attainment of the sublime in which the subject seems to have moved beyond the confines of the physical.

In Western culture, the orgasm can also be seen to be an important symbol of the sanctity of a particular relationship; for example, how many Hollywood films represent the well-suitedness of a couple through their attainment of mutual and simultaneous orgasm? Or conversely, how often do films show us the failure of a relationship through the evident sexual dissatisfaction or disappointment of one of the protagonists? Orgasm can be a symbol of true love: mutual emotional connection can find its physical outlet in sexual satisfaction, but also excessive focus on orgasm can be an indication of psychological problems. Orgasm and sexual desire are supreme paradoxes in Western culture, both life-affirming but if not properly contained thought to have destructive and potentially malevolent power.

That sex is not just a private matter, or one of individuality, is apparent in the existence of thousands of books and articles written by academics, and professionals in medicine, psychology and sexology; the worries expressed by moral campaign groups, religious leaders, parents, teachers and politicians; the how-to articles which fill newspaper supplements and men's and women's magazines; the thousands of self help books dedicated to sex; and the plethora of websites which focus on sexual matters such as how to get more sex, do it right, avoid addiction, and decide your orientation – as well as the millions dedicated to arousing desire. These multiple sites, political, popular and private, where sexuality is debated and practised indicate that sex, far from being a matter of personal choice or private interest, is of significant importance in modern culture – a site of regulation, improvement and social engineering as well as a source of considerable angst and entertainment.

In 2006, then prime minister of Britain, Tony Blair suggested that

> there are areas in which the State, or the community, no longer has a role or, if it does have one, it is a role that is completely different. It is not for the State to tell people that they cannot choose a different life-style, for example in issues to do with sexuality. (Blair, 2006)

A statement such as this maintains the fiction that there is a public/private divide when it comes to sexual practices, yet Tony Blair's New Labour government (like those before it and those in other nations) agonized over the sexual activities of its citizens, from questions of sexual health, sex education, appropriate relationships, the regulation of commercial sexual practices, the role of the internet in encouraging 'unsafe' and 'illegal' activities through to the place of same-sex relationships in modern democratic culture. Thus our focus here needs to engage with the ways in which sexual practices are shaped and understood through discourses of regulation and policy – health, education and economics – especially where the designations of appropriate and inappropriate lifestyles, attitudes and relationships are key to an understanding of the nation's public face and its most intimate secrets.

This is not to say that legislation plays the leading role in the policing or fostering of sexual behaviours. As Frank Mort has argued, the legal system is really a 'moral thermometer' (Mort, 1987) rather than the single driver or restraint of changing sexual mores. Most often, it seems that governments lag behind other concerned groups when it comes to sexual matters. Our fictional representations, especially films and television dramas, evidence a growing interest in exploring sexual identifications and it is fair to say we see more lesbian and gay identified characters than ever before. Even so, such characters are still absolutely outnumbered by heterosexual roles, and almost always are greeted with a great deal of brouhaha which suggests we're still not entirely comfortable with 'alternative lifestyles' even as *images*. Reality television and documentaries *have* explored the complexities of sexual desire and sexual identification while there has been a notable increase in the availability of sexual material on the high street and on the internet, ranging from what some have termed the pornographication of print media to the mainstreaming of sex aids and sex toys. In the last decade, the film *Brokeback Mountain* (dir. Ang Lee: 2005) (which portrays (relatively) explicit same-sex sexual activity between two men) attained recognition at the box office and won numerous Academy Awards, so it may seem as if we have moved into a new era that recognizes sexual diversity and the freedom to explore sexual choices.

Sexual freedom is a key theme in public discussions of sexuality and changing sexual mores, particularly in the West where history is mobilized to create a story of desire trapped by the needs of capitalism and civilization. So the story goes, our natural desires for sex and for pleasure have been constrained by civilizing processes (Elias, 1969, 1982) – those social and cultural injunctions which determine what is 'good' behaviour (for example, the banal aspects of natural functions and bodily decorum in matters of sex, eating, drinking and excretion) – and that in laying down those rules for self-management, society determines both what we do *and* the ways in which we understand what we do, our selves and our bodily desires. Such arguments also form a part of the critique of capitalism which, in the works of writers like Herbert Marcuse (1987), is an alienating force which attempts to suppress natural desires such as erotic feelings in order to ensure that bodies are available for economic labour and production. These ideas underpin many of the claims about the Victorian era in Britain as the high point of repressive and repressed attitudes to sexuality. You will no doubt have heard stories that suggest the Victorians were entirely prudish: that they covered their piano legs because they might inflame 'sexual' interests; that all young women were expected to be absolutely ignorant of sex before marriage and that they should 'lie back and think of England' once they were married; that Queen Victoria could not conceive of the existence of lesbians and that the art critic John Ruskin was so horrified by his wife's pubic hair that he ran screaming into the street on their wedding night. These are all great stories but they have little basis in fact and may, as historian Matthew Sweet (2002) suggests, be stories told to support the picture of the twentieth century as the great period of liberation.

There are lots of histories of twentieth-century British sexuality highlighting the rapid changes of the last half of that century. In particular the 1960s brought the 'sexual revolution' and new codes of sexual behaviour rejecting the strict morality of state-sanctioned marriage. The story goes that in three decades, from the end of the Second World War to the beginnings of the 1970s, Britain threw off Victorian prudery and embraced sexual liberation. In these histories, Britons of the 1940s and 1950s were paragons of sexual continence, never engaging in any sexual activity which wasn't married and heterosexual – 'the moral world of 1950s Britain, at least as far as the statute book was concerned, was barely altered from that of a century earlier' and consumed by 'overriding terror of almost literally unspeakable, but hugely potent horrors' (Green, 1998: 311). Indeed, Brits were so unsexy that author George Mikes poked fun at them with his one-line chapter which read 'Continental people have sex lives, the English have hot-water bottles' (Mikes, 1958). But by the end of the 1960s, everything was different! The British were using contraceptive pills, enjoying free love and pretty much having a swinging time of it.

That history is a bit of an exaggeration: as historian Paul Ferris points out, there was plenty of sex outside marriage in earlier decades of the twentieth century and anyway, 'the ideals [of continence and chastity] had never been more than declarations of intent' (Ferris, 1994: 121). If sales of diaphragms, condoms and sex manuals throughout the 1920s to 1960s are anything to go by, hot water bottles were not the only thing the British took to bed with them in the dark days before the 1960s set them free. Surveys show that 'nearly half of the women born between 1924 and 1934 admitted that they had engaged in pre-marital intercourse' (Sandbrook, 2007: 484). This doesn't mean to say that people thought sex before marriage was morally acceptable, but it does suggest that 'even in the supposedly tedious, terrified 1950s many people could not resist breaking their own moral codes' (ibid.). Even if the fifties and the decades before them were not as repressed as some have claimed, the sixties did usher in a period of change in relation to sex and its representation. New laws were passed in this period extending rights to divorce (1971), getting rid of theatre censorship (1968), legalizing abortion (1967) and decriminalizing homosexuality (1967). But those laws had their foundations in the 1950s. Lord Wolfenden's Report (published in 1957) focused on the twin 'problems' of prostitution and homosexuality and argued that 'private morality or immorality was a private affair' and that the state's role was 'the preservation of public order and decency', rather than interference in the behaviour of consenting adults in private (Moran, 1996; Sandbrook, 2007: 487). It is this principle that underpins the modern attitude to sex and the state in the UK (and in many other Western nations). Even so, that quote from Tony Blair that the state '*no longer* has a role' in the nation's bedrooms shows that sexual liberation was not quickly won. As Jeffrey Weeks has recently argued, it is an 'unfinished revolution' (2007: 7).

More importantly, whether or not the sixties were really the big break with 'Victorian' attitudes, they remain a particular reference point for our current understandings of sexual behaviour and sexual liberation. The sixties are remembered as a period of free love, freedom from unwanted pregnancies and the possibilities of self-realization through sexual experimentation. It is a story told time and time again in popular histories and popular culture, that sexuality and what we do with it is important to identity and in particular that there is something entirely 'authentic' in our pursuits of sexual pleasure. We have to 'be honest with ourselves', 'to come out', 'to stop living a lie', 'to follow the dream'. As we will discuss in the following chapters, many of our current practices draw on complex histories of repression and suppression to make the claim that, for example, masturbation is not only a case of pleasing yourself but also a means of exploring the liberating potentials of sexual experience freed from the repression of morality and normative conceptions of 'proper' sex as existing only for the purposes of procreation. This construction of modern sexualities emphasizes individualization, freedom, authenticity and honest self-expression.

But sexual freedom is not simply a matter of personal choice. There are areas of sexuality in which most people would still want the state to legislate. *Who* gets to have sex is not simply a question of two individuals meeting and deciding they fancy each other and wish to engage in some form of sexual interaction. One might think that we are entitled to have sex as soon as we are ready for it. Popular culture certainly subscribes to the myth that we live in an enlightened world where we can freely pursue sexual pleasure. Health professionals are agreed that children are reaching puberty earlier (although there are significant variations from child to child), and that therefore biologically, our bodies and specifically our sexual organs may well be primed and ready for sex (as in, able to reproduce) anywhere from 9 to 19 years of age – yet most parents would argue that a child's preparedness for sex is not just a matter of sexual maturity, but of emotional and cognitive maturity as well. All nations have their own idea of what constitutes an appropriate age for having sex for the first time, often tied to the legal age at which one can marry – and this can be as dependent on ideas of financial independence as much as emotional readiness for the 'responsibilities' of sex. Across the world there is no one age deemed suitable for engaging in sexual activity, as Table 1 indicates. Even within national boundaries there is no one standard. For example, the federal age of consent in America is 16 but in the state of Texas, children as young as 14 can marry as long as their parents agree.

Table 1 Age of consent in different countries

Argentina – 15
Bahamas – 16
Canada – 14
Colombia – male 14, female 12
Hungary – 14
India – 18
Indonesia – male 19, female 16
Peru – male 14, female 12
Tunisia – 20
UK – 16
US – federal age 16

In the UK, the law in England and Wales has allowed 16-year-olds to engage in heterosexual sexual activity since 1885 but only lowered the age of consent from 18 to 16 for homosexual relationships in 2000 with the passing of the Sexual Offences (Amendment) Act (2000) which also, for the first time, recognized lesbian sexual activity. The law in Scotland did not decriminalize male homosexual acts until 1980 even though in England and Wales such activity had been taken off the criminal register in 1963. Age of consent legislation is founded on a range of fears and concerns about the sexual, about potentials for abuse or exploitation, STDs, pregnancy and deviancy; very rarely does it recognize young people's own interests in sex or their agency (conflating children having sex with 'child sexual abuse') whatever one's sexual orientation. For example, in July 2009 the press in the UK and abroad had a field day with the story about the 'Pleasure' leaflet produced by Sheffield's Primary Care Trust for youth workers and others engaged in formal and informal sex education with teenagers. In media from *The Sunday*

Times to *The View* show hosted by Whoopi Goldberg (ABC: 1997–), the leaflet has been ridiculed for its suggestion that teenagers are entitled to sexual exploration and that masturbation might be good for teens to develop knowledge of their own bodies and their pleasures. These responses demonstrate that even as there is much talk of our more liberated attitudes towards sex, we still prefer to talk about teenagers' sexual interests in terms of deviancy and prevention rather than agency and/or pleasure. The idea that agency and pleasure are not important to sexual health has been widely critiqued; for instance, Holland *et al.* argue that 'for a young woman to negotiate safe sex in a heterosexual relationship, she has to be empowered both to develop a positive conception of female sexuality and able to put this positive conception into practice' (1992: 143). Healthy sexual development isn't, then, simply a matter of waiting until one is legally able to have sex: as McKee *et al.* observe, 'preventing unwanted sexual encounters is a key element of healthy sexual element – but it is far from being sufficient for an understanding of the important elements in that development. There is more to healthy sexual development than simply preventing abuse. Important positive skills and understandings must be developed' (2010: 16). In the matter of age of consent law we can see a clear delineation of who is to be considered sexual and who is not; the state has a defining role in recognizing sexual selfhood.

Sexual citizenship is a fairly new idea in sexuality studies, coming to the fore in the mid-1990s, but has sparked considerable interest since then. The term is linked to political, economic, social, legal and ethical studies and demonstrates the close link between the supposedly private activity of sexual behaviour and questions of public interest. Citizenship is about recognition – for example, the recognition of the right to practise sexual activity, as in gay and lesbian rights. Citizenship is a formal recognition of place in the social sphere. The state protects its citizens, guarantees their welfare and rights and in so doing, binds citizens together as a social group with common interests. Equally, if the state is going to look after you, then you need to understand the obligations of being a 'good citizen'. This can mean recognizing the important scaffolds of the society you live in – for example, the centrality of the family. Too often, there is a conservative emphasis in discussion of sexual citizenship: as well as conferring rights, individuals are understood to have responsibilities. In our culture, as Bell and Binnie explain,

> [t]he twinning of rights with responsibilities in the logic of citizenship is another way of expressing compromise – *we will grant you certain rights if (and only if) you match these by taking on certain responsibilities*. Every entitlement is freighted with a duty. (2000: 3)

Bell and Binnie argue that sexual citizenship demands a modality of privatized, deradicalized, de-eroticized and *confined* practices: kept in place, policed and limited. So, for example, it is extremely easy to argue for the right to practise any activity, not otherwise illegal, performed between consenting adults in private but that emphasis on 'in private' has been a very effective means of controlling 'non-normative' sexualities. For example, despite the legal freedoms enjoyed by many gay men and women today, many feel it is still not safe to hold hands or kiss in public – a freedom heterosexuals in the Western world take for granted. Thus same-sex relationships do not always enjoy the same measure of freedom for public display, and many have suggested that the requirement to keep one's pleasures and relationships private maintains different levels of citizenship – we are all equal, but some are more equal than others.

Many theoretical and political traditions challenge this notion of citizenship. For example, feminists have argued that women are not given full status as citizens: that in the exclusion of women from particular kinds of social and political office, they are more widely constructed as second-class citizens and that this has impacts for their understandings of themselves as sexual agents (Eichner, 2009). Moreover, in the development of identity politics, the figure of the citizen becomes a kind of limit rather than the ultimate achievement. Citizenship is often discussed as if it has no real relation to the sexual sphere, but in all cultures being a citizen is inflected with sexualities. From our understanding of the family through exclusion from institutions such as the military or the Church on the basis of one's sexual orientation, sexuality and civil personhood are inextricably linked. Take for example the recent extension of partnership rights to same-sex couples in the UK and the on-going (as we write) debates across America regarding same-sex marriage (the federal government does not currently recognize same-sex marriage, but such marriages are recognized by some individual states). The new millennium saw Lord Lester introduce a private members' bill – the Civil Partnership Bill – to the UK House of Lords, recognizing the entitlement of gay and lesbian couples to most of the various rights and responsibilities (including inheritance, next of kin, etc.) accorded to married heterosexuals. To ministers it was a case of recognizing the stability of many gay and lesbian relationships. As Meg Munn, Minister for Women and Equality, put it, 'We know there are people who have been together maybe 40 years and have been waiting for the chance to do this kind of thing, because of the important differences it makes to their lives' (BBC Online, 2005).

In the UK, the first registrations for civil partnership were allowed on 19 December 2005, and media coverage of the first partnership ceremonies was extensive – especially for Sir Elton John's lavish event. Within a year, 18,059 civil partnerships had been celebrated. Civil partnerships can be seen as the achievement of full sexual equality for gays and lesbians in the UK, but they have not been welcomed by all gay activists – for example, OutRage! activist Peter Tatchell has been very critical of the law as creating a form of 'sexual apartheid' which does nothing to change sexual politics:

> Instead of legislating a second rate version of marriage for gays only, the government could have created a truly modern system of partnership rights for everyone – gay and straight – covering all relationships of mutual care and commitment. (Tatchell, 2005)

Although the Bill extended the rights of inheritance to non-heterosexual relationships, it did little to change the seeming importance of those relationships to civil society in the UK. Instead, it can be seen to have said that as long as your relationship looks like and behaves like the traditional family set-up you can have an approximation of the legal protections given to the family but your partnership won't have the same legal status as a marriage in law (the UK government is currently consulting on this and intends to amend the law before the 2015 election). And it is precisely these ideas of visibility, responsibility and rights which are reflected, interrogated and ignored in the popular culture representations and practices we will address in later chapters. Media and communication technologies are widely used as information resources about sex, giving us access to other experiences, lifestyles and interests. In what follows, we suggest that in a changing landscape surrounded by media, sex is not simply a matter of personal experiences and relationships but is central to culture and to our understandings of others.

Further Reading

Sweet, M. (2002) *Inventing the Victorians* (London: Faber & Faber).
Weeks, J. (2007) *The World We Have Won* (London: Routledge).

Why Theory?

Part I

Introduction to Part I

'Why theory?' is a question often put to us by students who have come to university to learn how to become journalists or filmmakers, or to work in the media industries. One reason they have difficulty in understanding why theory is part of their degree programmes is that there are a number of different meanings or uses of the term. We want to digress a little to consider three of these, in order to make clear the distinctions between them and to show why theory matters. Firstly, an everyday use of the term 'theory' is to imply that there is a rationale for something that has no real relationship with our experiences of the practicalities of life. For example, we might say 'in *theory*, the National Health Service means that medical treatment is free for everyone', meaning that it is an abstract idea that is not borne out by the fact that, in England, we have to pay for our prescriptions. In other words, 'in theory' here means the idea is of no value in the real world. Given this popular usage, it is understandable that some students believe that theory modules have nothing to do with the 'real world'.

Another commonplace use of the term is to imply that theory is constraining rather than liberating or progressive. We might say to someone 'forget the theory and follow your instincts' to encourage them to be creative or to think outside given rules and regulations. Hence, using this working definition of the term, 'theory' is something that holds us back or hinders us. And yet, as you will see, if we use the term in its academic context nothing could be further from the truth.

A third way of defining theory is a more academic one referring to research and methodological approaches to a topic. But this can often be confused with the first definition as a set of abstract ideas that have no practical effects or uses. Indeed, another reason that some students ask 'why theory?' is because they do not realize the extent to which theory already governs our own beliefs, values and practices. Whether we know it or not, theory informs how we think and act, but also which questions we might ask. And this is also affected by which theories are in the ascendancy.

For example, rape (the compelling of a man or woman through physical force to engage in some form of sexual act) is universally condemned. And yet there are many theories as to why it occurs (e.g. some girls dress too provocatively or tease men; alcohol causes some men to become violent; pornography is to blame; some men are born evil; and so on). Similarly, there are many theories as to how rape should be dealt with (e.g. prison is the best solution; prison is no solution; men should receive maximum prison sentences; that there are different kinds of rape and they should be treated differently). So theory should not be regarded as fact, but rather as an attempt to *explain* something. Which theory you subscribe to will depend upon your view of reality and the ideas you have access to. For example, most feminists would question the theory that rape is caused by women's behaviour or dress, arguing that such explanations propose that it is women's fault that rape occurs. The idea that women bear some responsibility for rape comes from a curious amalgam of ways of thinking and understanding male/female sexual relations. Biological concepts of natural 'instincts' and 'drives' have been utilized to suggest, for instance, 'higher' sex drives in men, or that male urges become 'unstoppable' and therefore when a man commits rape he's just acting according to 'human nature'. Thus women are supposed to ensure that they do nothing to 'provoke' men's 'natural' urges for sex. These ideas are underpinned by moralist codes that insist that a woman ought to manage her sexual feelings to ensure she finds the right man to marry in order to have children. We like to think we're more enlightened about women's sexuality today but this idea of women's culpability hasn't gone away and resurfaces in media representations (often, but not always, unintentionally). For example, the ways in which journalists cover a rape incident are often underpinned by the suggestion that 'she [the victim] may have done something to provoke the attack'. They may mention the fact that the victim was walking in an unsafe area and, while it might seem like good advice to say 'stay away from unlit streets', this suggests that by doing so the victim laid themselves open to attack. This blaming of the victim may be a product of journalists' codes of practice of representing both sides, or may be a part of giving the story more 'edge'. There is no doubt that some newspapers focus on salacious details so that, for example, the attractiveness of the rape victim becomes a central part of the story, and so the idea that being pretty or sexy somehow motivates rape comes across loud and clear even as the report, more generally, emphasizes the horror and viciousness of an attack. Many commonly held theories of sexuality are underpinned by outdated ideas about morality, biology (for example, references to animal behaviour which propose a natural difference in sexual interest between males and females (see Anne Fausto-Sterling, 1985)), and fear.

In this book we introduce you to a number of theories and theorists on sexuality. Some names such as Sigmund Freud will probably be known to you, even if you are not sure what his work entails. Others, such as Michel Foucault, may not be as familiar, but in media and cultural studies he is an important influence. As you will see, these theories and theorists often disagree with one another. What they do agree upon is that sexuality is a human condition to be studied. Certain theories may seem more apt than others when applied to particular examples. Unquestionable truth is not necessarily attainable through the study of theory. But many of the theories we will cover in this book have produced ideas and ways of understanding whose influences are widely felt outside the therapy room or university.

As we've already explained, theory is not abstract, out there in the realm of ideas with no material effect on the outside world. It is based on research and has social effects. Take Freud, for example. Aspects of his ideas already have the authority of 'facts', as we shall see in Chapter 2 and in Chapter 8 on teenage sexuality. Indeed, we argue that the take-up of his work has often had a detrimental effect on cultural perceptions of sexualities and of individuals. But whilst some theories – feminist explorations of women's work, for example – have led to social changes that are now taken for granted (such as equal pay), other theories still exist mainly in the realm of academia.

An engagement with theory can radically question our understanding of sexuality, and hence enhance our ability to investigate critically popular culture in all its forms – whether that be the production, representation or the consumption of it. Theories of sexuality have provided us with a range of approaches with which to understand the media in terms of sexuality. So should you wish to write a final year dissertation on, say, television's representations of gay men, or perhaps want to make a practical project on an aspect of gay subcultures, you will have a wealth of theories on which you can draw rather than relying on stereotypes. Theory is about the sharing and re-working of ideas.

But theory can be difficult and many students feel intimidated by the very thought of it – another reason why they ask 'why theory?' This is especially so when reading the works of original thinkers – you may quite reasonably feel that you do not have the time to read the complete works of Freud during the course of a module or your degree. Hence our chapter on his work attempts to explain both his ideas and their importance to the broader field of media and cultural representations.

Understanding theory means your work will contribute to the field of research on sexuality and sexual representations. Even if that means you only demonstrate knowledge and understanding of existing theories you will, nevertheless, produce something that is unique if you apply it to your own examples. Most importantly, to those of us assessing your work, you will not fall into the trap of merely describing something such as *Will and Grace* or *The L Word*, but will utilize theory in order to analyse it. It will prevent your own personal impressions of the world from dominating your discussion, and will help you create a strong argument supported by theoretical evidence.

We want you to realize that above all else theory is empowering: how often have you wished you could reply to some bore you've been stuck next to at a party when their ideas are misguided or, worse, insulting? Theory gives you strength in argument, articulation and the confidence to express your views. A famous theorist of language studies, B.F. Skinner, said that education is what you are left with when you think you have forgotten everything you learned

(1964: 484). What he meant by this is that knowledge is not just about remembering, or memorizing facts and figures, or knowing which button to press on a camera. It is about understanding how we came by the values, beliefs and ideas that become integral to who we are and how we relate to those around us, and hence how we might represent them in our practices.

Michel Foucault and the 'Invention' of Sexuality

Chapter

1

Michel Foucault's *The History of Sexuality* is the foundation of contemporary queer theory, which we address in Chapter 3, but it also forms the backbone of studies of sexuality more generally. Foucault had originally anticipated that this work would be a six-volume set, but his untimely death prevented its completion. Although dense and often difficult, the three volumes of *The History of Sexuality* are worth engaging with in order to encounter Foucault's ideas at first hand. This chapter cannot possibly summarize the entire work and so simply aims to introduce some of Foucault's main arguments and to consider how these can aid critical analyses of representations of sexuality and sexual practices.

Foucault's most important contribution to sexuality studies is his comprehensive and insightful reading of the texts of nineteenth-century sexology illustrating the ways in which sexuality cannot be understood simply as a matter of biology. Foucault argued that sexuality, or more expressly what we often term 'sexual identity', far from being innate and immutable, was the product of cultural discourses. Discourse is a term which Foucault employs a lot in his writings and refers not simply to speech but to the context and manner in which words and ideas are exchanged – who gets to say what, how and when, and with what effects. The significance of an idea largely depends on the context in which the idea is being discussed and what other ideas it is being related to. Moreover, the way in which a subject is discussed is not 'neutral' but complexly connected to questions of power. In *The History of Sexuality*, Foucault suggests that 'what is at issue is the over-all discursive fact by which sex is put into discourse. My main concern will be ... the polymorphous techniques of power' (1990a: 11).

As we briefly suggested in the introduction to this book, sex is often described as 'repressed' or 'regulated', or made into a 'secret' or 'taboo', and there is a way in which this contributes to a construction of sex as a part of ourselves which we ought to liberate: if only we could be honest about what we like or do sexually, we could 'free' ourselves of 'hang-ups' or 'bad feelings'. But Foucault disagrees with the claim that sex has *only* been repressed and silenced. Instead, he suggests that talk about sex has intensified and proliferated since the eighteenth century, 'it is by making sex into a secret that we are incited to talk about it' (1990a: 34–5) and that our ideas about the 'secrets' of sex have changed over time. While the Church was the main power in Western societies, priests expected confessions to divulge the smallest temptation or desire in order that their parishioners could repent their sins and become 'good'. In the nineteenth century, with the rise of medicine and psychiatry, sexual behaviour became an increasingly important object of study and, with this intensification and proliferation of discourse, the emphasis moved from morality to cases of sexual 'perversion' – child sexuality, homosexuality, and so on. Individuals were still expected to 'confess' but they did so in the interests of 'health', 'science' or the 'family'.

Increasingly, sex became an object of knowledge. While other cultures have treated sex as an object of erotic knowledge (developing an *ars erotica*: an art of sensuality where it is important to understand how to give and receive pleasure), Western culture treated sex as a *scientia sexualis*: an object of distanced, scientific investigation. Thus, Foucault argues scientific discourse mixed with the religious form of confession to shape ways of talking about sex. Individuals were still expected to 'confess', to divulge sexual desires and practices as their darkest secrets, but now these confessions were codified into medical or quasi-scientific forms.

Therefore Foucault argued that sexual identity was the product of cultural regimes or discourses, and shows, rather brilliantly, how European and American medical and psychiatric literature of the nineteenth century treated, for example, sexual variability. What we think of as our sexual identity – heterosexual or homosexual – is, Foucault argues, a category of knowledge only understandable within a specific culture, paying attention to the common sets of assumptions and conceptual parameters that underpin particular arguments, diagnoses and characterizations of sexual behaviours and practices. In other words Foucault argued for a constructionist view of sexuality, that is, a view that sexuality is produced within and through our ways of thinking and talking about sex. This approach is commonly termed 'Foucauldian constructionism'.

Constructionism is the opposite of essentialism. Essentialism argues that identity is innate, inherent or, as its name implies, an essence. An essentialist would argue that certain character traits are specific to human beings, often divided up into behaviours or characteristics that are supposedly naturally 'male' and 'female', and that these do not vary across historical periods or geographical areas. For example, an essentialist may claim that it *is* human nature for people to compete with each other for success, and that men are naturally more competitive than women. This competitiveness would be viewed as an essential trait of 'mankind', something that is always there, irrespective of context. Whether the subject chooses to act on this 'essential trait' or not is a different matter, but the essentialist would argue that the trait would always be there. With regard to sexual orientations,

[e]ssentialist approaches ... whether they be evolutionary approaches or approaches that rely on hormones, genetics, or brain factors – rest on assumptions that (a) there are underlying true essences (homosexuality and heterosexuality), (b) there is discontinuity between forms (homosexuality and heterosexuality are two distinct, separate categories, rather than points on a continuum), and (c) there is constancy of these true essences over time and across cultures. (Delamater and Shibley Hyde, 1998: 16)

Constructionism argues differently. Constructionism claims that our identities are dependent upon the culture in which we are located, and that identity can therefore change or alter depending upon context or location. A constructionist would argue that particular concepts or practices may appear to be 'natural' but that they are simply created by the culture in which they are located. According to constructionism, human beings interact as part of a specific culture and it is through this interaction that various practices, beliefs or ideas become institutionalized and *made* into traditions or ways of judging others. To use a simple example, a specific style of eating – say, using fingers rather than a knife and fork – may be deemed uncouth or bad manners in one particular culture, while in a different context it may be viewed as quite acceptable. In the former context the person eating with their fingers would be 'identified' by other people as being uncouth or vulgar. However, in another culture this person may not be deemed uncouth because eating with the fingers is not deemed a vulgar act at all. Constructionism therefore argues that specific performances or acts in which human beings engage have different significance in different cultures, and it is from these acts that human beings attain identities in different contexts. The two positions, essentialist and constructionist, are in constant conflict, as Celia Kitzinger argues:

Social constructionism does not offer alternative answers to questions posed by essentialism: it raises a wholly different set of questions. Instead of searching for 'truths' about homosexuals and lesbians, it asks about the discursive practices, the narrative forms, within which homosexuals and lesbians are produced and reproduced ... it can never be rendered compatible with the essentialist project. (1996: 150)

Foucault argued that sexual identity was a cultural construct – sexuality was the product of a culture labelling specific sexual acts. It is important to emphasize that Foucauldian constructionism does *not* argue that a person *learns* their sexuality from the culture in which they are located. A person does not 'learn' to be gay or straight because of the culture in which they are situated. Rather, Foucault argued that sexual acts signify differently, dependent upon the culture in which they are located. Just like the varied understandings of 'eating with the fingers', specific sexual acts have different significances in different cultures, and the identity constructed by these acts will also vary according to context. Constructionism, therefore, argues that it is culture that labels specific acts, attributes to these acts a specific sexual identity, and assigns that identity to a particular personage.

To help clarify, here are a few examples. In contemporary Western culture, if a man engages in sexual activity with women he is identified as 'heterosexual', while engaging in sexual activity with men evokes the label 'homosexual', and engaging in sexual activity with both men and women renders him 'bisexual'. However, in earlier eras, sexuality was not identified in this way. In Ancient Mediterranean cultures, for example, sexual identification was not divided into 'heterosexual' and 'homosexual' as it is in contemporary Western culture. In Ancient Greece, an adult Greek male could have sexual relations with anyone, provided his sexual partner was his social inferior and provided he maintained the active role during sexual penetration (Halperin, 1990). The objects of the adult Greek male's attention were therefore his 'social inferiors': women, slaves and boys. Rather than identifying sexuality in terms of which gender a man had sex with, Ancient Greek culture was concerned firstly with *how* a man had sex (he was expected to be active/penetrative during sex) and secondly with *whom* he had sex, in terms of social class rather than gender. In contemporary culture, the act of two men engaging in sexual activity together is understood as 'homosexual'. In Ancient Mediterranean culture the act did not signify this identity.

Even in contemporary culture we find examples where sexual acts signify differently from the way they do in contemporary Western society. To emphasize once again, in contemporary Anglo-American culture we identify sexuality in terms of the gender of the sexual object choice. In much of Latin American culture, however, sexuality is not defined in terms of who someone has sex with but *how* someone has sex. As Tomas Almaguer points out (1991), in Chicano culture, sexuality is defined in terms of what someone *does* in bed rather than with whom. In Chicano culture if a man plays an active/penetrative role during sexual activity he is identified as heterosexual irrespective of whether he is penetrating a woman or another man, and only the man who is passive during sexual activity is labelled as 'homosexual'. In contemporary Anglo-American culture a man is labelled as homosexual if he has sex with another man – irrespective of which acts are performed.

To offer another example, tribes in Papua New Guinea have various 'rite of passage' ceremonies – or initiations into manhood – where teenage boys perform fellatio on the older male members of the tribe in order to succeed to adult manhood (see Halperin, 1990; Herdt, 1994). In contemporary Western culture the act of a man performing fellatio on another man signifies the identity 'homosexual', but in the particular cultures of individual tribes this act is understood very differently and has specific meanings and historical associations which are fundamental to becoming an adult and properly *masculine* member of the tribe.

Thus the concept of having a 'sexual identity' is historically and culturally mutable, and is not dependent upon innate attributes. Constructionism pays attention to how specific cultures understand or produce knowledge about sex. In this respect, it is culture (and its knowledge systems) which labels/identifies sexuality. People have always performed specific sexual acts, but how these acts signify will vary across cultures and historical periods.

Foucault also points out that the 'labelling' of sexual acts as indicative of a specific identity is a relatively recent occurrence. There is evidence that in earlier eras Western culture was not obsessed with regimenting and labelling sexual acts (see Sinfield, 1994a). In Shakespeare's time people may well have performed varied sexual acts but the idea of claiming a specific identity from these acts would not have been as important as it is to subjects in contemporary culture. Therefore when critics try to argue that Shakespeare was homosexual (Wells, 2004), they are making a redundant point. Shakespeare couldn't have been homosexual because the term did not exist (Sinfield, 1994a). Men in the Elizabethan era may well have engaged in sexual acts with other men but they would not have claimed an identity from these acts. This may seem strange to us in our contemporary culture but, if we think about it, is it not odd that we claim an identity from a short act engaged in relatively infrequently or, in the case of some people, never?

Indeed, this is one of Foucault's key questions – how is it that we have come to see sex as being so important to understanding who we are? He argues that the explanation lies in the relationships between sex and power and knowledge. While many historians look back over previous centuries and suggest that power operates as a force of repression and restriction, Foucault criticizes that 'juridico-discursive' conception of power and suggests instead that power is *productive* as well as repressive; power is multi-faceted and omnipresent, everywhere and working in all directions. For Foucault, sexuality isn't some natural essence that power represses, but rather a conduit of power, a means by which power is exercised and deployed. In his explorations of nineteenth-century writings on sexuality, Foucault identifies four major areas of concern: the sexuality of children, women, married couples, and 'perversions'. These four areas were endlessly talked about, by politicians, priests, doctors and teachers, who described, analysed and confessed to sexual acts, desires and interests which were then taken to add up to the truth of the self. Thus Foucault writes:

> It is in fact through sex – in fact, an imaginary point determined by the deployment of sexuality – that each individual has to pass in order to have access to his own intelligibility, to the whole of his body, to his identity. (1990a: 155–6)

This cultural practice of labelling sexual acts, and citing them as testament to a specific identity, can be related to the Industrial Revolution and the growth of the urban working class. The late 1800s saw the formation of big, inner city factories that required the movement of a vast number of peasants and rural workers from the countryside to the city to operate the machinery. Understandably, this caused considerable emotional and mental turmoil for these workers who had been used to labouring in relative isolation on the open land, and who were now toiling inside in hot, cramped and very noisy environments. More importantly, as these cities grew, their social make-up changed; huge numbers of people lived in cramped spaces and started to engage in forms of socialization which would not have been possible in the relative isolation of a rural setting. The rise of urban factories was accompanied by the expansion of pubs, opium dens and, most importantly, prostitution and a general loosening of sexual restraint. Groups of people who had been used to living in small communities (where their behaviours could be overseen by the parish priest, family members, neighbours and bosses – working on a country estate, for example) found themselves surrounded by thousands of other workers, all living in very close proximity but more anonymously than before. No wonder they sought out entertainments and ways of socializing, much of which could lead to greater sexual opportunities and, of course, associated problems (such as the spread of sexual diseases and unwanted pregnancies). As a result, both the Church and governments looked to control behaviours and to identify specific activities as 'acceptable' while policing the 'unacceptable'. Indeed, the word 'immoral' became very popular from this period onwards and, as Frank Mort argues, it 'signified all the practices of working-class life, leading to ungovernable and disruptive behaviour' (Mort, 1987: 37). Drinking, brawling, prostitution and unmarried sex had long been considered 'immoral' behaviours in a religious context, but now they also became associated with these new formations of urban working-class life which needed to be controlled in the interests of 'business', 'health', 'law and order' and 'the family'.

The Church had aimed to regiment sexuality into appropriate forms for spiritual salvation, but the state and medicine required sexual regulation for more social reasons. Ironically, this began not with injunctions against urban working-class behaviours, but by identifying the ways in which relatively affluent and middle-class families *ought* to function. As Foucault suggests:

> The bourgeoisie began by considering that its own sex was something important, a fragile treasure, a secret that had to be discovered at all costs… The first figure to be invested by the deployment of sexuality, one of the first to be 'sexualized', was the 'idle' woman. She inhabited the outer edge of the 'world', in which she always had to appear as a value, and of the family, where she was assigned a new destiny charged with conjugal and parental obligations. (1990a: 120–1)

Sexual acts started to attain new social significance depending on 'where' they were performed and with whom. Within the confines of marriage and for procreative purposes sex was deemed acceptable, while anything else was decreed to be 'immoral'. Drawing on the biblical belief in women's potentially disruptive role as sexual tempters but linking this to discoveries about the transmission of infections, there was a strong agenda to control female sexuality – regimenting women into 'good' women differentiated from 'whores' and 'sluts'. The term 'loose woman' referred to a woman whose corset and boots were loosely tied in order to facilitate sex. A 'good' woman would always have her corset and boots 'straight laced' because this would hinder access to her body. Moreover, in legislation such as the Contagious Diseases Act of 1864, 'bad' women became identified as the 'vectors' (means of transmission) of sexual diseases to men, solidifying ideas of female sexuality as socially disruptive. The industrial era also saw the first concerns with the strict regimentation of children's sexuality and the prevention of masturbation. This period saw the labelling and stigmatization of 'perversity' – notably homosexuality. No longer simply 'sordid' or 'depraved' acts, sexual acts between men were now read as identifying a specific person – a person to be controlled and reprimanded.

Foucault cites 1870 as the year when the term 'homosexual' was invented, a date other historians contest (see Bray, 1988). He was not saying that same-sex acts had not existed prior to this date, but that the idea of 'the homosexual', a man defined by those acts, comes into being at that point.

> The nineteenth-century homosexual became a personage, a past, a case history, and a childhood, in addition to being a type of life, a life form, and a morphology, with an indiscreet anatomy and possibly a mysterious physiology… Homosexuality appeared as one of the forms of sexuality when it was transposed from a practice of sodomy onto a kind of interior androgyny, a hermaphroditism of the soul. The sodomite had been a temporary aberration; the homosexual was now a species. (1990a: 43)

Thus, the late nineteenth century saw a *reconceptualization*, via various forms of writing and talking about same-sex sexual activity, which produced an identity and ways of thinking about that identity. As Foucault explains, this labelling of sex was implicit in regimes of power in which practices, behaviours and people could be connected as sexualities that could be explained and quantified and, most importantly, placed in a social hierarchy. As sex became increasingly a matter for science and understood as an instinctual biological and psychic drive fundamentally linked to identity (see our discussion of Freud in the next chapter), it was also feared as a potentially disruptive or destructive force which needed to be regimented. Sexual behaviours became classified across scales of 'normal' and 'pathological' sexual instincts (Dreyfus and Rabinow, 1982: 173). Thus, in speaking and worrying about sex, Foucault suggests, modern society sought to control the behaviour of individuals and groups through *standards of normality* which were assessed by criminologists, medics, psychologists and psychiatrists.

Foucault argued that modern power functions through classifying, marginalizing and therefore ranking these various sexualities in moral terms. Whenever labelling takes place it creates hierarchies, as one category must be at the top of the ladder and another must be at the bottom (we discuss this in more detail later). This labelling of sexualities allowed a degree of control over the newly formed urban mob in the interests of 'society' and created divisions within this group, most notably the concept of the 'good' family unit, set in opposition to the 'deviant' or 'perverse'.

As we briefly touched on in our main introduction, there is a popular belief that the Victorian era was very prudish and frightened of acknowledging sexuality. Foucault, by contrast, argued that, from the Industrial Revolution onwards, there was a great incitement to 'talk' about sexuality. Through this urge to acknowledge sexuality, to label good and bad forms of sex, unorthodox sexual interests or practices become 'secrets'.

This concept of dissident sexuality as the *open secret* (something supposedly secret but in fact generally known) in the Victorian era is illustrated by one of the most famous court cases in history: the trial of Oscar Wilde. A celebrated author and playwright, Wilde appeared in court three times during 1895 – first when he brought a libel case against the Marquess of Queensberry who, angry at Wilde's close relationship with his son Alfred Douglas, had accused Wilde of 'posing' as a 'sodomite'. Wilde withdrew his libel charge but was then arrested for acts of 'gross indecency' and prosecuted at the Old Bailey. In the first of his criminal trials the jury could not reach a verdict, but in the second, after a number of young, often working-class, men testified to Wilde's sexual activities, he was sentenced to two years in prison. His career and marriage were over. Arguably, Wilde was one of the first publicly identified homosexuals in modern Western culture. In fact, it is fair to say that Wilde entered the courtroom for his second criminal trial accused of committing *acts of sodomy* but left the courtroom identified as *'a sodomite'*: the acts had now become an identity. Most importantly, this homosexual identity was now conflated with the Wildean persona.

In his book *The Wilde Century*, Alan Sinfield explores Wilde's cultural significance. Sinfield explains that Wilde's persona was that of the 'dandy'. Dandies were upper-middle class (not aristocratic) men distinguished by their attention to fashion, flamboyance and, most importantly, their effeteness and effeminacy. Sinfield points out that in the Victorian era effeminacy was not thought to be a signifier of homosexuality but instead was the symbol of upper-middle class interests in aesthetics and the pursuit of pleasures.

> The Wildean Dandy – so far from looking like a queer – was distinctively exonerated from such suspicions. Because of his class identification, or aspiration, he above all need not be read as identified with same-sex practices. (Sinfield, 1994b: 71)

Effeminacy signified upper-middle class aspirations of grandeur, an interest in beauty, in elegance. As such, effeminacy would not have been anything to be proud of – but it did not denote homosexuality. After his trial, however, the identity of the sodomite/homosexual was pinned on Wilde and, as such, the public started to read his dandyism and effeminacy as a signifier of his homosexuality. Wilde was one of the first 'celebrities' in European culture (he was much parodied in popular texts ranging from Gilbert and Sullivan's operettas to newspaper cartoons) and so the public were very much aware of the Wildean persona. Indeed, as fashion historians have documented, after Wilde's public disgrace, many London dandies became very worried about how they should dress and perform in public in case their effeminacy labelled them as another Wildean sodomite. This idea became so ingrained in public perception that when film started to represent homosexuality it was able to draw upon the formula 'effeminacy = homosexuality' in order to identify gay characters on the screen (see Chapter 4).

This worrying about whether or not one *appears* effeminate illustrates another aspect of Foucault's explanation of sexuality: the ways in which *bio-power* – 'an explosion of numerous and diverse techniques for achieving the subjugations of bodies and the control of populations' (Foucault, 1990a: 140) – operates on modern individuals. To fully understand this, we need to turn to another work by Foucault – *Discipline and Punish* – in which he studied the practices of discipline and training associated with 'disciplinary power' that operated in particular locations, such as the military and schools, but most particularly in prisons – spaces where individuals could be watched/surveilled to ensure they behaved appropriately, and where they could be punished if they did not:

> What was then being formed was a policy of coercions that act on the body, a calculated manipulation of its elements, its gestures, its behaviour. The human body was entering a machinery of power that explores it, breaks it down and rearranges it... Thus, discipline produces subjected and practiced bodies, 'docile' bodies. (Foucault, 1977: 138–9)

Of course, what Foucault is suggesting is that discipline is a form of *training* of individual bodies but bio-power operates as a form of *regulating* social bodies. In his discussion of the 'panopticon' (a prison structure which enables a single guard to oversee many prisoners from a central watchtower) Foucault argues that surveillance works best when those being watched can never be sure that they *are* being seen, and so begin to behave at all times *as if* they are being observed. Constant surveillance, initially intended to discipline the body, takes hold of the mind as well to produce a psychological state of 'conscious and permanent visibility' (1977: 201). Thus, individuals become their own 'overseers', constantly on the watch for their own infractions of the 'rules', and become responsible for their own disciplining of their bodies and behaviours. In relation to sexuality, individuals become invested in regulating their own behaviours in line with the medical, moral and cultural definitions of 'normalcy' and internalizing the various ways that 'bio-power' sought to regulate sexual bodies for the 'good of society'. Hence people begin to regulate their own practices in line with the ideas of what is 'good' or 'healthy' or 'normal' sexual behaviour.

One further point needs to be made about Foucault's ideas of power. Foucault argues that sexuality was involved in a network of power dynamics – through the labelling of sexuality, specific groups could be identified and put in their place – yet, where there is power there is always resistance. Foucault cautions 'we must not imagine a world of discourse divided between accepted discourse and excluded discourse ... but as a multiplicity of discursive elements that come into play in various strategies' (1990a: 100). The formation of the homosexual subject facilitated the development of a unified group who could, through what Foucault termed 'reverse discourse', claim the label as a politically useful identity. The identification of homosexuality as a *personality* created possibilities for sexual identity politics. As Foucault points out, the identification of 'the homosexual' as a person rather than a category of sexual acts facilitates both the rise 'of social controls into this area of perversity' (1990a: 101) and the birth of politics around that identity. As Foucault writes:

> There is no question that the appearance in nineteenth-century psychiatry, jurisprudence, and literature of a whole series of discourses on the species and subspecies of homosexuality, 'inversion', pederasty, and 'psychic hermaphroditism' made possible a strong advance of social controls into this area of 'perversity'; but it also made possible the formation of a 'reverse' discourse: homosexuality began to speak on its own behalf, to demand that its legitimacy or 'naturality' be acknowledged, often in the same vocabulary, using the same categories by which it was medically disqualified. (ibid.)

Perhaps the simplest examples of reverse discourse are the reclaimings of terminology used to label sexually 'inappropriate' behaviours. So, activists have reclaimed words which have been used in derogatory ways such as 'gay', 'dyke' and 'queer'. The derogatory meanings of these words don't necessarily change, but reclaiming puts the value judgements that go along with them into a more 'fragile' position where those who attempt to use them negatively can themselves be seen as cruel, bigoted or old-fashioned.

Gay and lesbian civil rights movements are examples of the deployment of reverse discourse. Victorian categorizations of homosexuality were first used to produce confession of 'perverse interests' in order to produce submission and conformity to heterosexuality. But the same categorizations, with a few modifications, have been used to argue for civil rights. The discourse of homosexuality as a shameful secret produced the 'closet', 'the love that dare not speak its name' and the fear of being exposed. But that, of course, gives rise to 'coming out' – the idea that the secret desires cannot be contained, and must be confessed and acknowledged. In being acknowledged, they become a source of pride rather than shame. Coming-out stories are often narrativized as a linear progression – from discovering, in childhood, that one is 'different' and often unhappy, followed by a discovery of *how* one is different, leading to understanding that one is not alone and that there is a community to which one belongs. Thus, coming out is both a key moment in self-discovery but also a means by which one joins a community and finds self-worth. The coming-out narrative has been central to the gay rights movement since the late 1960s (Plummer, 1995; Weeks, 2007).

Foucauldian constructionism can be a useful theoretical paradigm for analysing representations of sexuality and sexual practices. For example, an understanding of constructionist theories of sexuality is necessary for the critical analysis of representations where the characters do not seem to conform to accepted paradigms of either heterosexuality or homosexuality. The Oscar-winning film *Brokeback Mountain*, for example, requires a knowledge of how sexual identity is a cultural construct in order to fully understand the dilemma of the two leading characters. Based on the short story by Annie Proulx (1997), *Brokeback Mountain* portrays the love between two cowboys – Ennis (played by the late Heath Ledger) and Jack (Jake Gyllenhaal). The film offers a sensitive exploration of the difficulty these men have in reconciling the desires they feel for each other with their identities, and can be read as an analysis of how constrictive cultural identifications can be. Given that contemporary Western culture identifies all sexual acts between men as homosexual, what happens when someone does not want to claim that identity and all its cultural baggage (especially homosexuality as effeminacy)? The sexual activity between the two men is often violent and aggressive (at times it is difficult to tell whether they are wrestling or trying to have sex): they are trying to contain their passion for each other within a culturally acceptable form of male intimacy, namely wrestling/physicality.

Similarly, constructionism is useful when we consider various sexual practices such as sadomasochism (SM) (see Chapter 10). To emphasize once again, contemporary Western culture often identifies sexuality in terms of the person with whom someone has sex. In SM subcultures, however, people often identify sexuality in terms of sexual sensations or pleasures rather than with whom they experience these sensations. Many SM enthusiasts are happy to perform sexual acts with members of either sex. For them, the sex of the partner is not as important as the specific acts and their accompanying sensations. As we'll go on to discuss, this subcultural group within contemporary Western culture actively violates normative sexual identity politics and forges an alternative scheme of sexual identity. For many SM enthusiasts the practice of labelling people as heterosexual or homosexual has no relevance in their specific subculture.

Another example can be found in 'men seeking men' personal ads where posters often advertise themselves as a 'straight man who has sex with men'. For whatever reason, the poster does not want to assume the identity of 'gay man', perhaps because of the associated cultural signifiers (effeminacy) and lifestyle of homosexuality. Yet the 'straight man who has sex with men' undoubtedly interprets their sexual activities against the common perception in contemporary Western culture. Maybe this man argues that he cannot be labelled gay because he never kisses another man – only penetrates him. Perhaps he adopts the Latin American model and believes that because he is active during sex he should not identify as gay, as only passive/receptive men should claim that identity. Either way, a constructionist does not suggest this man is lying to himself – identity is contingent upon how acts signify in the culture. Constructionism opens up debates about what *constitutes* a sexual identity. Should we continue to label sexuality using the binary system of hetero- and homosexuality? How stable is this binary? Why do so many cultures seek to regiment identities into such narrow categories? These questions and more underpin the fascinating debates in queer theory that we turn to in Chapter 3. First, though, we look at one of the founding fathers of modern sexuality.

Further Reading

Downing, L. (2008) *The Cambridge Introduction to Michel Foucault* (Cambridge: Cambridge University Press).

Psychoanalysis and Sexuality

Chapter 2

In our last chapter we examined the discursive production of sexuality. We now want to look at one of the key discourses on sexuality emerging at the turn of the nineteenth and twentieth centuries, one which has made an essential contribution to the development of modern sexualities and their study. Foucault critiqued psychoanalysis as one of the regulatory discourses that helped create the binary opposition between 'normal' and 'pathological', and a form of power that locates the 'truth' of the individual in his or her sexuality. Psychoanalysis is perhaps one of the most difficult theoretical traditions to explore because it has infiltrated so many aspects of modern life from, as Meltzer observes, 'literature (to which it owes its myths), linguistics, philosophy, anthropology, history, feminism, psychology, archeology, neurology, to name some. And it is in the notion of "some", perhaps, that lies the crux of the problem. For there is in psychoanalysis an overt conviction that it exists as the ultimate totality, of which everything else is a part' (1988: 2). Thus psychoanalysis is a mode of thinking which crosses many disciplinary boundaries – it is a theory of the mind, of subjectivity and of sexual development, but also forms of treatment and therapy. It is also a theory used to engage with all manner of human activities such as art, film and literature, and it produces particular methodologies or ways of examining those activities. Clearly we cannot explore all its manifestations. This chapter considers key ideas and concepts in psychoanalysis, reviewing the main ways in which these have influenced the study of visual media and its representations of sex and sexuality.

Sigmund Freud (1856–1939) is the most important figure in psychoanalysis. Born into a Jewish family, Freud was raised in Vienna and lived there until 1937 when, in order to escape the Nazi invasion, he left Austria to live the last years of his life in England. Freud's most enduring contribution to contemporary life and cultural theory is his insistence that sexuality is the key to the formation of personality. However, in order to understand Freud's theory of sexuality, it is first necessary to explain his beliefs about the unconscious mind.

Although the notion of the unconscious was already in existence when Freud was developing his hypotheses, he popularized the idea of a mind divided into three parts: *the conscious*, which contains all the thoughts, memories and desires of which we are aware; *the preconscious* where we store those things of which we are aware, but which we give little attention; and finally *the unconscious mind*, which Freud argued is constituted of thoughts and images we are not aware of because they are illicit desires and memories which are too disturbing for our conscious mind to acknowledge. For Freud, the unconscious is the motivating force in our personality, and, although it consists of numerous drives (for example the death drive), the sex drive in the unconscious is the most important agent in the development of gender identity.

So what are the processes through which we develop gendered identity? According to Freud, these begin at a very early age. Freud believed that all young children, male and female, are initially bisexual and believe everyone has the same physical make-up. Then, from around the age of three, children become aware of differences between their mothers and fathers and also physical differences between genders: for boys that they have penises and for girls that they do not. And it is from this age, according to Freud, that children enter 'the phallic stage' of sexual development, becoming aware of their own, and others', genitalia. This stage in turn brings about the onset of an 'Oedipal crisis'. In Greek mythology, Oedipus is a king who unknowingly kills his father and marries his mother. Freud related this story to his own experiences of his relationship to his mother, father and older brother, and developed a set of models that account for the processes by which boys and girls develop their gendered identity.

Most Freud scholars are agreed that Freud's views on the Oedipus complex went through a number of stages of development (see Simon and Blass, 1992 if you want to read about this in detail) but to summarize, for Freud, the first erotic love object for both sexes is the mother. In terms of the little boy, he sees that his father is a powerful rival who could physically harm him, but at the same time recognizes that, like his father, he has a penis. This is something he 'owns' that girls do not, and this unconscious realization also leads to what Freud called 'castration anxiety' – the initial threat that his father will castrate him, which produces the lifelong fear of losing his penis. Then, partly through fear of the father and partly through the development of socialization, the boy switches to identify with his father as the same sex, and then transfers his sexual desires from his mother to other women.

Obviously, for little girls this process is more complex and involves more obstacles. Girls also begin life desiring the mother, but the little girl recognizes that, like herself, the mother does not have a penis, and this unconscious realization leads to what Freud comprehended as 'penis envy'. She must then switch her sexual desire to her father, believing that he can give her a baby and hence she can own a penis vicariously. However, the same dilemma that boys face in their attachment to the mother faces a girl in their attachment to the father, in that she already has a rival. So the girl must displace sexual desire for the father with desire for other boys, and identify with her mother as female.

Freud's schema may seem bizarre, but his influence on how sexuality is perceived must not be underestimated. For Freud, the unconscious is the motivating force in our personality and the sex drive is the most important aspect of the unconscious. As we said in the introduction to this book, it can be difficult to find an example of something in the media that does not include sexual imagery. Advertising, for example, seems to rely upon sexualized images to sell products; newspapers are often accused of using titillation rather than serious news stories to entice prospective consumers; music videos almost routinely feature scenes that some describe as soft porn. So it may seem that Freud was right to assert that sex is a key driver of all our choices, from the cars we want to buy to the politicians we elect.

However, Freud's influence has had some catastrophic ramifications for cultural perceptions beyond recognition of the sex drive. Notice how for both boys and girls, Freud argues that sexual development in the child begins with a desire for the mother. Boys must transfer their sexual attractions from their mothers to other women and girls from their mother to men in order to enter heterosexuality. For Freud, the Oedipal crisis must be resolved in these ways in order for men and women to operate as 'normal' heterosexual human beings. Indeed, it is this aspect of Freud's theory of 'normal' sexual development that has been utilized most often to construct the homophobic discourses that we discussed in Chapter 1. Another unhappy outcome of Freud's theory of sexual development results from the notion of 'penis envy', the reaction of a girl during her psychosexual development to the realization that she does not have a penis: 'She has seen it and knows she is without it and wants to have it' (Freud, 1925 in Bergmann, 1994: 177). Taken literally (as Freud intended), this idea has been used authoritatively in patriarchal culture (especially during the 1950s when there was a political move to place women within the home as housewives) to condemn women for wanting to be men if they aspired to a life that included a career, or did not include having children. Many scholars, particularly feminists, have been critical of penis envy as a concept (and psychoanalysis as a discipline), contending that the assumptions and approaches of the psychoanalytic project, and its take-up in culture more widely in medicine and cultural theory, are profoundly patriarchal, misogynistic and anti-feminist – especially in its conceptualization of women as 'imperfect' men.

These taken-for-granted aspects of Freud's ideas and his theory of sexuality are extremely problematic, and it has taken substantial re-readings of Freud for many feminists to embrace psychoanalysis as a tool for theorizing sexuality. One of the most influential re-readings was produced by a French psychoanalyst called Jacques Lacan (1901–81).

Lacan's re-readings of Freud moved psychoanalysis away from the realm of biology into the realm of language and culture. For Lacan, the early phase of development begins before we have language, whilst we are living in the realm of the 'imaginary' – in other words, when we make sense of the world through images. In this phase (as with Freud) neither boys nor girls differentiate between themselves and the mother. Indeed, the child has no sense of its own identity, or of where it begins as separate from its mother, and therefore has no sense of 'I' as distinct from 'You'. To put it in Lacan's terms, the child at this stage cannot distinguish between itself as a subject and others as object. For Lacan the first key development, which occurs between the ages of 6 and 18 months, is what he termed 'the mirror stage'. Here, Lacan was drawing on clinical accounts of babies that describe a child's fascination with its own reflection, as the child recognizes itself in its own image. He used these accounts to develop a theory of the way a sense of self is constructed. He wrote:

> I [...] regard the function of the mirror stage as a particular case of the function of the *imago*, which is to establish a relationship between the organism and its reality – or, as they say, between the *Innenwelt* and the *Umwelt* [the 'inner world' and the 'outer world']. (2001: 3)

According to Lacan, what the child sees in their reflection is an organized totality, a being in control – an illusion or image of complete wholeness. This is an immensely pleasurable experience, in that the child sees the ideal self and also recognizes itself as separate from its mother.

But at the same time this is misrecognition of the self. The child sees itself not as experienced but as seen from the position of another. For the child, recognizing itself as different or separate from the mother means that identification with this image involves a splitting into both subject and object: the self that looks (subject) and the self which is looked at (object). At this point it is useful to consider an everyday, material example of this experience. Suppose you are preparing for a job interview. Part of the routine in preparation for this is to check your appearance in a mirror before leaving the house. You will probably examine your reflection in the mirror as object, in other words as others will see you. You will check your hair, clothes, make-up, and so on. In order to be satisfied you generally need to be able to confirm to yourself that you look confident and professional. However, this image is rarely identical to how you feel as subject. You may feel nervous rather than confident, for example.

Lacan said that when a child enters the mirror stage, the sense of wholeness previously experienced with the mother (which Lacan called 'the moment of plenitude') is lost forever, and so this fragmentation of the self is also the moment of recognition of absence or distance from the mother. Lacan referred to this experience of loss of wholeness as a sense of 'lack' that initiates a desire, in both boys and girls, to rediscover that moment of plenitude. This desire, however, can never be fulfilled. Lacan saw this pre-linguistic phase as biological or natural; it is not until the child enters into language that they enter into culture, or what he terms 'the symbolic'.

Lacan called language 'the law of the father'. What he was alluding to is that language is the system of laws, rules and codes. Far from being neutral, language is the means by which a culture's ideology is transmitted, and as far as gender is concerned it is male-centred. Thus we acquire a gendered 'I' and 'You' but more than this, language also serves to reinforce the experience of lack, in that it fails to restore the sense of wholeness we desire. And so we experience further splitting from the moment of plenitude. What we are left with is a constant longing for the ideal, imaginary self. We attempt to achieve this through making meaning in language but language itself is inadequate, it does not fulfil our desire.

Through language we become speaking subjects. But language genders us as either male or female, and because language favours the male as norm, women's recognition of sexual difference is as the 'Other' who 'lacks' more acutely than men. For both boys and girls desire for wholeness must be repressed, and this repression creates the unconscious. Desire in the unconscious searches for that which is lost, but the quest can never be fulfilled, because it can only be undertaken via language. Lacan said that desire in the unconscious moves from signifier to signifier in search of that which is lost. This can be illustrated by the act of, for example, searching for a word in a dictionary. In the dictionary a word will be explained by other words, and sometimes none of them seem to encapsulate exactly what we are trying to say. Further, Lacan says we constantly construct narratives which attempt to fulfil us by moving towards closure or resolution, but these are never adequate and therefore we repeat the attempt again and again.

Why is Lacan's theory so influential? Firstly, it is an account of the subject that sees subjectivity as split or fragmented, and therefore it challenges notions of the unified self. Secondly, it can readily be related to textual analysis because we can examine how subjectivity is constructed through the symbolic of narrative. Further, males and females learn to perceive themselves as 'different' through the symbolic, or the law of the father, rather than conceiving this difference as being entirely biologically determined. But at the same time, Lacan suggests this position, founded as it is on repression, is radically unstable. Both femininity and masculinity are founded on lack, but Lacan argues that it is not literal lack of a *penis*, as suggested by Freud, but of the *phallus* as the symbolic power of patriarchy. Women, because they are marginalized in relation to men in the symbolic, experience a more acute sense of lack. Some feminists argue that this explains why women are more likely than men to feel an acute sense of lack of self-worth, and that this is manifested in cultural practices such as eating disorders and cosmetic surgery.

If we consider this in the context of the notion that consumption of popular culture is a means by which we attempt to achieve a sense of wholeness, it may now be becoming clear how reading stories can be seen as a quest for plenitude, achieved vicariously in their resolution. The popularity of romance has been explained as the quest for a return to the moment of plenitude or for the lost mother. Janice Radway (1984), for example, uses Lacan to explore popular romantic literature. She argues that the female readers of romance such as the Harlequin series (Mills & Boon in the UK and worldwide) are mainly mothers themselves who are expected to provide the nurturing of others. The hero in the text, then, stands in for the absent mother for whom the reader herself longs but can now only experience imaginatively through forms of regression. Thus Radway argues that romance functions as a quest to recover the lost mother. Indeed, Radway argues that most heroines in adult romance have absent mothers and either absent or weak fathers, while the hero in romance possesses motherly as well as masculine qualities, in that he cares for the heroine in a maternal way. Radway identifies the formal characteristics and narrative conventions of the genre, which usually consist of a central heroine who is either orphaned or abandoned by her mother. The hero, although initially quite curt towards the heroine, eventually demonstrates his ability to be nurturing and tender – a replacement for the mother.

Similarly, John Storey applies Lacanian psychoanalysis to explain the function of masculine romance:

> The ideology of romance holds that 'love' is the ultimate solution to all our problems. Love makes us whole, it makes us full, and it completes our being. Love in effect promises to return us to the moment of plenitude, warm against the body of the mother. (2001: 77)

Although we often conceive of romances as a particularly feminine genre, Storey suggests that both men and women seek the possible plenitude of the romance and uses the film *Paris, Texas* as an example of a 'masculine romance', suggesting it is 'a road movie of the unconscious, a figuration of Travis Henderson's impossible struggle to return to the moment of plenitude' (ibid.). The hero searches for his mother's roots in Mexico, then seeks his place of conception in Paris (Texas) and 'finally in an act of "displacement"', he returns his own son, Hunter, to his long-lost mother, Travis's ex-wife Jane. This is 'in symbolic recognition that his own quest is doomed to failure' (ibid.).

What does Lacanian theory offer sexuality studies? Firstly, it places gendered subjectivity at its core, but insists that the process of acquiring this subjectivity is not biological, but cultural. Secondly, it draws together ideology, the symbolic order, society and individual subjectivity. In short, it links ideology with individual identity. And finally, it insists that our gendered subjectivities are inherently unstable. We can never be whole, complete unified subjects. Subjectivity is founded on lack or absence, and this includes masculinity, as men and women both experience lack. For women, though, lack is more acute. The literal penis is not the key signifier of difference or superiority, but rather the *phallus*, which nobody can own – including men – is a metaphor for the law of the father, or patriarchal power.

Lacanian psychoanalysis also offers a way of reading texts. Laura Mulvey, in her important article 'Visual Pleasure and Narrative Cinema' (1975), drew on both Freud's and Lacan's psychoanalytic concepts to devise a key tool for feminist analyses of popular culture. Mulvey proposed that in film, characters function like Lacan's ideal image of the perfect self, offering the pleasure for the viewer of the illusion of wholeness. In film, power is conferred on the central character who looks, who is subject not object, and according to Mulvey, this power is normally bestowed upon men. For female characters this is different. Women in film tend to function as projections of men's desire – men's fantasy. Women are there, she argued, primarily to be looked at as objects rather than subjects.

Thus Mulvey developed an analogy between Lacan's mirror stage and Hollywood film. For the male spectator, the male protagonist functions like the mirror stage's ideal ego, or Lacan's ideal image – the perfect self, who offers to the spectator the illusion of wholeness. The structuring in film of point-of-view shots means that, like the mirror image, the male hero both *is* and *is not* the self. For example, the central male characters, say Harry Potter or James Bond, carry the action, carry the narrative and are active subjects rather than passive objects, representing the promise of that imaginary wholeness we strive for. And like language, films are structured along gendered lines. They are products, argues Mulvey, of masculine desire as well as anxiety centring on lack.

But Mulvey, and those who followed her, took this even further and used Lacan to explain the specific function of 'woman' in mainstream film. Mulvey argues that in mainstream cinema, women are always coded in terms of their 'to-be-looked-at-ness'. She said that women on screen always exist, not in relation to other women, but in relation to masculine desire.

This was not an entirely new idea. John Berger, in *Ways of Seeing* (1972), examined the function of naked women in art, and coined the term 'the male gaze' to refer to the ways in which women are constructed purely to offer pleasure for the male viewer. He wrote that women are 'depicted in a different way to men – because the "ideal" spectator is always assumed to be male and the image of the woman is designed to flatter him' (1972: 64). Berger's arguments are based upon men's social and economic dominance over women rather than on psychoanalysis but, borrowing from Berger, Mulvey said that in mainstream cinema the camera is an extension of the male gaze. She says that the gaze and the power it confers belong to the man – the male hero (and of course the male spectator). In short, in film, through production strategies such as the standard shot-reverse-shot, man is subject of the gaze and woman is object of that gaze. The shot-reverse-shot is a technique for filming conversations from one character's point of view by cutting back and forth from a close-up shot of the male character, then a shot of the woman he is looking at, and then cutting to another shot of the man's eyes. Mulvey argued that this camera technique not only invites the spectator's identification with the male character, it also gives the illusion of power to men and renders women powerless.

It is not difficult to find many examples of this strategy in popular culture, from classic cinema to contemporary music videos. For example, Sut Jhally's educational video *Dream Worlds: Desire, Sex and Power in Music Video* (1995) examines the representations of women on MTV. *Dream Worlds* vividly illustrates how the shot-reverse-shot is systematically utilized to construct women as 'sex objects' and argues that these representations convey 'a dangerous and narrow set of stories about what it means to be male or female; stories which impact how women think about themselves sexually, and how men think sexually about women'. Analysing scenes in film and television from this perspective allows us to note how often a female character is aware of a male character watching her and how she derives pleasure from his approval and desire for her. Berger says this is because women have been socialized into always thinking about their 'to-be-looked-at-ness' and seeking positive judgements of themselves in relation to how they look.

But women are not only objects of desire: they are also a source of threat. So although women are represented in film as potential sex objects they are, on the other hand, also often represented as monstrous. Utilizing Freud, Mulvey said that the male viewer is also looking at the woman as a castrated subject (metaphorically because of her 'lack') and hence she also represents the threat of castration. And film can deal with this in one of two ways: firstly, through a narrative that leads to the woman being controlled or punished; and secondly, by fetishizing her so that the female star becomes reassuring rather than threatening. In many narratives both these strategies are apparent, producing binary oppositions between two main female characters. Examples range from fairy stories such as *Snow White* (dir. David Hand: 1937) and her polar opposite the Evil Queen, to more contemporary films such as *Fatal Attraction* (dir. Adrian Lyne: 1987) where Glenn Close's 'dangerous' career woman is contrasted with Anne Archer's 'safe' wife and mother.

Of course there have been many critiques of Mulvey's hypothesis (for example Clover, 1992; Prince, 1996) and there are problems in the appropriation and application of Lacan's ideas. For example, if the gaze is male and the object is woman, where does this place the female viewer? Drawing on Freud's theory of early childhood bisexuality, Mulvey proposes a sort of transvestism whereby women also identify with the male hero as well as with the female object. Other researchers turned to the work of Nancy Chodorow (1999) to explain women's experiences as spectators. According to Chodorow, psychological processes are developed through our experiences of a culture in which women carry responsibility for childcare. Because girls are perceived, by the mother, in terms of sameness and as an extension of the self, a girl's sense of self is less differentiated than that of boys who define themselves as more separate and distinct from the world. Mothers are the first significant other for both sexes, but whereas boys are encouraged to construct a sense of self through separation from the mother in order to establish a masculine identity, girls are encouraged to construct their selfhood through identification with the mother as female. For Chodorow, the female identifies with the father without ever losing this identification with the mother, which means that because the woman's sense of self is more fluid, less differentiated and more adaptable than men's, they are able to identify with a variety of subject positions.

Nevertheless, despite these explanations, there are still unanswered questions around spectatorship. As Myra Macdonald points out, in a critique of Mulvey's argument,

> [m]ost surprisingly, given her own emphasis on the play of erotic and sexual desire, [Mulvey] sidesteps the impact on viewing of the spectator's sexual orientation. To characterise Madonna, Debra Winger and Sharon Stone as equivalent objects of the male gaze is to elide the very different pleasures which may be on offer not just to lesbian and heterosexual women but also to homosexual and heterosexual men. (1995: 29)

The most robust criticism focuses on the dominance of Mulvey's method of textual analysis in 1970s film studies and its exclusion of social factors that shape audiences and their responses to film. Mulvey's theory proposed that gender is the only factor influencing how we read or respond to a text. But of course our identities are negotiated through other factors such as age, ethnicity and class. For example, black working-class males are often marginalized in films too. So a black male viewer may not identify with the white middle-class hero; indeed, he may identify more with a black female character. Moreover, there are considerable problems with the notion of 'identification' as the primary way in which we might engage with cinematic, or other cultural, representations.

Of course Mulvey was formulating these theories in the 1970s and 1980s. Much has changed in mainstream film since then, and indeed Mulvey herself has revisited her original article in order to develop and clarify her ideas (1981). We now have more female-centred genres or 'chick-flicks' that specifically address a female viewer, such as *Desperately Seeking Susan* (dir. Susan Seidelman: 1985), *Thelma and Louise* (dir. Ridley Scott: 1991), *Bridget Jones Diary* (dir. Sharon Maguire: 2001), *27 Dresses* (dir. Anne Fletcher: 2008) and *Bridesmaids* (dir. Paul Feig: 2011). But in any case, Mulvey's approach only 'works' with particular films and fails to recognize the ways in which women were directly addressed by films such as *Black Narcissus* (dir. Michael Powell and Emeric Pressburger: 1947), the whole genre of melodrama and women's evident interests in male film stars (Hansen, 1986). More recently, in advertising particularly, there has been a profusion of images of men constructed as 'objects of desire'.

Nevertheless, feminist psychoanalysis remains a key approach, especially for texts that construct a 'male gaze' and address a male viewer. While it is no longer the dominant method of analysis, nor is it perceived as providing all the answers in our quest to gain an understanding of a text, nonetheless it remains an influential and important approach.

Further Reading

de Laurentis, T. (2010) *Freud's Drive: Psychoanalysis, Literature and Film* (London: Palgrave Macmillan).

Thornham, S. (1999) *Feminist Film Theory: A Reader* (Edinburgh: Edinburgh University Press).

Queer Theory and Postmodern Sexualities

Chapter 3

'Queer' was a term once widely used as a taunt to insult people of alternative or non-normative sexualities. However, in the 1990s, activist groups such as OutRage! in Britain and Queer Nation in the USA started to appropriate the word as a positive form of identification. This re-appropriation of 'queer' was predicated upon various considerations. Firstly, there was a form of linguistic deconstruction at work. The word 'queer' – like all words – carries no particular meaning outside a specific context or culture. Calling someone 'queer' may be intended as abusive, but if the abused person claims the word as a positive identity then the attacker has had their ammunition removed.

Yet claiming the word 'queer' as a positive identity is not as simple as removing it from the lips of the attacker. As many theorists have argued (Butler, 1999; Munt, 2008) 'queer' always remains freighted with its history of abuse and discrimination. In self-identifying as queer, the subject acknowledges all the years of shame and discrimination the word denotes, but claims a pride in now identifying with the label. As such, 'queer' is still a difficult identity tag and many people feel it should only be employed as a self-appellation: it is acceptable for queer people to use the label about themselves, but if someone else labels them as such then it still has the connotation of abuse. Therefore 'queer' remains a particularly volatile label, often explosively political in its usage.

Activist groups also chose 'queer' as an identity label because it could be easily employed as a more inclusive umbrella term. Unlike the specific labels of 'gay', 'lesbian' and 'bisexual', 'queer' can include any non-normative expression of gender or sexuality, including transgenderism and transsexualism. 'Queer' popular politics has its roots in a growing disillusionment, during the 1980s, with gay liberation and lesbian feminisms which were criticized for assuming a singular gay identity based on gender or sexual object choice, and which too often seemed to ignore other aspects of identity like race and class (Jagose, 1996; Spargo, 1999; Sullivan, 2003). During the same decade, the AIDS crisis brought sexual *practices*, rather than identities, to the fore – the labels 'gay' and 'lesbian' were rejected as too restrictive and,

43

crucially, seemed to enable the dangerous misrecognition of AIDs as a 'gay' disease. Tamsin Spargo observes that 'in popular culture, queer meant sexier, more transgressive, a deliberate show of difference which didn't want to be assimilated or tolerated' (1999: 38). Jagose suggests that queer theory differs from gay liberation by 'avoiding the delusion that its project is to uncover or invent some free, natural and primordial sexuality' (1996: 98).

Sullivan suggests that to define queer theory is a 'decidedly un-queer thing to do' (2003: 43), but we do need to explore some of the academic arguments about queer theory as well as its more populist approaches to issues of identity and sexuality, its intentions to denaturalize sex, gender and sexuality and its development of Foucauldian ideas discussed in Chapter 1. It can be difficult to decide whether queer is a form of analysis or a popular politics, a way of thinking or a way of being – and, at times, it can seem like a club which keeps a very strict rein on its memberships.

The term 'queer' itself literally means 'strange' or 'odd' and stems from the Latin 'torquere' (to twist). In this sense, Jagose claims that 'queer ... can have neither a fundamental logic nor a consistent set of characteristics' (1996: 96) yet as a theory, queer has found a place in academic institutions and is very comfortably at home in numerous books and articles. Even so, identifying as 'queer' suggests a distinct political stance – decidedly and proudly antinormative – and an intention to denaturalize all issues relating to sex. But we should be clear that queer politics and theory are not concerned with establishing a 'queer' versus 'normative' binary in which some people identify as 'queer' and others are designated 'normal'. The very point of queer politics lies in its challenge of the whole idea of 'norms', to challenge what Butler calls 'foundationalism' – where phenomena are understood as causes, when they might actually be effects. For example, it is assumed that women's heterosexual desires are focused on bodies sexed as masculine but if we 'queer' this, we would ask whether the presumption of heterosexuality *requires* that bodies are sexed? For Spargo, 'mobilising "queer" as a verb ... unsettles assumptions about sexed and sexual being and doing' (1999: 40). To do so is not to get rid of binary terms such as homosexuality and heterosexuality, or nature and culture, but to draw attention to how difficult they are to maintain and how they have been constructed in specific historical and cultural ways.

Thus, 'Queer is less an identity than a critique of identity' (Jagose, 1996: 131). Queer politics forces a reconsideration of what is considered 'normal', 'natural' or 'appropriate', exposing these as *constructs* rather than fundamental and unchanging facts. Within queer studies a distinction should be drawn between the terms 'normal' and 'normative'. For the purposes of queer cultural studies, 'normal' denotes something biological and medically necessary. For example, it is 'normal' that a person's heart should beat a certain number of times a minute, or that person will become sick and possibly die. 'Normative', however, denotes something culture decrees as 'normal' but which is not biologically or medically necessary. For example, it is not biologically necessary for a couple to be married in order to have children, although most Western cultures have institutionalized marriage as the ideal arrangement for a procreative couple. Therefore marriage is something which is not 'normal', it is 'normative' – the preferred mode. Queer theory contends that fixed ideas about gender and sexuality are never 'normal', they are 'normative', and it is the exposure of this construct that queer theory aims for.

In Chapter 1 we considered Foucauldian constructionism and its proposals that sexual identity is contingent upon context and location. Queer theory also takes up that agenda and posits that identity is not innate and fixed, but a product of cultural regimes. As Stuart Hall summarizes, the contemporary subject is

> conceptualized as having no fixed, essential or permanent identity. Identity becomes a 'moveable feast': formed and transformed continuously in relation to the ways we are represented or addressed in the cultural systems that surround us. It is historically, not biologically, defined. The subject assumes different identities at different times, identities which are not unified around a coherent 'self'. (1992: 277)

As Hall argues, identity is culturally mutable rather than essential or innate. Drawing on Foucault and his ideas of the ways in which power operates to produce identities, queer theory argues that there is no original, repressed sexuality waiting to be liberated – sexual identity is an *effect*, or a construction, of culture. Homosexuality is produced in and through discourse, so that it can be policed and so that heterosexuality can be defined against it. Hence queer, as both theory and method, refuses to categorize people or things according to binary oppositions – for example, heterosexual/homosexual, nature/culture, masculine/feminine or natural/artificial – because those very categorizations need to be deconstructed to expose the ways in which they are mutually dependent on each other even as they are sites for struggle over meaning. Instead, we should ask: Why do these definitions matter and to whom? How do they arise? And how have they shaped 'moral and political hierarchies of knowledge and power?' (Spargo, 1999: 47) The two main critics who developed the debates about identity in relation to gender and sexuality are Judith Butler and Eve Kosofsky Sedgwick.

First published in 1990, Judith Butler's *Gender Trouble: Feminism and the Subversion of Identity* has been acknowledged as the first major text in the debates now known as queer theory. Although Butler wrote *Gender Trouble* as a feminist project, the book's exposition of gender instability and how heterosexuality is universally privileged has been of great importance for queer studies. *Gender Trouble* is a difficult and complex work, not helped by Butler's often convoluted writing style (Spargo (1999) termed her writing opaque and intentionally difficult). Nevertheless, as with Foucault's *The History of*

Sexuality, it is worth taking the time and effort to engage with *Gender Trouble*. This chapter attempts to summarize Butler's most quoted idea, the concept on which much of queer theory is predicated: gender performativity.

In her influential thesis, Butler argued that gender is a self-reflexive, performative effect. In an often-quoted passage, Butler asserts that 'there is no gender identity behind the expressions of gender; that identity is performatively constituted by the very "expressions" that are said to be its results' (1999: 33). Performativity is a term first developed by the philosopher John Austin, who argued that language could be divided into two broad categories: the constative and the performative (1962). The constative is descriptive language – a saying that describes what is already there. An example of a constative utterance might be 'It's a sunny day'. The performative, on the other hand, is a 'saying' or 'doing' which constitutes a 'being' when exercised within an accepted matrix of conventions and witnesses. The most often-cited example of a 'performative' utterance is the marriage ceremony where a priest or vicar *pronounces* a man and woman to be husband and wife. This utterance or gesture alters the ontological status of the male and female subjects standing in the church before the vicar – they are no longer simply a man and a woman, now the vicar has *pronounced* them to be husband and wife. However, performativity cannot exist in a vacuum. It can only make sense within an established and accepted social matrix. If the proverbial 'man on the street' pronounced the male and female to be husband and wife then the utterance would mean nothing. Similarly the performative always requires witnesses who validate its legitimacy within this accepted culture.

Therefore, it is important not to confuse performativity with performance – as some early critics of Butler's work did. Performance is voluntary and applied (the actor is on the stage 'performing' King Lear and understands his actions as a *conscious* performance) while performativity has an anti-voluntarist (unconscious) aesthetic which cannot be separated from the concepts of iterability (where an action feels entirely natural and spontaneous but is already-and-always known and repetitious) and ritualization (actions which have symbolic value). Hence for Butler, gender is a set of acts and rituals that we repeatedly practise – everyday examples could include washing with scented soaps or manicuring our nails – we understand these daily acts as expressions of our gender (we bathe with scented soaps *because* we are girls and like to smell 'nice'), but Butler suggests that our repeated practice of them is more than an expression of gender; it helps to create gender. If Foucault warned against seeing sex as a 'fictitious unity ... a causal principle' (1990a: 154), Butler argues that 'natural sex' is the 'effect of the apparatus of cultural construction designated by gender' (1999: 11). Through these repeated practices, we establish and reinforce that we are girls or, by not doing them and doing other things instead, that we are boys.

Butler, in her sequel *Bodies that Matter*, stresses that 'performativity must not be understood as a singular or deliberate "act", but rather as the reiterative and citational practice by which discourse produces the effects that it names' (1993: 2). If this were not the case, Butler speculates, the subject could simply go to the wardrobe, put on a 'gender of the day' and then take it off at night (1993: x). Therefore the subject does not just turn performativity on and off at will. Indeed, one of the earliest examples of a performative utterance is when the midwife delivers the newborn baby and pronounces 'It's a girl!' This pronouncement has created the baby's identity but is not so much a label as a threat. Implicit in the performative utterance 'It's a girl!' is the threat that the baby should now proceed to act out girlishness, that her parents should ensure that she 'does' girlishness (buy the appropriate colour clothes, toys, etc.) so that the child is interpellated into the correct and normative gender regime. As such, gender performativity is something which contemporary culture polices right from the subject's birth. That being said, however, there are occasions on which gender performativity can be queered and specific acts can show that although gender is policed and regimented by contemporary culture, it is not natural or innate.

In order to illustrate how all gender is performative, Butler cites the entertainment spectacle of drag which, she argues, exposes gender as a form of ritual: 'in imitating gender, drag implicitly reveals the imitative structure of gender itself – as well as its contingency' (1999: 175). Where much previous feminist criticism read drag as a mockery of the idea of essentialized femininity, Butler suggests that drag demonstrates there is *no original* or inherent femininity to be caricatured or mocked. Drag exposes gender as only *performative* effects. Drag shows that everyone – male or female – is simply 'doing' gender and that although we learn from an early age that certain genders are 'supposed' to be mapped onto certain sexed bodies, this is not biological or natural.

The problem with Butler's argument, however, is that it cites only a drag act of supreme persuasiveness. Butler's theory is certainly applicable to a drag act where the gender parody is seamless and imperceptible. The frisson or thrill of such an act lies in its exposure of gender as imitative and not related to chromosomal sex. Unfortunately other drag acts (such as the classic British end-of-the-pier type drag show or much 'family' entertainment on television), where the artist is perceptibly a man in woman's clothes (usually a big, burly man wedged into a floral frock), can have the opposite effect, supporting the essentialist view that gender is indeed inextricably linked to chromosomal sex.

Many critics misinterpreted Butler's theories, and often conflated day-to-day gender performativity with theatrical drag, which Butler merely offered as an *example* of performativity. Sheila Jeffreys, for example, asks:

> When a woman is being beaten by the brutal man she lives with is this because she adopted the feminine gender in her appearance? Would it be a solution for her to adopt a masculine gender for the day and strut about in a work shirt or leather chaps? (1993: 81)

Jeffreys' rhetorical question is intended to render Butler's argument ridiculous, but in suggesting that Butler thinks gender can be 'adopted' she misunderstands Butler's anti-voluntarist argument. Such a misreading of Butler may well have more to do with Butler's difficult writing style – her 'barbed-wire prose' (Medhurst, 1997: xxiv) – than the academic ability of her readers. Nevertheless, perhaps it does need to be spelt out: Butler is *not* arguing that gender can be assumed or discarded at will, nor does her work suggest 'subvert gender in the way that I say, and life will be good' (1999: xxi).

Although Butler was writing from a feminist perspective, her work not only revised feminist politics but also had a tremendous influence on emerging queer studies. The defining characteristic of sexual object choice had traditionally been thought to be gender. The word 'heterosexuality', traced back to its roots in Ancient Greek and Latin, is made up of the concepts of otherness (hetero = other) or difference, and sex. It is the gender difference (masculine/feminine) which is thought to be the scaffold of hetero-erotics. Masculinity is attracted to its binary opposite – femininity. Aretha Franklin sings that 'You make me feel like a natural woman' (Atlantic Records: 1967) because she is with a man whose masculinity sparks off against her femininity. The juxtaposition and difference between the two creates a sense of the 'natural' order of heterosexual attraction. Butler terms this the 'heterosexual matrix' and points out that 'the institution of a compulsory and naturalized heterosexuality *requires* and regulates gender as a binary relation in which the masculine term is differentiated from a feminine term, and this differentiation is accomplished through the practices of heterosexual desire' (1999: 30). Put simply, Butler is arguing that for heterosexuality to appear as 'natural' it requires the gender binary to also seem essential or natural.

But what happens if this gender binary is destabilized? What happens if gender is exposed as a performative effect through spectacles such as drag or camp? If gender is the scaffold for heterosexual desire, and gender itself is shown to be merely a performative effect, then heterosexuality is challenged. Much queer art has therefore tried to represent gender as a 'regulatory fiction' (Butler, 1999: 180), to force viewers to realize that gender may actually be a flimsy scaffold for eroticism. If a heterosexual man is watching a 'quality' drag act and finds the drag-artist, who is flawlessly 'doing' femininity, 'sexually attractive', then this may challenge that viewer's sense of sexual identification requiring him to reconsider how something as 'fictional' as gender can be a scaffold for eroticism. What does *having* a heterosexual identity actually mean?

Recently, a number of popular cultural representations have explored aspects of 'queering' heterosexuality through the deconstruction of gender. The virtual reality dating show *There's Something about Miriam* (Sky1: 2004) addressed this very issue, although not necessarily well or to radical political effect. A dating show with a twist, *There's Something...* took a group of eligible bachelors and had them compete for the attentions of a beautiful woman called Miriam. The twist was that Miriam was not biologically female but instead was a man 'doing' a flawless act of femininity. Labelled 'the cruellest reality show idea yet' (Mohan, 2003), Miriam's performance was not revealed until the end of the series, and much of the 'humour' and suspense of the programme rested on the assumption that the male contestants would be shocked by the 'revelation'. They were indeed shocked. In fact, screenings of the series were delayed by court actions taken by the contestants. There is little evidence that the edifice of heterosexuality was significantly rocked by this demonstration of its 'instability' and, indeed, many commentators suggested the programme reaffirmed trans-phobia (fear of transgendered persons). As Petra Boynton (2004) observed:

> The whole premise of *There's Something About Miriam* was not a celebration of transgendered life. It was designed to elicit horror from the winning contestant discovering that his dream date had a penis.

The queer project poses interesting questions for students of sexuality – if gender is the scaffold for eroticism, but gender is simply a performative effect, then what *is* sexual identity? How natural and fixed is heterosexuality when sexual desire can be inspired by a performative effect? Queer representations therefore ask if desire is necessarily circumscribed by the gender of the sexual object choice. And, if desire is predicated upon gender, how can desire be viewed as stable if gender is a flexible fiction?

An alternative slant on this 'queering' of heterosexuality is offered by the work of Eve Kosofsky Sedgwick, a literary critic, whose hugely influential *Epistemology of the Closet* was published in the same year as *Gender Trouble*. Sedgwick's theories about sexuality have exerted a profound influence on cultural studies approaches to sexual identity and developed Butler's agenda within queer theory. Labelled the 'queen of queer studies' whose work 'can be seen as initiating the field of queer theory' (Campbell, 2000: 159), Sedgwick is clearly an important thinker although often criticized for her indulgent queer readings of classic texts (see Siegel, 1998: 36). For example, her readings of Henry James's novels claim that

> there is an argument to be made that James's anal erotics function especially saliently at the level of sentence structure … whose relatively conventional subject-verb-object armature is disrupted, if never quite ruptured, as the sac of the sentence gets distended by the insinuation of one more, and just one more and another, and another and impossibly just one more qualifying phrase or clause. (102)

Thus, in James, Sedgwick claims to find a form of 'fisting as *ecriture*', a way of writing which conveys to readers a sense of being probed anally. Her claims to find masturbation in Jane Austen (*Sense and Sensibility*'s Marianne Dashwood isn't nervous or excitable, she's masturbating) caused quite a stir amongst literary scholars but others believe Sedgwick offers valuable insight to sexuality debates. In particular, in her numerous writings exploring the relationships between homo- and heterosexualities she shows that homosexuality – far from being the bogeyman of modern, bourgeois culture – is actually heterosexuality's defining other. Sedgwick's project has been the destabilization of normative heterosexuality and of the homo/hetero binary through two main agendas.

Firstly, Sedgwick reworks Foucault's 'constructionist' versus 'essentialist' argument into the paradigms 'universalizing' versus 'minoritizing'. The minoritizing approach sees homosexuality as something relevant only to a specific or distinct minority. On the other hand, the universalizing approach reads homosexuality as pervading, in one way or another, the entire spectrum of sexualities in modern culture (Sedgwick, 1990: 1–2). 'Universalizing' and 'minoritizing' are therefore not exact synonyms for 'constructionist' and 'essentialist' but offer a more malleable theory. The minoritizing view offers an identity politics founded on the sense of immutable sexual identity but the universalizing view, rather than focusing on the idea of identification as an effect produced by culture, suggests that sexual desire moves in excess of the limiting labels of *any* sexual identification. Arguably, it is impossible to regiment sexual desire at all, despite what mainstream culture tries to do. As Sedgwick writes, 'sexual desire is an unpredictable powerful solvent of stable identities' so that 'apparently heterosexual persons and object choices are strongly marked by same-sex influences and desires' (1990: 85). Sedgwick also reworks Foucault's argument that sexuality is the effect of networks of power into the symbol of 'the closet', which she sees as 'the defining structure for gay oppression in this century' (1990: 71). Sexuality and, more importantly, knowledge of sexuality are intrinsically linked to the web-like structures of power pervading modern culture. Homosexuality holds an important relation to the 'wider mappings of secrecy and disclosure' (1990: 71) and to issues of public and private that maintain a sexual hierarchy throughout the Western world. 'Queers' are deemed 'tolerable' provided they remain conveniently closeted. The closet is a figure of speech for the self-imposed (but often compulsory) silence a person maintains around their sexual orientations (see, for example, the 'don't ask, don't tell' rules which operated in the American military until very recently). People are 'in the closet' if they don't 'confess' their homosexuality or they hide it by 'passing' as heterosexual. Being 'closeted' is not necessarily a choice: it may only be safe to tell friends that one is gay while maintaining an appearance of heterosexuality to employers. And not telling does not mean that others will not presume to judge on the basis of dress or appearance. Throughout her writings, the closet is an important symbol of the 'open secret' of sexuality pervading Western culture and everyday life, and it is this symbolic resonance of the closet which makes Sedgwick's work so useful to analysis of popular texts.

For example, the 'closet' appears to great effect in Ang Lee's *Brokeback Mountain*. After Jack's death, Ennis visits his lover's family home and from within Jack's bedroom closet we view Ennis's grief. Ennis goes to the closet and finds two shirts hidden there, one his own, the other Jack's; hanging together they symbolize the lost love and the depth of feelings which could never be publicly acknowledged.

Secondly, and most importantly, Sedgwick develops Butler's thesis on gender as the scaffold for desire to question why the sole defining feature of sexual identity has historically been the gender of the subject's sexual object choice. As we have considered already, there are examples where it is not the gender of the object choice but rather *how* someone has sex that is considered the defining attribute in sexual identification. Sedgwick points out that there are many other features that may be the defining agency in sexual desire instead of gender (1990: 31). Some people may enjoy only group sex and engage in threesomes. Others may eroticize age difference and be 'cradle-snatchers' (attracted to those younger than themselves) or 'daddy-seekers' (attracted to older, father figures), while others may eroticize body attributes as in muscle-worship.

Indeed, we could develop this argument further and consider other ways in which sexuality could or perhaps should be identified rather than in terms of the gender of the sexual partner. For example, some people like to have a lot of sex while others do not and prefer it only infrequently. Others define themselves as asexual, because of their preference not to engage in sexual activity at all. Why do we not classify sexuality in terms of frequency of sexual acts rather than with whom we perform these acts? Surely that would make just as much sense? In that respect, a heterosexual couple who only ever engage in oral sex could be classified as having more in common with a gay couple who also only engage in oral sex than with another heterosexual couple who only engage in penetrative genital sex. All these variations signify other potential ways of classifying sexuality, so is it not remarkable that contemporary culture regiments sexuality only in terms of the gender of the sexual object choice?

In light of this argument, Sedgwick's most (in)famous contribution to queer theory has been her revival of a category from archaic sexology: the onanist or 'chronic masturbator'. Sedgwick wrote that she herself did not identify as homo- or heterosexual because for her, sexuality is not predicated upon sexual object choice, but on practice. Therefore, in light of Sedgwick's argument, are we often not too reductionist in the way we label sexual identity? For example, if a straight-identified female straps on a dildo and penetrates her male partner, can this 'queer' activity be labelled 'heterosexual'? Although the activity is between a male and female couple, the practice violates the traditional performance of heterosexuality. Similarly, if a straight-identified woman gains erotic pleasure from watching hardcore gay porn, is it not reductionist to label her desire 'heterosexual'?

The effect of both these Sedgwickian approaches – universalizing versus minoritizing, and the calibration of sexuality outside the axis of gender – is to fracture the hetero/homo binary and challenge the importance of sexual identity politics. The goal of Sedgwick's project is to destabilize heteronormativity, shifting the emphasis from traditional identity politics to a broader examination of how sexual taxonomies (systems of classification) are labelled and regimented by the cultural landscape.

So how might you take this forward into your own studies? As with many theoretical perspectives, queer suffers from its own tensions. As a way of thinking about sexuality and the deconstruction of identity, queer spends a lot of time constructing its own sets of identities as 'eccentric, ab-normal' (Spargo, 1999: 40). Queer can also include attacks on assimilation politics and has been critiqued for its seeming acceptance of 'deviants' such as sadists and paedophiles. However, this is to mistake the *analytical* purpose of queer theory, which is to expose and denaturalize the discursive constructs that inform debates and identities associated with 'deviant' practices, rather than to claim such practices are, in themselves, 'queer'. It can seem, sometimes, that queer theory is only for certain people – Sullivan suggests that it is often implied that 'all heterosexuals are situated in a dominant normative position, whereas all queers are marginalised and consciously and intentionally resist assimilation of any kind' (2003: 48–9). However, queer can offer ways of understanding how most people's lives and practices are categorized and judged. Smith suggests that queer theory is a 'strategy, an attitude... Queer articulates a radical questioning of social and cultural norms, notions of gender, reproductive sexuality, and the family' (1996: 280). Hence, in its insistence that no sexual identification is natural, normal or unified, queer can have application for all of us.

To conclude, it is worth noting here that many media representations have started to respond to such 'queer' dynamics. As the chapters in the next part will address, a number of recent television shows and films have featured sexual dynamics that can be seen to twist or 'queer' the established hetero/homo binary. A show such as *Sex and the City*, for example, may focus predominantly on heterosexual sexual activity, but much of this is often quite 'queer' in that the characters engage in unconventional sexual acts that don't quite 'fit' within traditional expectations of heterosexuality. Likewise, the hit sitcom *Will and Grace* focuses on slippages or strange relationships which do not quite fit within the hetero/homo scheme, such as the 'queer' eroticism which exists between the gay-identified Will and his straight female friend Grace, or the 'queering' of normative heterosexuality by the polysexual Karen Walker. A hit show such as *The L Word* may be considered groundbreaking in its depiction of a community of lesbians whose characters' 'coming-out' experiences are not depicted as painful and who challenge the idea that sexuality is innate or fixed. The following part, 'Representations', will consider these texts and issues in detail.

Further Reading

Giffney, N. and O'Rourke, M. (2009) *The Ashgate Research Companion to Queer Theory* (Farnham: Ashgate Publishing).

Kohnen, M. (2012) *Queer Representation, Visibility, and Race in American Film and Television: Screening the Closet* (London: Routledge).

Peele, T. (2011) *Queer Popular Culture: Literature, Media, Film, and Television* (Hampshire: Palgrave Macmillan).

Representations

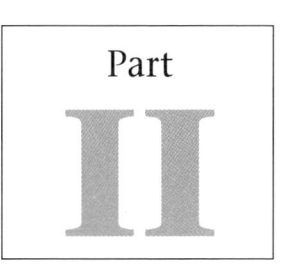

Part II

Introduction to Part II

'Representation' is one of the most important concepts in media, film and cultural studies. Indeed, 'representation studies' often make up a big part of any media/cultural studies course and, not surprisingly, a considerable number of books have been written on this area of criticism alone. When examining 'representations' there are a number of issues to be considered. Although these areas are pertinent to all debates in representation – especially gender, race and class – they have a particular relevance to sexuality studies. The following brief introduction aims to outline two key concerns in representation studies with considerable relevance for the study of sexualities.

Representation as re-presentation

First, it is important to remember that no matter how realistic or natural a representation is, it is never simply a window onto the world or a direct, unmediated reflection of something. Instead, it is always a re-presentation. In other words, the producer of the image has re-presented something in a particular fashion. In this respect, representations are *never* 'innocent' – they do not just suddenly happen by accident – but are always a construct in accordance with specific sets of politics and ideas.

For example, consider one of the most commonplace, easily identifiable representations: the family wedding photograph. Even this simple representation is never a window onto the world or a replication of reality but instead has been constructed in accordance with a set of specific codes, conventions and politics. The wedding photograph aims to represent the idea of the happy family. It is a celebration of a joyous day when a couple are joined together in matrimony and two separate families are united. Ideally, everyone in the wedding photograph will look happy and contented, whether or not this is actually the case. Perhaps Aunt Agatha absolutely loathes and despises Uncle Arthur, so much so that she feels physically sick in his presence. The photographer, however, will not permit this ill-feeling to be apparent in the photograph as it would violate the conventions of the 'happy family'. If the photographer is competent they will notice the displeasure demonstrated by Aunt Agatha and Uncle Arthur and will instruct them that they must re-present themselves – 'Smile please!' – so that they look happy and convivial. In other words, the photographer will re-present these bodies so that they accord with the conventional expectations of the wedding photograph.

Secondly, it is important to remember that the photographer will draw upon generic conventions – a specific set of codes which are common to this type of photography and which we, as viewers, have learned from experience how to read. For example, it is traditional that the bride and groom will be positioned at the centre of the photograph. This is a tradition allowing viewers to interpret which couple is the bride and groom. However, this positioning is not simply a matter of easy recognition – it also suggests how this couple form the centre of the newly united family group. In this photograph, marriage is, quite literally, the centre of family life – one of the most important rites of passage for the couple and their families. Similarly, it is also expected that any little children (pageboys and flowergirls) will be positioned at the front of the photograph. Usually, if there is one pageboy and one flowergirl, they will be positioned in a pose echoing that of the bride and groom. Although this is, on one level, simply an aesthetic requirement (the little ones must be at the front of the group or they will not be visible) there is also a particular politics suggested by this arrangement in that the pageboy and flowergirl at the front mirror (in miniature) the bride and groom, thus suggesting what marriage is all about: the bride and groom will marry, have children who in turn will grow up, marry and have children of their own. The particular politics of heterosexual union are therefore suggested – although at an implicit level – by this simple image.

Most media texts share the same implicit concern with reinforcing the traditional dynamics of heterosexuality as the wedding photograph. For the student considering representations of sexualities, it is important to remember that, like the wedding photograph, normative, heterosexual union is implied in nearly all mainstream representations. Underpinning most narratives are the politics of heterosexual union in which a couple will marry (or be expected to marry) and produce children. Take, for example, one of the most popular films ever made: *Jurassic Park* (dir. Steven Spielberg: 1993). Without a doubt one pleasure in this film is being able to marvel at its amazing special effects – not least the incredible dinosaurs. However, even in this rollercoaster action film, the politics of traditional heterosexuality are very much implied.

The film starts with the hero – Dr Grant (played by Sam Neill) – as a bad-tempered academic who hates children. This is demonstrated through the way he frightens a boy with a gory description of how a velociraptor kills and devours its prey. However, by the end of the film Dr Grant has become a surrogate father figure to the two children, and the final image of the film shows Dr Grant, Dr Ellie Sattler (Laura Dern) and the children flying to safety in a helicopter. Dr Grant places his arm around the boy, and the image resembles a nuclear family. The point is that, even though *Jurassic Park* is an action film, it is still underpinned by the politics of normative heterosexuality.

Heterosexuality underpins almost every representation, but is usually represented in a very narrow fashion in which its normative mode – marriage and family – is portrayed as normal and natural. Any form of 'aberrant' heterosexuality – such as people who live non-monogamous, non-child-rearing lives – will, like Dr Grant in *Jurassic Park*, change their ways by the conclusion of the narrative. Alternatives do occur but can often end in a form of punishment (even death) as in, for example, the many Hollywood representations of the 'femme fatale' – the 'dangerously' sexual and unattached woman who creates mayhem, particularly in the film noir genre. As we discuss in a later chapter, some representations do attempt to challenge narrow prescripts of 'acceptable' heterosexuality by representing alternative lifestyle paradigms: we use *Sex and the City* as a particular example. However, to summarize, ideas of normative heterosexuality (in other words, heterosexual marriage and children) underpin most mainstream representations. These may be slightly more explicit, as in the family wedding photograph, or implicit, as in a film like *Jurassic Park*, but either way they are nearly always present.

There is another key point in representation studies that needs to be addressed. A second meaning of representation is the idea of something being *representative of* a specific group or set of ideas/politics. Here the representation stands in for something, be it a specific group of people or specific ideologies. For example, for every university course there will be a student known as the 'student representative'. This is the student who *stands in for* the entire student body at departmental meetings. It is this student's job to voice the particular concerns and issues of the undergraduate cohort. The rep is expected to have discussed teaching and pastoral issues with the other students, and assimilated their worries and concerns, with a view to re-presenting these to the faculty. 'Re-presenting' is a key point here, as the student rep, if he or she has any diplomacy at all, will very likely re-phrase or re-draft the student concerns with some delicacy and tact. While a student might have viciously attacked a particular module or lecturer, the student rep will re-present this complaint in a more appropriate fashion. In this respect, the student rep performs the first function of representation as discussed above. However, the student rep is also 'standing in for' the student cohort. This is important when we remember that perhaps the people whom the student rep is addressing – senior academics, administrative staff – may have no first-hand knowledge of these particular students. Therefore, this student rep 'stands in for' and becomes the representative of *all* the students. The impression the academics have of the student body in its entirety is distinctly coloured by the student rep. If he or she is confrontational or combative, this creates an impression that all students are like this. On the other hand, if the student rep is diplomatic and sensitive, he or she conveys a more positive impression of the whole student cohort.

This aspect of re-presentation – the standing in for a particular group – has particular relevance when we consider the representation of non-normative sexualities in the media. Many viewers may have little knowledge of, for example, gays or lesbians, to the extent that some may *never* have knowingly met a gay- or lesbian-identified person in their life. In this respect, the viewer's only encounter with sexual minorities may well be the re-presentation on the screen, which then stands in for *all* gays and lesbians. If these re-presentations are continually negative or caricaturish portrayals, these can affect public perceptions. This is particularly important when we remember that sexuality is different from other areas of representation because of one key point: sexuality doesn't show. Unlike, say, race or ethnicity, sexuality is not visible in one's physicality. Heterosexuality is the taken-for-granted sexual interest, implied in every mainstream representation. Therefore, when a producer of an image wants to re-present non-heterosexuality, they draw upon particular conventions and ways of showing this to viewers. In order to identify a character as gay or lesbian, mainstream representations have drawn upon specific symbols that viewers have, through time, learned to interpret as signifying a gay or lesbian identity. The most common of these is gender transitivity, in which gay men are 'effeminate sissies' while lesbians are 'butch dykes' (as we elaborate later).

Therefore, representation studies – especially in relation to sexualities – is a politically loaded area. To dismiss a media image with 'it's *only* a representation' is to miss this important fact. Mainstream representations have played a significant role in the 'naturalizing' of a particular form of heterosexuality while demonizing others, and have a continuing role in creating perceptions of sexual minority groups, especially lesbians and gays. This is not to say that *only* the media have done this but to emphasize that representations should not simply be dismissed as inconsequential or irrelevant.

The following chapters address the representation of sexualities in a range of media texts but with a particular focus on popular television texts. In all the chapters, we pay particular attention to how these representations function, how they are coded and what these codes may mean, and we do so with an awareness of how they often 'stand in for' particular minority groups. This part commences with a discussion of homosexuality in Chapter 4, overviewing the traditions and codes employed in the representation of homosexuality in film and media. Chapter 5 considers the history of the representation of lesbians on television and concludes with an analysis of the popular TV drama *The L Word*. Chapters 6 and 7 discuss a particularly difficult area in the critical study of representations of sexualities – heterosexuality – using *Sex and the City* and *Entourage* as examples of television's attempts to portray hedonistic heterosexualities. Finally, Chapter 8 considers the representation of teenage sexuality; in recent years a number of literary texts have addressed this issue directly, and the chapter examines two of the most popular representations – *Point Horror* and *Twilight*.

Chapter 4

Representations of Homosexuality

Case Study: *Will and Grace*

Given that sexuality, unlike other identities such as race, does not 'show', as we saw in the previous chapter, how can a specific character be represented as lesbian or gay within a television or film narrative? In the documentary *The Celluloid Closet* (1996), based on Vito Russo's book of the same name (1987), Richard Dyer cites an example from a very early Hollywood movie – a Charlie Chaplin film – in which a character caricatures homosexuality by 'swishing around in the most effeminate way'. Dyer points out that this idea of 'homosexuality as demonstrated through effeminacy' must already have been so engrained in the public perception that the viewers of this very early film knew exactly what this 'swishy mime' was supposed to signify. Therefore, although the media has helped reinforce and even perpetuate the idea of homosexuality as demonstrable through gender transitivity, it did not invent or create this formula.

As we noted in Chapter 1, Michel Foucault argued that when homosexuality was first labelled as an identity, rather than specific acts, it was characterized by what he termed an 'interior androgyny, a hermaphroditism of the soul' (1990a: 43). Sedgwick also employs a similar image in her suggestion that gender transitivity is a form of 'inversion, *anima muliebris in corpore virile inclusa* – "a woman's soul trapped in a man's body" and vice versa' (1990: 87). This trope preserves the idea of 'heterosexuality' as essential to desire – that is, that in *any* sexual coupling, there should be one male and one female self. This gives rise to the belief that anyone (whether male or female) who desired a man must be feminine and likewise that anyone who desired a woman (whether male or female) must be masculine (as we discussed in Chapter 3).

The earliest representations of homosexual characters on screen were what we now refer to as 'sissies'. The word 'sissy' is the abbreviation of the archaic term 'sister-boy' and it describes a male character who is effeminate in a very obvious, often pronounced fashion. The sissy was and continues to be a sure source of humour in mainstream representation – effeminate queens have peppered the narrative of many comedy films and television shows seemingly

61

serving very little function other than a humorous extra, something wedged into the narrative to provide some comic relief.

It is not entirely clear, however, what viewers were laughing at when they saw the 'sissy'. Many will have laughed because of homophobia – viewers saw the signifiers of homosexuality (effeminacy) and laughed at the 'homosexual' on the screen. Yet there is a further reaction of 'effeminophobia' in which viewers respond to the effeminacy represented in the text (see Richardson, 2009). The effeminate man provokes strong reactions: firstly, he is demonstrating that femininity is not the exclusive property of female bodies and by implication that masculinity is not the inherent or innate property of male bodies. The sissy is a male body 'doing' femininity, and so makes explicit how gender is a performative effect. In so doing the sissy denaturalizes gender and deconstructs masculinity and femininity. Brian Pronger (1990: 227) uses the metaphor of the rollercoaster to describe the effects the spectacle of effeminacy may provoke. When riding a rollercoaster a person is disoriented because opposites previously assumed to be stable – up/down and left/right – suddenly become violently confused. The result is disorientation that some find thrilling, while others find it less pleasant. Similarly the spectacle of effeminacy confuses opposites (masculine and feminine) in a rollercoaster fashion. For some this is exciting, for some it is moderately disquieting, for others it may be offensive. Of course, in a comedy, that rollercoaster ride provokes humour, and where you have the kind of misunderstanding and misrecognition that characterizes a lot of situation comedy, it may be difficult to separate out precisely what is generating the belly laughs.

Another factor in the spectacle of the effeminate man (sissy) is the question of misogyny. The effeminate man is, after all, behaving 'like' a woman and therefore renouncing his masculine privilege and moving down the gender ladder. Indeed, if we consider many of the effeminophobic terms of abuse such as 'sissy', 'girlie', 'pussy', these all suggest that a man is 'like a woman' but this can only be a term of abuse if femininity is deemed inferior to masculinity. In a world of true gender equality, saying that a man is 'like a woman' would be no insult at all. So it may be the case that what many viewers laugh at when they watch effeminacy on screen is a socially acceptable form of misogyny. The effeminate character allows male viewers to laugh, guilt free, at 'womanliness'.

Finally, the popularity of the sissy can also be accounted for due to his 'de-sexualization'. As Lily Tomlin, narrator of *The Celluloid Closet* explains, the sissy 'didn't seem to have a sexuality, so Hollywood allowed him to thrive'. If we remember that gender is assumed to be the defining attribute in eroticism (Chapter 3) then a character that sits between genders does not 'fit' into the sexual equation and, by this reckoning, is un-attractive. Richard Dyer aptly terms gender transitive lesbian and gay characters as 'the inbetweens' (1993: 33) in that they were often 'tragic, pathetic, wretched, despicable, comic or ridiculous figures' (1993: 37). Many representations showed sissies as alone and unloved. Although often lecherous and keen to find sexual encounters, sissies were represented as pathetic, unattractive creatures unable to attain any sexual contact. In this respect, viewers need feel no danger that they may have to witness same-sex sexual activity when the figure of the sissy is an 'inbetween' who will undoubtedly remain alone and condemned to celibacy.

The sissy became, and continues to be, a very popular character in mainstream cinema and television, although rarely ever three-dimensional in their presentation. Stereotypes are constructed by taking something – a character trait, a way of walking or speaking, or an ability – which may apply to a percentage of a group, and presenting it as indicative of the group as a whole. In the case of homosexuality, stereotyping marks an identity that is not outwardly visible, rendering homosexuals as recognizable and distinct from the majority. In short, stereotypes often make visible the invisible. Stereotypes are not always negative ('the French are good cooks' is a stereotype which is obviously not negative, for example), nor are they always 'about' the powerless, though they always relate to power in some way – Tessa Perkins cites the 'upper class twit' as a particular favourite in prime-time British comedy (1979). Nor are they always entirely inaccurate: if we consider the stereotype of the 'dumb blonde' we have to realize that there are a great many people in the world who are blonde and a great many people who are also 'lacking in intelligence'. These factors will inevitably overlap and there may indeed be a great number of 'dumb blondes' in the world. The power of stereotypes lies in the ways in which, in this example, blondeness and dumbness are tied up in a particular kind of politics about gender, because the dumb blonde is almost always female. Thus, 'it implies more than hair colour and intelligence. It refers immediately to *her* sex, which refers to her status in society, her relationship to men, her inability to behave or think rationally, and so on. In short, it implies knowledge of a complex social structure' (Perkins, 1979: 139).

For many activists, stereotypes of minority groups must be rigorously challenged, and a key concern about stereotypes in the media is that their ideological function is particularly problematic when viewers have little or no knowledge of the group being stereotyped, and therefore have little or no experience or information to counterbalance those representations.

More worrying is the suggestion that stereotypical representations could foster self-loathing in incipiently gay viewers. The impact of mainstream representations is perhaps especially important in the realm of sexual identity. Feminist media critics have shown how popular culture tends to reduce representations of women to either sex objects, dutiful daughters/housewives or sexually dangerous (mad, bad) women who are usually tamed or punished by the end of the narrative. Obviously it may be difficult or frustrating for female viewers to see so little diversity in the representation of women, and the images they see can be demeaning or degrading, but it is highly unlikely that female viewers have no knowledge of other women living in their neighbourhood. However, for many young gay viewers, that is often exactly the situation. Many gays and lesbians grow up in isolation, closeted, having little or no connection with other gays or lesbians. Often, for many gay teens, the only other gay people they can identify with are fictional representations on-screen. For young gay teens, seeing homosexuality represented only as an object of disgust/ridicule in the form of the stereotypical sissy or the dyke could encourage self-loathing.

Even so, we do need to be careful about some of our claims about stereotypes. Firstly, we may be able to agree that stereotypes function to categorize our world and to shape our perceptions of it, but that doesn't mean that they have an absolutely instrumental role in our collective consciousness or ways of relating to people we have only ever met through representations. For example, Richard Dyer suggests that

> stereotypes can be both a complex and a formative mode of representation. We are accustomed to thinking of them as simple, repetitive, boring and prejudiced group images which, should they supposedly be about ourselves, we angrily reject. We mistake their simplicity of formal means (a few broadly drawn, instantly identifiable signs endlessly repeated) and evident ideological purpose (to keep/put out-groups in their place) for a simplicity of connotation and actual ideological effect ... [but] a stereotype can be complex, varied, intense and contradictory, an image of otherness in which it is still possible to find oneself. (1993: 74)

What is key here is *how* the stereotype is offered to us, what *kind* of representation we are viewing and what *kinds of stories* they are telling.

Often, homosexuality is represented in opposition to traditional normative heterosexuality. As well as being represented as gender transitive, gay men have also been represented as lecherous and dangerously predatory. One of the earliest public information films about homosexuality was entitled *Boys Beware* (prod. Sid Davis: 1961) and represented the 'homosexual' as a monster, preying on unsuspecting young boys in the hope of 'seducing' them into 'sordid' activity. The film is notable for the way it conflates homosexuality with child molestation (the term paedophilia would be used today, but wasn't in wide currency in the 1960s) and suggests that the homosexual is a vampire-like creature lurking in the shadows ready to pounce on an unsuspecting victim. *Boys Beware* was a public information film, but in fiction too there has tended to be a focus on the 'problem' of homosexuality. In representations, heterosexuality usually leads to close and satisfying coupledom; homosexuality, by contrast, is often represented in characters who are unable to secure any sort of long-lasting, meaningful relationship.

We can't offer a comprehensive history of gay and lesbian representation here but from the early 1980s, media representations of homosexuality began to change. Soap operas, dramas and sitcoms featured 'straight-acting' gays who were often represented in monogamous relationships. A common storyline in soap operas was the 'coming-out narrative' in which a previously straight-identified character discovered that he had feelings for another male character and then went through the heart-wrenching ordeal of 'coming out' (see Allen, 1995). The newly emerged gay character would experience a few episodes of loneliness before meeting the 'man of his dreams' and moving into a marriage-like relationship. As Simon Watney comments, in these representations, a man loses a wife to become some other guy's wife (1982). Most importantly, these representations were often sanitized and de-sexualized. The so-called relationship was presented as little more than a flatmate relationship and, until very recently, expressions of sexual interest – even actions as simple as two men holding hands – were not represented. Too often, characters have been gay 'in name only'. The narrative might assert that a character is gay but nothing in his actions or lifestyle suggested this meant anything more than dressing well or living stylishly.

The 1990s saw something of a change in media representations of gay men, most controversially with the British drama series *Queer as Folk* (Channel 4: 1999–2000). This groundbreaking drama has been the subject of much academic analysis (see Davis, 2007; Munt, 2000; Thornham and Purvis, 2005), not least because of its explicit detailing of sexual activity from the very first episode. In an unforgettable opening sequence, *Queer as Folk* showed Stuart Jones, a 30-year-old, middle-class gay man, 'pick up' the 15-year-old schoolboy Nathan, take him home and introduce him to assorted sex acts. In many ways this episode was true to the political nature of queer – particularly in its focus on sexual acts (such as rimming and anal sex) which are considered taboo by many, and thus not normally portrayed in mainstream media. The programme showed characters flaunting their sexual interests and rejecting any idea of behaving 'acceptably', the character of Stuart, in particular, refusing to 'behave himself' in order to be 'tolerated', and clearly rejecting any idea of assimilation. *Queer as Folk* was remarkable in its explicitness (although no subsequent episode would be as explicit as the first). It pushed the boundary of acceptable representation further than it ever had been. *Queer as Folk* is important, not just as a TV series with gay characters, but because it was incredibly popular across the wide demographic of the 'quality television audience', indicating that when television production companies want to take risks there are significant audiences that will be receptive. Moreover, the series demonstrated that well-written and well-played gay characters can carry a drama.

The 1990s also saw the creation of the first 'gay' sitcom: *Will and Grace*. Notwithstanding *Ellen* (ABC, 1994–98) (see Chapter 5), this sitcom was the first to feature a gay-identified lead character, Will Truman. Will is a middle-class, good-looking, straight-acting Manhattan lawyer. The sitcom focuses on the relationship he has with his straight, female flatmate Grace Adler, a beautiful, middle-class interior designer. The other two characters in the show are

Jack McFarland, Will's best friend – an effeminate, unemployed actor – and Karen Walker – a spoiled socialite who dabbles with the novelty of doing a day's work as Grace's personal assistant. Inevitably, *Will and Grace* has been the subject of considerable academic debate (Battles and Hilton-Morrow, 2002; Castiglia and Reed, 2004; Keller, 2002; Mitchell, 2005; Quimby, 2005; Shugart, 2003). *Will and Grace* is a complicated show and critics are divided in their interpretations of it, some reading it as very conservative while others see something transgressive and queer in the show. Such dispute demonstrates that popular television, in order *to be* popular, must appeal to a wide variety of audiences and that we need to be aware of the ways in which those audiences may have very different kinds of response depending upon a variety of factors; as audience studies have shown (Briggs, 2009; Wood, 2009), representations are rarely to be understood in one way only. 'Ordinary' viewers debate and dispute television all the time, arguing whether a character ought to behave the way they have or whether a show is funny or dull, and much more besides. In the following discussion of *Will and Grace* we are not offering a definitive exposition of what the series *means*; instead we offer some ways of thinking about the kind of representation it is.

Many critics have noted that the representation of Will Truman (he is a 'true man', get it?) conforms to assimilationist gay politics that seeks enfranchisement and acceptance by arguing that homosexuals differ from heterosexuals *only* in their sexual object choice. Will is white, upper-middle class, good-looking, responsible, career-orientated, interested in building a monogamous relationship with the right guy and, most importantly, straight-acting. Will's 'straight-acting-ness' is emphasized by his juxtaposition with the queeny Jack McFarland who is not only flamboyantly effeminate but also unemployed and promiscuous. Indeed it is possible to read Jack's effeminacy as a metonym for all the other 'undesirable' attributes of this character, especially his joblessness and his promiscuity. Yet even a cursory review of internet message boards where fans discuss the show will reveal that many viewers find Will to be extremely bland and uninteresting while Jack is the character who not only gets the most humorous lines in the show but also gets into the most exciting narrative situations. Indeed Castiglia and Reed point out that Will's relationship to metropolitan gay culture is often represented as one of intense pain and difficulty so that Will always 'seems oddly and unhappily isolated, locked into a heterosexual-seeming relationship with Grace' (2004: 163–4). Jack, by contrast, despite failing to achieve professional success, always seems happier and more comfortable in metropolitan gay culture, especially revelling in its subcultural style codes and promiscuity. Therefore, although Will's character seems a *positive* representation in that he has the success and good looks, in the context of the show, this often appears as dull and uninteresting compared to the queer dynamism expressed by Jack.

Related to this is the relationship between Will and his straight female flatmate Grace. Remarkable as it may seem, much of the series' imagery represents Will and Grace as a heterosexual couple. Battles and Hilton-Morrow point out that 'Grace is clearly being positioned as Will's wife' throughout the sitcom and that 'they routinely perform roles associated with couples, particularly married heterosexual partners' (2002: 93). There are two ways of interpreting this representational strategy. One way is to read it simply as the traditional family narrative of situation comedy. Most sitcoms revolve around the personal tensions of a family or family-like unit and *Will and Grace* can be read as simply conforming to this narrative strategy and representing an alternative family unit. Indeed, as Battles and Hilton-Morrow argue, it is even possible to read Jack and Karen as occupying the role of children within the family narrative: 'Jack and Karen are continually infantilized, occupying the slot of children to Will and Grace's narrative slots as parents' (2002: 97). One of the popular situational jokes in *Will and Grace* is to represent the quartet in the car together with Will and Grace sitting in the front like mummy and daddy while the 'children' sit in the back. These naughty children inevitably misbehave so that Grace has to turn round and chastise them with the familiar parental threat that if they cannot behave they will turn the car round and go straight home.

This positioning of Will and Grace as parents to the naughty children Jack and Karen may be more than simple adherence to situation comedy formulae. As various critics have argued, this representation of Will and Grace as couple removes the difficulty of representing same-sex sexual activity on the screen. Indeed, throughout the series Will is rarely seen with a man and, when he is, this relationship looks to be little more than a close friendship. More touching, kissing, nuzzling and holding goes on between Will and Grace than ever occurs between Will and another man. Karen Quimby points out that this is important for enabling *disavowal* of the sexy-ness of sexuality, that is the 'psychic mechanism routinely invoked in response to gay people and gay culture' (2005: 717). Quimby argues that this positioning of Will and Grace as a couple allows viewers to acknowledge Will's gayness (the narrative asserts that Will is a proud, gay man) but also to 'disavow this difference through the heterosexual fantasy that visualizes Will and Grace's eventual coupling' (ibid.). In other words, Will is gay in name only and so 'gayness' can be acknowledged but absolved of its discomforting, material issues, especially the question of what he does in bed. Indeed, many gay viewers find Will's performances unbelievable for a metropolitan gay man. Even basic details such as gay fashion and style are often erased from his performances so that he 'looks' to all intents and purposes like a straight heterosexual man. In one episode Will is shown going to a gay club while attired in polo shirt and chinos. In an episode of *Sex and the City* ('Pick-a-Little, Talk-a-Little', S.6, ep.4) Carrie criticizes her boyfriend-of-the-moment Berger for a sartorial inaccuracy where his novel's Manhattan heroine wears an outdated hair accessory known as a 'scrunchy', on the grounds that no fashionable New York woman would be seen dead in a scrunchy. Similarly, many gay viewers find it equally incredible that a so-called Manhattan gay man would wear a polo shirt for an evening of clubbing.

Will's 'straightness' has also been read as a representational strategy, which critics have labelled 'gay male privilege' (Shugart, 2003). Shugart argues that by representing a gay man as having unlimited access to a straight female (many episodes show Will hauling Grace around like a doll, holding and touching her in ways which would not be appropriate for a non-sexually intimate couple) a heterosexual male fantasy is affirmed for straight viewers. Shugart suggests that

> due to their homosexuality, they (gay men) can touch women with impunity in inappropriate ways and inappropriate contexts – this may entail overt, very intimate sexual touches, public contexts, or access to women who would conventionally be construed as sexually unavailable. This consistent pattern cultivates a perception of gay male sexuality as an extension of heterosexual male privilege; the access and license portrayed in these representations is tantamount to a degree of sexual entitlement that is, notably, no longer readily available to heterosexual men. (2003: 83)

For Shugart, *Will and Grace* represents a return to a 'pre-feminist' type relationship in which women were portrayed as needy and overly dependent on their male partner. Indeed Grace is often represented as utterly incompetent and very dependent upon Will for everything. On most occasions it is Will who picks up the bills, Will who guides Grace in making difficult decisions and Will who organizes all the activities the pair engage in. By cloaking this relationship in the veil of 'gay man/straight woman' the sitcom offers a pre-feminist relationship which may well, as Shugart argues, be a representation of 'heterosexual male privilege' that heterosexual men are no longer able to access.

Connected to this is the open articulation of homophobia (or at least homophobic taunts) in the sitcom. Many of the characters make jokes about gay culture which, if not coming from the mouth of a gay man or a gay-friendly woman, would be deemed homophobic. Jack, for example, continually ridicules lesbian culture, especially lesbian style. In one episode ('Jingle Balls', S.4, ep.12: 2001) Karen accuses Jack of thinking 'everything's gay'. He replies, 'I once saw this thing on lesbian seagulls on *Animal Planet*', [and pointing to his hair] 'Yeah, they had short feathers here, and then real long feathers back here'. The seagulls were 'obviously' lesbian because their feathers resembled a hairstyle known as 'the mullet' – a popular stereotype of lesbian iconography perhaps only surpassed in notoriety by the dungarees. This bitchy remark against lesbian style would probably, if articulated by a non-gay identified person, be regarded as offensive. Other potentially lesbian-phobic remarks include references to lesbians' supposed aggressive tendencies (Jack warns a male friend that 'they bite'), lesbian shoe wear (the 'walking sandals') and lesbian body odour problems. Danielle Mitchell therefore argues that many of these jokes enable 'guilt-free expressions of homophobia because they are expressed through the mouths of gay figures' (2005: 1062). Similarly when Will makes fun of Jack's effeminacy and 'flaming queen-ness' (in one episode he even laments that Jack is 'such a fag') how is this different from early representations of sissies other than the fact that the enunciator of the taunt is now gay-identified? We could see these as examples of 'reverse discourse' (as we discussed in Chapters 1 and 3) but given all of these factors it is hardly surprising that a number of critics read *Will and Grace* as a highly conservative show which not only reinforces negative images of homosexuality but revises archaic, pre-feminist gender politics.

While *Will and Grace* can be read as a very unthreatening show, complicit in hegemonic gender and sexual politics, and attempting to elide gay sexuality from the narrative so that its lead character is gay 'in name only', it can also be read as particularly transgressive, or queer. In contrast to the previous interpretations, other critics read the relationship between Will and Grace as a queer challenge to ideas of normative heterosexuality. The relationship between Will and Grace is essentially a 'fag-hag' relationship. The 'fag-hag' refers to a single straight woman (the 'hag') who has a close personal friendship with her gay male friend (the 'fag'). Although recently reclaimed by some critics (Thompson, 2004), the term is derogatory to both the woman – presumably so unattractive that she can't find a relationship with a heterosexual man (hence the 'hag') – and the gay man (a 'fag') who is unable to find a boyfriend and so must make do with the affections of a frustrated woman. In short, both fags and hags were thought to be pitiful, pathetic creatures. However, recent representations have revised this image by representing attractive gay men and straight women who have no problem securing sexual partners of their choice but voluntarily choose to spend time with each other because this relationship brings happiness and true companionship.

In the critically acclaimed film *My Best Friend's Wedding* (dir. P.J. Hogan: 1997), central to the story is the 'fag-hag' relationship, and in particular the 'safe eroticism' (Dreisinger, 2000) between Jules (Julia Roberts) and her gay best friend George (Rupert Everett). As Susan Bordo (1999) points out, more touching and nuzzling takes place between Jules and George during the film than ever takes place between Jules and her male love interest. In the final sequence Jules, having finally lost the man she had been pursuing, dances with George, laughing and smiling. Far from being two unattractive, pitiful people stuck together because they cannot find anything else, the narrative affirms the joy and pleasure offered by their emotionally rich relationship. Bordo argues convincingly that *My Best Friend's Wedding* is a return to the screwball comedy formula, especially the type of film for which the actor Cary Grant became famous. As Bordo points out, 'sex was not the focus of the screwball comedy' (1999: 162); instead it was the pleasure of flirtations and fun between the central male and female characters. Given the increasing sexual frankness of contemporary popular representations, fictional flirtations between a straight man and a straight woman lead inevitably to sex. One way of recapturing the pleasure of the screwball comedy is to recast the Cary Grant character as a gay man. Arguably, *Will and Grace* offers a similar pleasure to *My Best Friend's Wedding*, and Quimby suggests that what makes this sitcom so special is its portrayal of a 'queer love that exists outside that exclusive and exclusionary frame' (2005: 726) of normative heterosexuality. Will and Grace's queerly erotic relationship challenges society's very narrow prescripts of heterosexuality and homosexuality.

Indeed, Quimby argues that *Will and Grace*, far from being a conservative show, can, on occasions, be read as critiquing or satirizing normative heterosexuality. The spoiled socialite Karen Walker is the only married character in the show but constantly refers to her marriage to Stanley as a financial arrangement. Seemingly without any emotional attachment to her husband Stanley or her two step-children, Karen's life revolves around a diet of pills, alcohol and, most importantly, spending Stanley's vast wealth. Stanley never actually appears in the show and fulfils that narrative strategy of the 'off-screen freak' who becomes ever more revolting in descriptions by the on-screen characters (a similar technique is used to evoke the monstrous Maris in *Frasier* (Paramount: 1993–2004)). The obese, toupee-wearing, halitosis-afflicted, sexually insatiable Stanley appears increasingly gruesome in descriptions throughout the series, and Karen makes it clear that marriage, for her, has little or nothing to do with love or sexual desire, but is solely a means to access Stanley's wealth. This reduction of the ideal of normative heterosexuality to a form of financial exchange is an example of how *Will and Grace* may not be as conservative as it first appears, but challenges normative conventions.

Similarly, Karen Walker may be the 'queerest' character in the show. Not only does she have no sexual interest in her husband, Karen openly flirts with lesbianism. On various occasions it is suggested she has had female lovers: Martina Navratilova makes a guest appearance as a former lover in one flashback episode ('Lows in the Mid-Eighties', S.3, ep.8) and in another, Karen tells Deirdre, a lesbian character, 'Stay back, bulldozer, I'm engaged' to which Deirdre replies, 'You were last time, too!', implying Karen isn't always exclusive in her attentions ('East Side Story', S.6, ep.17). Karen also hints at relationships with Goldie Hawn and Candice Bergen, as well as kissing and touching Grace or Rosario whenever opportunities present themselves. These constant references to previous and future lesbian encounters, as well as intimations of a porn-star past, flirtations with BDSM and Karen's other 'unusual' sexual interests, give an indication that sexual desire is not as easily compartmentalized as mainstream culture might like to insist.

In conclusion, *Will and Grace* is noteworthy as the first successful sitcom with a gay-identified lead character and for its address of gay culture. Whatever view we take, it is clear that it is difficult to judge any text as either wholly positive or negative. As the following chapter will explain, the very fact that gay and lesbian characters are *present at all in popular culture* is progress.

Further Reading

Davis, G. and Needham, G. (2008) *Queer TV: Theories, Histories, Politics* (London: Routledge).

Dyer, R. (1993) *The Matter of Images* (London and New York: Routledge).

Keller, J.R. (2002) *Queer (Un)Friendly Film and Television* (Jefferson: McFarland and Company).

Representations of Lesbians on Television

Chapter 5

Case Study: *The L Word*

In this chapter we offer a brief cultural and historical overview of the representation of lesbians on television. The chapter begins by reflecting on recent television history before moving on to a detailed analysis of the groundbreaking series *Ellen* and *The L Word*. Both series were critically acclaimed but are also important landmarks in the politics of lesbian representation. This chapter refers to work within American and British cultural studies exploring the relationships between feminism and popular TV, and these series' representations of lesbians.

As we discussed earlier, a crucial point to bear in mind is that many television viewers may have little or no personal knowledge of lesbian women, only ever encountering them occasionally as re-presentations on screen. For most of the history of television, lesbian sexuality has remained firmly in the closet. However, it would be too simplistic to assert that lesbian sexuality has never appeared on television or that lesbian-coded characters have never popped up from time to time. Nor is it to say that audiences do not construct lesbian readings from texts, whatever the intention of the producers. As we saw in Chapter 4, texts can support various reading positions. Nevertheless, the relative absence of overtly lesbian-identified characters on television is indicative of the challenge that lesbian sexuality poses to the dominant discourses of heteronormativity we discussed in Chapters 1 and 3.

Statistical studies on lesbian and gay representations carried out by GLAAD (Gay, Lesbian Alliance Against Defamation) found that lesbian and gay TV representations amounted to less than 2% in US schedules in 2005/06 (available at the website GLAAD.org). The story is very similar for UK television. Even today, it would seem odd to see a same-sex couple feeding their children in a TV advertisement for breakfast cereal. (As recently as 2008, an advert for Deli Mayo featuring two men kissing (shown only in the UK) was pulled after the American Family Association put pressure on Heinz to withdraw it (Sweney, 2008).) GLAAD conclude that this absence is a misrepresentation of the real world, and of the audiences who watch television programmes.

Representation of gay men is rare, but GLAAD's statistics revealed that lesbian representation is even rarer; indeed, a quick glance through any television guide reveals an acute sense of ambivalence towards lesbian women. For example, while Graham Norton, Dale Winton and Paul O'Grady are all highly paid, openly gay male television presenters, there are no British lesbians with similar media visibility.

Useful though such statistics are, they cannot capture the quality or importance of representations when they do appear. For example, on both sides of the Atlantic, reality television genres have included lesbian women, but such programmes tend towards voyeurism and the exhibition of 'freakery' in their representations (Dovey, 2000). The on-camera displays of turbulent relationships between those who differ from the heterosexual norm is often a common theme in daytime chat shows, such as *The Jeremy Kyle Show* (ITV: 2005–) or *The Jerry Springer Show* (NBC: 1991–), and reality programmes such as *Big Brother* (Channel 4 [UK]: 2000) but these can hardly be claimed to be uniformly *positive* representations.

Of course, there have been some notable exceptions during the last few decades, including the British TV drama *Oranges are Not the Only Fruit* (BBC: 1990), an adaptation of the critically acclaimed literary work by Jeanette Winterson, which tells the story of a lesbian girl growing up in a repressed, religious community. *Tipping the Velvet* (2002) is another example of a BBC adaptation of a successful book. Based on Sarah Waters' period novel and set in Victorian London, the drama had an explicitly, even defiantly, lesbian narrative centred on the turbulent lives and loves of male impersonator music hall star Kitty Butler and her lover Nan Astley.

Despite the depressing figures for lesbian-centred drama, it is possible to construct a list of popular TV genres that have included supporting lesbian characters. For example, in *Friends* (Warner Bros: 1994–2004), the phenomenally successful US sitcom about a group of heterosexual twenty- to thirty-somethings, Ross's ex-wife, Carol, left him to live with her lover Susan. Although Carol only appears in fifteen episodes (out of 238), she is a character whose storyline weaves through every season – we see her bring up a child with Susan and eventually the two women marry, in an episode broadcast in 1996. Similarly, there have been a small number of regular lesbian characters in British and US TV soaps. *Brookside* (Channel 4: 1982–2003) character Beth Jordache (played by Anna Friel) is famous for British television's first lesbian kiss in 1995, and *Emmerdale*'s (ITV: 1972–) character Zoe Tate 'discovered' her lesbianism in 1993, becoming the first lesbian character on a UK soap. Welcome though these representations have been, the characters are often constructed as outsiders, lonely and isolated from lesbian groups, and their coming out is usually a long, painful process (although it should be acknowledged that this is one of the beauties of a soap – that a story can build over time, both creating dramatic tension and increasing audience empathy).

Nevertheless, as we discussed in Chapter 4 in relation to homosexuality, the painful coming-out narrative is a staple, in which a previously straight-identified character such as Zoe in *Emmerdale* realizes that she has sexual feelings for another female character and goes through a very painful process of coming out to the straight community in which she lives and socializes. The emphasis is on the difficulty of coming out, rather than on the positive aspects of the experience, for example discovering one's sexual interest and the possibility of those feelings being returned.

Eventually, in most cases, lesbian desire becomes a less important aspect of her identity as the character 'develops'. As Warn observes, 'Television has painted a lonely existence for lesbians – the handful of lesbian characters you do see only interact with straight characters, never with other lesbians (unless they're dating them)' (2006: 6). Further, unlike the stereotypical effeminate gay man who pops up in the narrative of many television shows as comic relief, the stereotypical lesbian is often a lonely, embittered spinster.

It is to US television that we must turn to see more innovative representations, although it is perhaps a measure of how small the victories have been that one series broadcast in 1997 still retains its stand-out status in the roll call of television depictions of lesbian women. In Season 4 of the sitcom *Ellen*, actor and writer Ellen DeGeneres outed her fictional namesake to an audience of 36 million:

> Before *Ellen*, same-sexness was an interruptive, marginal force in the sitcom, its duration limited to one-off figures in 'very special' episodes and supporting characters. Ellen's coming out episode was momentous because it promised to make queer life something other than an interruptive force, something potentially assimilated into the repertoire of romantic and personal situations replayed weekly on primetime sitcom. (McCarthy, 2003: 93)

The series won an Emmy award and provoked a huge response from the public but, sadly, this success was not to last. ABC cancelled *Ellen* after one further season, due, at least in part, to falling viewing figures. However, as Huff argues, *Ellen*'s ultimate 'failure' was that it 'became a programme about a character who was gay every single week and that was too much for people' (Huff, cited in McCarthy, 2003: 91).

After the demise of *Ellen*, television lesbians returned to the closet. Despite a rise in new, women-centred genres both in the UK with *Mistresses* (BBC: 2008–10) and in the US with *Sex and the City* and *Desperate Housewives* (ABC: 2004–12), these either marginalized lesbian characters as thematic digressions or simply avoided gay-centred narratives altogether. Ironically, after *Ellen*, television production seemed to focus on gay men. Indeed, journalist Christine Champagne argues that *Ellen*'s 'groundbreaking move ultimately paved the way for shows like *Will and Grace* and *Queer as Folk* focusing on men's lives, with lesbians playing supporting roles' (2004). *Queer as Folk* first arrived on British television in 1999, and the US channel Showtime produced an American version set in Pittsburgh. But even though *Queer as Folk* included a lesbian couple to enable a storyline centred on Stuart, the main character, becoming a father, critics argued the lesbian characters were one-dimensional and focused on motherhood, rather than lesbian desire or romance.

At the point when *Queer as Folk* was enjoying high viewing figures in the US, Ilene Chaiken, an executive at Aaron Spelling Production, pitched her idea to the network Showtime for a long-running series about a group of lesbians. The success of *Queer as Folk* helped persuade Showtime that a series centred on lesbians could win similar viewing figures. Chaiken, herself a lesbian, went on to create, write and produce the hit show *The L Word*. Its success indicates that viewers are receptive to a show which explores the everyday lives and loves of women who desire women, but does lesbian visibility automatically result in positive perspectives?

The L Word first aired in America in January 2004. Its importance as a TV event lies in the fact that it is the first television series to be exclusively focused on a group of lesbian characters and their relationships. As we said in the introduction to this part, in order to identify a character as lesbian, mainstream representations have drawn upon well-worn symbols of gender transitivity, in which lesbians are portrayed as butch dykes. *The L Word* attempted something different. Its characters are an ensemble of middle-class, beautiful women, belonging to a newer set of codings encapsulated by the term 'lipstick lesbian'. Despite the prevalence of the dungaree-wearing dyke stereotype, lesbian women come in all shapes and sizes, with many embracing the typical aspects of what is considered feminine: long hair, make-up, and clothes that show off their bodies. The term 'lipstick lesbian' came to the fore in the early 1990s when fashion magazines and advertising seemingly woke up to the 'discovery' that lesbian women could be as fashionable and sexy as their heterosexual sisters. These are the women who populate *The L Word*.

So who are the characters? Marina is owner of 'Planet', the coffee house where characters meet; Bette is an art curator; Dana a professional tennis player, Jenny a writer; Shane a top hairstylist and Alice a successful journalist. The main characters are all lesbian, with only a handful of heterosexual characters whose regular appearances serve narrative convenience rather than driving the storylines. For example, Tim is a neighbour of the central couple, Bette and Tina, but he functions as a foil for the storyline that involves his girlfriend, Jenny, who 'comes out' during the course of the first series.

Like other female ensemble texts (*Band of Gold* (ITV: 1995–97), *Mistresses*, *Sex and the City*), *The L Word* celebrates the value of all-female communities and female friendship, but similarly it is problematic in terms of its class signification (as we discuss in Chapter 6). For example, with its focus on successful careers, middle-class lifestyles and the opportunities these provide for shopping and wearing designer clothes, living in fabulous apartments, and eating in chic restaurants, *The L Word* suggests women are enjoying the 1970s feminist aims of equality – in fact, all the spoils of a lifestyle denied to most working-class women today.

Despite its expansion of lesbian iconography, many feminist critics and lesbian viewers were not entirely happy about *The L Word*'s exclusions, particularly the absence of 'butch' women on the show. Moreover, they feared that *The L Word*'s explicit sex scenes were, far from breaking taboos about lesbian desire, simply pandering to heterosexual males and their fantasies of 'girl-on-girl-action'. Indeed, a recent intertextual reference to the show illustrates this point when the character Gregory House from the US series *House* (Fox: 2004–12) said that he watched *The L Word* on mute. The criticism that the show is really *for* straight men draws on similar suspicions that have dogged representations of female same-sex desire for decades (in particular, criticisms of lesbian pornography which, it is argued, is easily co-opted for male pleasure).

Are these fair criticisms? The series' focus on a lesbian subculture that is the least threatening and safe for prime-time television is hardly a surprising feature when we consider the historical lack of mainstream media representations of lesbian sexuality. The continuation of a series depends upon not alarming television viewers, advertisers and sponsors. But even so, there is more to this representation than the fact that it is centred on lesbian characters. Leaving aside its sexual politics, *The L Word* is in step with wider cultural representations of women in US TV dramas such as *Sex and the City* that also emphasize the conventional aspects of femininity in their depiction of potentially threatening kinds of women. In other words, the series representation of beautiful 'power lesbians' is also in line with TV drama's preoccupation with career women with considerable disposable incomes such as in *Sex and the City* and *Mistresses*. Further, as in those examples, the aims of second-wave feminism (such as equal pay, equal legal rights and reproductive rights) look as though they have all been achieved in *The L Word*. At the same time, the series distances itself from the typical media image of the man-hating feminist lesbian.

As to the question of whether the programme privileges the male gaze, Sedgwick describes a scene from the show's first episode: 'the viewer watches two young women strip and plunge into a backyard pool, romping amorously in a scene that would not be out of place in soft-core girl-on-girl pornography aimed at heterosexual men or couples' (2006: xx). But this does not mean that *The L Word* necessarily panders to male voyeurism. The non-lesbian character watching the scene is another woman: 'The voyeuristic framing of the scene is even accentuated: we observe it mainly from the point of view of the fascinated woman next door as she crouches behind a fence' (ibid.). Thus female, heterosexual surveillance is introduced in the first episode of *The L Word* and is used throughout the series as a means to explore sexual desire and lesbian identity. The heterosexual woman, Jenny, who provides the viewers' point of view in this scene, becomes at first fascinated with her desirable neighbours and her feelings for them; and then, by the end of the series, comes to identify as a lesbian herself.

Through an analysis of Jenny's journey that culminates in her entry into the lesbian 'family', we can see the ways in which the series constructs sexuality as fluid rather than fixed. The narrative charts Jenny's construction of a lesbian identity as one of sexual *awakening* rather than a painful process. The characters use the phrase 'coming out' to mean 'coming in', to denote Jenny's entry into and visibility in the lesbian community.

At this point it is necessary to return to the key term in the title of this chapter – *representation*. Ultimately, representation is a human process that aims to create a convincing illusion of reality. Realist codes, including *mise-en-scène*, are the means by which programme-makers tap into our understandings of the world. *Mise-en-scène* is a film studies term which refers to everything a camera reveals in a scene. If we focus on the *mise-en-scène* of *The L Word*'s coffee house 'Planet', we would look to every detail that has gone into its construction: furniture, wall coverings, paintings and the colour of the walls. These seemingly petty details are important to our recognition of the kind of space 'Planet' is and the kinds of people who are likely to frequent it. Just as in our own lives we judge people (often unconsciously) by their style of dress or their possessions, so too in television representations we decode props and costumes recognizing that these are signifiers of characters' 'tastes' and social status (Bourdieu, 1986) and are thus intimately related to class, sexual orientation, age and ethnicity. Set design isn't simply a matter of providing an attractive backdrop; it is important to the realism of a representation. Imagine, for example, the effect it would have on our impressions of the characters and the world they inhabit to exchange the modern, chrome tables and chairs of 'Planet' for the upholstered benches and wooden tables found in the 'Rover's Return' in *Coronation Street* (ITV: 1960–).

Different genres use different realist codes depending on what we know about the world outside the text, or *cultural* codes, and what we expect from a work of fiction belonging to a particular genre, or *fictional* codes. Cultural and fictional codes are both constructs, and any appearance of naturalness stems from a text's relationship to the codes – the language – of television. 'Verisimilitude' is a term used in film and cultural studies to describe the extent to which a text generates credibility or the appearance of being real. Steve Neale (2003) distinguishes between fictional and cultural verisimilitude. For example, *The L Word* draws heavily on fictional verisimilitude. This means that the show refers to what we know about the conventions or rules of a fictional world, and so we understand what happens in the narrative as belonging to the genre of the female ensemble drama. This allows the programme the freedom to transgress the boundaries of cultural realism and construct a world that is not necessarily 'authentic'.

Nevertheless, *The L Word* is also constrained by the conventions of cultural verisimilitude – what we know and understand from discourses circulating around and outside the text (from other cultural texts such as reality programmes, documentary, newspapers and so on) – to make the day-to-day lives of this community of lesbians appear like real-world experiences and relationships. As audiences, we have to be convinced that, even though we know the community is not literally a real one (in that the characters are played by actors, the story is scripted, and the environments are 'sets'), in all other respects it seems as real as, say, the lesbian communities we may encounter in our own lives or via other representations. The dilemmas, difficulties and situations the characters face should also bear resemblance to those that occur in the real world.

So what are the defining features of *The L Word*? The first important characteristic is the fact that the characters do not operate in the realm of pretence or 'the closet'; rather, the women are at ease with their sexuality, living openly gay lives in and out of the workplace. This is not a show focused on the trials and tribulations of coming out. While gay culture has traditionally been represented as operating outside heteronormativity (gay male characters often reject monogamy and romance), lesbians are more likely to be represented as conforming to the stereotypical heterosexual woman's aim of finding 'true' love. So it is not that surprising that the first series of *The L Word* placed the romantic ideal of finding Ms Right and a satisfying monogamous relationship centre-stage. However, rather than this being reproduced as the show's message, the search for normative romantic love is questioned. For example, within the lesbian community, Bette and Tina enjoy the prestigious parent-figure roles because they represent the archetypal 'married' couple. But, even if the other characters envy their apparent stability and commitment to one another, Bette and Tina's relationship is not depicted as ideal or problem-free.

While other characters remain unaware, viewers were alerted, in the first episode, to the cracks in the 'marriage' when Bette arrives late for a meeting with Tina and their relationship counsellor. In the scene, Bette is introduced as the breadwinner (a traditionally 'male' role) whilst Tina is the full-time, stay-at-home 'wife', and we learn that Bette is so distracted by career ambitions that she is oblivious to Tina's emotional needs. Bette, bored with her stay-at-home, asexual partner who talks only about pregnancy, enters into a passionate adulterous relationship with a female colleague. Thus Bette and Tina's relationship replicates the power relations and division of labour in more traditional, heterosexual marriages but in its variation of the traditional dyad – male/female to female/female – the narrative opens up a wider commentary on power and gender politics. The show critiques the institution of *marriage* by exposing the ways in which it is tied up in restrictive societal and economic structures, demonstrating that marital infidelity is intimately related to social roles rather than essential male/female characteristics. *The L Word* explores the potential for gay 'marriage' to be just as constraining and repressive as heterosexual marriage.

Another key element of the series is its setting within a community where lesbian residents have their own public space, 'Planet', seemingly separate from heterosexual meeting places. This West Hollywood setting has been the focus of considerable critical attention. Critiques of female-centred fictions have noted that such narratives are 'generally located within an easily identified material world, both in terms of its consumer landscape and of its social and physical geography' (Knowles, 2004: 38). 'Chicklit' fictions, as they are often referred to, are almost always set in capital cities such as London or New York although the heroines are rarely born or brought up in those places. Little information (by way of dialogue or storylines) is given about the characters' backgrounds, and few clues are given regarding their journey to the city. We know little more about the character Carrie Bradshaw in *Sex and the City* and her friends' histories or families at the end of the final series than we do in the first. The only explanation for their motivations in moving to the city is Carrie's oft-repeated claim that New York is the best place in the world to be single and have sex. Similarly, in *The L Word* it is clear that West Hollywood represents an escape from small-town prejudices and family – and viewers will be aware that Los Angeles is widely regarded as a welcoming and established gay environment. However, charges have been made that *The L Word* offers an entirely fictionalized representation of the 'gay city' and that this lesbian-friendly characterization of West Hollywood is based upon 'real and imagined physical attributes with social and personal characteristics of gay *men*' (Forest, 1995: 133). As Forest points out:

> The geographies of gay men in West Hollywood certainly differ from the geographies of West Hollywood lesbians. The highly visible public expression of gay men in West Hollywood in contrast to lesbians is a case in point. Authors of some studies argue that lesbians are less visible because they have a relatively private orientation. More compelling are studies that have focused on the fact that lesbians, like women in general, have less access to capital, earn lower incomes, and have a higher risk of violence in public places. (ibid.)

Thus *The L Word* offers a fantasy environment that bears no relation to most women's (whether gay or straight) experiences of the city. Hankin (2002) has argued that popular representations of the lesbian bar can work to *contain* rather than expand lesbian spatial liberation. *The L Word*'s lesbian community, and hence its visibility, is centred on the chic coffee house that converts into a nightclub in the evenings. However, in West Hollywood itself, although there are certain bars with 'lesbian-friendly' reputations, they are usually rented for one evening a week or, very occasionally, leased for longer periods of time. Truly lesbian-friendly or lesbian-only spaces are few-and-far-between. As Retter argues, 'lesbian "territorialisation" was and continues to be significantly different from that of gay men . . . queer space and territory is profoundly male-orientated' (1997: 326).

One viewer's response describes her frustration when she failed to find 'Planet', or any place like it, in the real West Hollywood: 'West Hollywood is still first and foremost a boy's town, and no matter how much I worked the lesbian grapevine, I could not conjure a coffeehouse as central and communal as The Planet. What can I say? Television lies' (Krochmal, 2005). This viewer's irritation lies in her recognition of the gap between the 'inauthentic', idealized represented space in *The L Word* and the spaces within the 'real' West Hollywood.

Through generic, rather than cultural, verisimilitude *The L Word* resists pressure to be 'authentic' but is it misguided to uphold the importance of authenticity and social realism at a time when the media are only just beginning to address lesbian identity? Does it matter that a viewer cannot find the 'real-world' 'Planet'? As Kelly Hankin has argued in her exploration of the representations of lesbian bars, other commonly referenced spaces and characters, such as those in *Sex and the City*, are examined via aesthetic and emotional criteria rather than social realism. More importantly, she says, compulsion to authenticate can function voyeuristically and often has a homophobic imperative – as documentary evidence of the 'sordid' lifestyle of a subculture. She gives the example of the film *The Killing of Sister George* (1966) which was shot in a studio, but when a lesbian bar scene was required the director, Robert Aldrich, wanted an 'authentic' place. With this in mind, he chose a decrepit, seedy backroom, providing viewers with a voyeuristic look at 'others', thereby also confirming the idea that sexual minorities only ever congregate in 'nasty' spaces.

Yet, as feminists have argued for decades, space is fundamental to any consideration of women's relationships, and access to power and community. When the viewer complains that she cannot find 'Planet', this is surely not just about finding a nice place to have a coffee. We could link this to Virginia Woolf's (1929) plea that women need their own spaces in order to realize their potential – that space enables creativity, confirms belonging and, crucially, allows mobility (Woolf, 1984). The space does not have to be literal (although that surely helps) and in that sense we think it is worth engaging further with this idea of *The L Word*'s 'inauthentic' geographies, and to do so via the work of Ien Ang (1985). In her seminal work on audiences' relationships with the TV series *Dallas* (CBS: 1978–91) Ang is very critical of empiricist realism or consideration of a text in terms of whether or not it is an authentic reflection of the wider social world. For Ang, soap opera texts are best understood via what she terms 'emotional realism'. Drawing on the work of Roland Barthes (1968), Ang argues that emotional realism operates at the level of connotation:

> It is striking; the same things, people, relations and situations which are regarded at the denotative level as unrealistic, and unreal, are at the

connotative level apparently not seen as unreal at all, but in fact as 'recognisable'. Clearly, in the connotative reading process the denotative level of the text is put in brackets. (Ang, 1985: 42)

What's important to recognize here, and referring back to the viewer who couldn't find 'Planet', are the ways in which viewers find, in certain dramas, a sense of possibilities – emotional, physical, imaginative – which they want to embrace. The viewer who was disappointed in not finding 'Planet' complained that television lies, but is it not precisely the attractiveness, the hope, the possibilities of its representations of a real and tangible space for her within a community of other like-minded women that surely constitutes her disappointment? The point is not that she was fooled into thinking that 'Planet' *really* exists, but that in the real world where sexuality is lived out, having space and community and being visible really matter (see discussion of sexual citizenship in our main introduction). The space to be in a community of lesbian women – having fun, having life-dramas, experiencing oneself as safe, secure and welcomed – *is* important, and this is why it matters that there are representations of sexual minorities. Being able to move around the city means you belong. Being visible in ways that resonate with your own experiences matters enormously, and that's why these are not just representations, they are symbolic. If, as we discussed in Chapter 3, 'the closet' symbolized the requirement to keep one's sexuality secret, then 'Planet' could symbolize a new-found freedom to be out and proud.

Thus, many lesbian cultural critics have been enthusiastic about *The L Word* and the ways in which it works to reveal the lives of its characters without judging or punishing them. Dolan writes:

> How could I not find myself cathecting with stories whose narrative arcs take interesting, funny, graceful leaps of faith straight into the messy center of lesbian relationships? The show communicates something of what it means to have a sustaining kinship network separate from families of origin that winds into and out of sexual and emotional attachments not necessarily defined by domesticity ... the friendships among these women sustain them through their estrangements with others who can never quite claim them. ... Their birth families judge them, mooch from them, or avoid them, but their slights prove incidental to the characters. They gather in public places ... to define and debate their lives. The show represents lesbians forming each other through their own interactions, looking out at the rest of the world through the support of their own circle of influence and understanding. (2005)

In ways comparable to *Friends*, the series constructs its ensemble of characters as individuals with different personalities who are committed to their 'family'. As Jennifer Vanesco puts it in her article 'The Good Word about *The L Word*':

The best thing about *The L Word* is that there are enough lesbians on the show to help straight people see that we're individuals. And to remind ourselves that even though we may have many things in common we should not stuff ourselves into stereotypical boxes because we're not actually all the same. After all, there are Shane girls and there are Mariana girls. (2004)

The viewer of *The L Word* may not find 'Planet' in the streets of West Hollywood or belong to a community of beautiful, affluent lesbians, but other essential elements – such as emotional ties, desire and sexuality – give it an affective truth.

Further Reading

Akass, K. and McCabe, J. (eds) (2006) *Reading the L Word: Outing Contemporary Television* (New York and London: I.B.Tauris).

Hankin, K. (2002) *The Girls in the Back Room: Looking at the Lesbian Bar* (Minneapolis: University of Minnesota Press).

Ingram, G.B., Bouthillette, A. and Retter, Y. (eds) (1997) *Queers in Space: Communities, Public Places, Sites of Resistance* (Washington: Bay Press).

Wilton, T. (ed.) (1995) *Immortal Invisible: Lesbians and the Moving Image* (London: Routledge).

Representations of Heterosexuality 1

Case Study: *Sex and the City*

Chapter 6

Thinking about 'heterosexuality' can be difficult. It is hard to analyse something that is found everywhere and forms the very fabric of contemporary Western culture. As Monique Wittig famously stated, 'to live in society *is* to live in heterosexuality' (1992: 40). Indeed, heterosexually identified people have the luxury of not even having to consider 'heterosexuality' as an identity at all, in much the same way that white people have had the privilege (until recently) of not having to consider themselves as raced. It has only been since the rise of queer theory that heterosexuality has been considered as merely one form of sexual identity, from a myriad of other possibilities, rather than the norm or the definitive.

Although heterosexuality is the dominant mode of sexuality, Western culture attempts to regiment this sexuality into a particular form termed 'heteronormativity', which can be understood as a monogamous relationship that produces children. As Michael Warner summarizes, 'Western political thought has taken the heterosexual couple to represent the principle of social union itself' (1993: xxi).

As students of media and popular culture, it is important to note that most (if not nearly all) media representations depict heteronormative relationships. As Susan Hayward noted, 'mainstream Hollywood cinema's great subject is not sexual identity but heterosexuality and more precisely the family' (2006: 129). Indeed, as the introduction to this part has already pointed out, the idea of the 'family' (i.e. the goal of heteronormativity) is found in most mainstream representations, although not necessarily presented as problem-free. Most romantic comedies are structured around the formula boy meets girl, boy falls in love with girl, boy loses girl but then finds her again at the end. This happy-ever-after resolution suggests that the couple will settle into a monogamous relationship and produce children. Variations on this heterosexual life-script are usually represented as a source of ridicule, danger or even horror. Promiscuity, for example, is rarely validated in media representations. Having multiple sexual partners, rather than committing to one person, is shown to lead to general unhappiness or a lack of fulfilment.

Media's condemnation of promiscuity, however, has not been the same for both sexes. While sexually promiscuous women are usually identified as depraved or disturbed and labelled 'nymphomaniacs', promiscuous men have always received less negative attention. Indeed, many representations even exalted the sexually promiscuous heterosexual male (such as the fictional character Casanova whose name has acquired adjectival properties in much the same way as Dickens' Scrooge). As we saw in Chapter 1, this concern with regimenting heterosexuality into appropriate expressions (i.e. Church-sanctioned monogamy) was a tool in engineering public control in the newly formed industrial urban centres. One of the targets for control was female sexuality. As such there has always been a huge distinction between the regimentation of female and male heterosexuality. While the Casanova type is a romanticized figure whose unbridled passions are exciting and decadent, the promiscuous female is a monster to be tamed and controlled.

Even so, the celibate, single female is also an object of pity or derision – often viewed as a pathetic creature unable to attain or maintain a relationship with a man. The very successful film *Bridget Jones's Diary* details how this control of female sexuality into acceptable life-scripts is still very much an issue in contemporary culture. Bridget Jones is a thirty-something, single, heterosexual woman living in contemporary London. Although shown surrounded by supportive friends and living in her own flat (by central London standards that is certainly quite a privilege), Bridget is frightened that she'll never find a man. The film contains many humorous sequences providing their own critique of contemporary culture's obsession with regimenting female sexuality. In one sequence, Bridget (working as a television reporter) has just viewed a video clip of herself sliding down a fire-station pole, and the camera, positioned at ground level, gives an unflattering view of her voluminous backside. After various rewinds and replays of the videotape Bridget decides, with a sigh of despair, that her backside is comparable to the size of Brazil and she is a national laughing stock. Indeed, being a 'laughing stock' for this one action can be read as a metonym for how Bridget feels for being a thirty-something single woman in contemporary culture. The very next sequence further emphasizes her status as 'laughing stock': attending a dinner party, Bridget finds it is populated by, as she terms it, 'smug marrieds'. As the only single person there, a 'special' seat has been reserved for her at the end of the table – so she won't disrupt the sequence of couples positioned around the dinner table. The camera offers Bridget's point of view as she sees all the couples staring at her like a firing squad. Her fellow diners banter about poor Bridget and her singledom, and one character asks why there are so many single, thirty-something women. Bridget tries to deflect his rude question with a joke that perhaps underneath their clothes all single women are covered in scales. Nobody laughs. Bridget's joke is a little too close to the truth that contemporary culture still views these women as freakish in some way. The idea that women could be happy outside a heteronormative relationship is rarely seen in popular representations. Normative heterosexuality is always represented as monogamy and one tool which engineers this monogamy is the regimentation and policing of female (hetero)sexuality.

One of the few shows to 'continually test ... and question ... what constitutes heteronormativity' (Jermyn, 2009: 25) has been the award-winning HBO dramedy (drama-comedy) *Sex and the City* (*SATC*). Loosely based on the Candace Bushnell novella (1997) of the same name, *Sex and the City* examines the sexual relationships of four heterosexual, upper-middle class, white, Manhattan-based women. The characters are Carrie Bradshaw, a newspaper columnist and character narrator of the show; Miranda Hobbs, a corporate lawyer; Charlotte York, who runs an art gallery, and Samantha Jones, a successful PR agent. The series has received a considerable amount of affectionate academic attention, as many critics have found the show a goldmine for debate about sexuality and the gender politics of representation. Like many other HBO dramas, *SATC* can be viewed as an example of 'quality' television drama – its high-budget production values, beautifully scripted episodes and exquisitely shot sequences can be labelled 'cinematic television'. These shows are not studio-bound, and draw upon the writing and directorial talents of people more often associated with film than with television.

Sex and the City has also been praised for offering alternative viewing pleasures beyond narrative and character. For example, the clothes worn in the show undoubtedly give much pleasure to viewers and, as some critics have argued, 'fashion' may be read as the fifth character in the show (Bruzzi and Church Gibson, 2004). This was particularly evident in the recent film *Sex and the City: The Movie* (dir. Michael Patrick King: 2008) which, aiming for a '15' rather than '18' certificate, chose to tone down its sexual scenes, compensating by revelling in the display of sumptuous fashion. Indeed, in a narrative style similar to a Busby Berkeley musical, the display of clothes acted as 'show stoppers' – occasions when the narrative was temporarily suspended so that viewers could fully delight in the spectacle of gorgeous dresses.

Although glamour and style and their attendant pleasures could be found in many high-gloss American soap operas (the ABC super-soap *Dynasty* (1981–89) would be the prime example), *Sex and the City* offers a more detailed interrogation of fashion. *Dynasty*, for example, was dominated by one unique 'look': all the clothes were designed by Nolan Miller, famous for his wrap-around dresses which emphasized a woman's curves. In contrast, costume manager Patricia Field successfully turned *SATC* into television's 'hottest catwalk' by giving its four leading ladies a variety of fashions to display and play with. Moreover, *Sex and the City*'s costuming offers its own investigation of *haute couture* through Carrie Bradshaw's innovative and often quite controversial fashion deconstructions.

As Bruzzi and Church Gibson suggest, Carrie has two unique strategies for creating her distinctive look: an aggressive mixing of designer clothes with vintage items to deliberately 'undercut a classic look' (2004: 118), and the combination of very expensive clothes accessorized with cheap and even slightly tawdry items. Carrie's trademark in this respect is a fabric corsage or a piece of trinket jewellery, such as her 'Carrie' nameplate necklace, which she always wears in a particularly ironic or playful fashion. Although Bruzzi and Church Gibson comment that *SATC* clothes are often 'spectacular', perhaps Carrie's deconstructive fashion ought to be read as a metaphor for what the show achieves as a whole. Carrie's playful experimentations with fashion are surely allied to the ways in which the show itself experiments with feminine heteronormativity. Carrie is, after all, a cultural critic whose newspaper column (extracts of which serve as the voice-over narration) is concerned with analysing and considering sexual acts and how these affect or even effect her sexual identity and those of her three friends. Just as Carrie's 'outrageous styling' (Jermyn, 2009: 31) tests the parameters of fashion, so her column interrogates how sexual identity is fashioned.

Almost every form of sexual act has been portrayed on *Sex and the City*. So it is hardly surprising that *SATC* is most noted for its explicit representations of the weird, wonderful and, most importantly, multiple permutations of sexual activity. In each episode, Carrie and her friends encounter some new form of fetishism or 'perversity', or an unusual innovation which many viewers might not even have heard of. For the first time, television viewers could watch and listen to explicit expositions of 'water-sports', cunnilingus, rimming, anal sex, digital anal sex, sex in public and tea-bagging (dangling testicles into a partner's mouth – hence the image of the 'tea-bag'). Interestingly, although some of these activities were presented for comedic effect, sometimes they were employed to actively interrogate how society attributes specific sexual identities to individual acts.

Heteronormativity does not merely refer to appropriate lifestyles premised on sexual attraction but to the appropriate performance of sexual desire through specific acts. In one episode, Miranda's current lover breaks up with her after she reminds him how much he likes her to insert a finger into his anus. Within heteronormative Western culture, a male body taking pleasure in anal penetration of any kind is understood as a homosexual preference. Even though prostate stimulation could heighten orgasm in all male bodies, whatever their orientation, the activity and enjoyment of anal/prostate manipulation has been deemed the preserve of gay men and to be avoided by 'straight' men. An episode of the adult cartoon *Family Guy* (Fox: 1999–) is a good example of this. Peter Griffin (the family guy of the title) is traumatized by a simple prostate examination conducted by his GP, and in his hysterical imagination Peter builds the medical prostate exam into the act of male rape (S.5, ep.1). In *SATC*, Miranda's boyfriend enjoyed but was not prepared to acknowledge, outside the bedroom, the pleasure gained from Miranda's fingers massaging his prostate as this act is, within contemporary culture, understood to indicate a specific sexual identity he would rather not claim.

This 'queering' of sexual identity – obliging viewers to question how culture attributes specific acts to particular identities – is perhaps most forcefully demonstrated by the most sexually innovative of all the characters, Samantha Jones. Samantha is remarkable in the way she often distils sexuality down to simplistic, physical elements. Samantha always refers to sex in the crudest of terms. She never uses the term 'making love' but prefers 'fuck' and, on one occasion when Charlotte is unable to bring herself to say the word 'ejaculate', Samantha interrupts with a host of vulgar synonyms – 'cum, spunk, shoot-his-wad' – much to Charlotte's displeasure. More importantly, for all of Samantha's relationships she always focuses on the specific, physical pleasures she gains from sexual intercourse – irrespective of whether these are wrought by a male or female partner. During Season 4, Samantha embarks on a sexual liaison with a woman, delighting in newfound pleasures with an emotional dimension she has rejected in her interactions with men. As we saw in Chapter 3, sexual attraction is – within the normative schema of hetero and homo – premised upon gender, in that we eroticize our partner's gender, their masculinity or femininity. However, as Sedgwick points out it would be just as possible to eroticize the sensations of an activity rather than the gender of the partner.

However, although the idea of sexuality premised on gender attraction is challenged by her focus on physical sensations, Samantha also challenges heteronormative life-scripts by rejecting traditional monogamy. In the girls' farewell performance in *Sex and the City: The Movie* Samantha decides to end her long-term relationship with model/actor Smith. According to heteronormative culture, being in a relationship with a gorgeous, male-model partner should make any woman happy, yet Samantha becomes depressed. In a complete reversal of the Bridget Jones model, Samantha comfort eats because she is in a relationship, not because she is single. When Samantha breaks up with Smith, she regains her happiness and, in the final sequence, she reclaims her identity as 'single, fifty and fabulous' and indeed, as Jermyn argues, the whole series can be read as a 'celebration of single womanhood' (2009: 95).

In its representation of a woman who is not only active and desiring but also an *older* woman, *SATC* offers a distinct challenge to traditional conceptions of femininity. Samantha repeatedly celebrates her 35th birthday, but viewers are in no doubt that she is a *little* older than that. Previous representations of the older and desiring woman showed her as a camp joke (a 'type' Raquel Welch has made her own) or else a predatory, vampire-like creature (Mrs Robinson from *The Graduate* (dir. Mike Nichols: 1967) is probably the best example, though we could also point to the monstrous Bubbles from *Little Britain* (BBC: 2003–06)). Either way, middle-aged women with sexual desires were represented as something terrifying or humorous, and always as a defining 'other' to the 'good' woman. Thus Samantha – as a single, desiring, older woman who is also a sympathetic character – is a landmark figure.

Samantha is also the character who most particularly embodies the pleasures of hedonistic eroticism – in *Sex and the City: The Movie* there are few sexual scenes and the majority are those in which Samantha watches her sexy neighbour as he cavorts on the beach, showers, and has sex with different women every night of the week. The sequences portray the thrills of seeing a desirable body for the first time, and the excitement of wondering whether or not he would be interested. Far from suggesting that the only true goal of meeting someone would be the relationship, these sequences glorify the exhilarating thrill of the chase. Indeed what Samantha finds intensely pleasurable about life is not the prospect of meeting her 'true love' but the excitement of encountering so many eligible, gorgeous men.

Given its focus on openly sexually desiring women, it is hardly surprising that much of the critical attention given to *Sex and the City* has focused on its (post)feminist politics (Brasfield, 2006; Cramer, 2007; Tropp, 2006). One of the most interesting of these discussions is Jane Gerhard's (2005) essay addressing the 'queer postfeminism' of the show. Gerhard makes the point that the (post)feminist politics of *Sex and the City* are influenced by the paradigms of 'queer culture'. Although some lesbians and gays may be reproducing heteronormativity by engaging in marriage-like civil partnerships, many have established alternative forms of partnership. Some engage in 'open relationships', where a couple agree to allow sexual relationships outside their partnership (couples either 'play together' or 'play apart'), while many others never form lasting sexual relationships at all, instead enjoying emotional support through their network of friends and communities. As Gerhard observes, *Sex and the City* co-opts these paradigms in its representation of female characters who provide friendship and support for each other while their sexual relationships may come and go. Charlotte, the most conservative of the quartet, makes this explicit in one episode when she suggests, 'Don't laugh at me, but maybe we can be each other's soul mates. And then we can let men be just these great, nice guys to have fun with' ('The Agony and the Ex-tacy', S.4, ep.1). This adoption of queer cultural paradigms by heterosexual women *is* innovative, but it is also one of the reasons why so many critics have dismissed the *Sex and the City* women as metaphors for gay men (Merck, 2004). The argument has some value, but Merck's reading seems reductive of complex representations which indicate how metropolitan, upper-middle class, post-feminist culture may co-opt different cultural agendas, such as queer lifestyles, to carve out new forms of feminine – and, possibly, feminist – existence.

And so we come to another important element in *SATC*'s representation of female heterosexuality: Manhattan and its 'class' signification. Here 'class' signifies in two ways: having the economic privilege to permit and afford living in Manhattan – the most expensive location in the world – and having the level of cultural awareness or metropolitan sophistication to make one's way there. Although the show does indeed validate alternative forms of female heterosexuality, it makes one proviso – the location. New York City, and especially central Manhattan, has a long-standing connection to alternative sexualities (see Chauncey, 1994). It was in New York that the first gay liberation riots started (at the Stonewall Inn, 1969) and after the Second World War, when most European cities had been decimated, New York sought to position itself as the artistic and cultural capital of the Western world. Popular representations of New York have changed remarkably in the past thirty years. Where it was once represented as a sordid, seedy den of depravity (as seen in films like *Midnight Cowboy* (dir. John Schlesinger: 1969) and *Cruising* (dir. William Friedkin: 1980)), it is now represented as gloriously diverse and 'queer'. A veritable hive of crime, prostitution and lunacy in the 1960s, parts of Manhattan could be truly terrifying, but recent representations have shown the very opposite. The transformation of New York's image can be seen in the comparison between the 1960s film *The Out of Towners* (dir. Arthur Hiller: 1970) and its recent remake by director Sam Weisman (1999). While the early version showed the danger of New York that led the out-of-town couple to decide that they would much rather stay in quiet, safe suburbia, the remake emphasized the dynamism and eclectic vivacity of the capital city which, though strange and disturbing at first, becomes thrilling and enticing for the out-of-town couple. *Sex and the City* stresses the importance of place to its characters' identities. Many episodes end with Carrie's voice-over proclaiming the glory of New York. As in *The L Word* and its celebration of West Hollywood (see Chapter 5), *Sex and the City* foregrounds the pleasures of viewing beautiful buildings and scenery. A leading critic of heritage cinema, Andrew Higson, labels this approach 'pictorialism', where cinema aims to offer many of the pleasures made possible by landscape paintings (2003: 39). *Sex and the City*'s sequences of daily life in Manhattan revel in the glorious vistas of the city.

This celebration of place is particularly important in relation to sexual identification. The series affirms Carrie's and her friends' sophistication and glamour, intimately connected to their location *in* Manhattan – if they were *not* located in Manhattan would they signify differently? If located in heteronormative suburbia, where all of the other residents were married with children, would four 'middle-aged' women, picking up men on a regular basis, signify as they do in their privileged Manhattan location? If located within a provincial setting, or other less 'queer' cities, Carrie and her friends could, at best, be considered outrageous or labelled as depraved. In many ways this exemplifies Foucault's argument that sexual identification is the product of a specific culture and that sexual activities will signify differently dependent upon culture or context (see Chapter 1). Indeed, New York (like other metropolitan centres) has been a beacon for alternative sexualities and sexual lifestyles, and many choose to live there simply for the knowledge that this vibrant, multicultural society will permit people to live alternative sexual lifestyles that would not be condoned in more provincial areas (Buckland, 2002).

This metropolitan sophistication and acceptance is not without its class dynamics. Living in Manhattan is very expensive and, as *Sex and the City* regularly shows, finding a habitable apartment is a difficult task even with a significant budget at one's disposal. More than simple economic class, *Sex and the City* also stresses a certain level of sophistication commensurate with living in Manhattan. Sophistication, as used in this respect, is not a synonym for academic education, but cultural 'know-how' – having knowledge of the codes and regimes of *style*, as the series' dominant metaphor of fashion makes clear. Carrie Bradshaw's outrageous fashion deconstructions (corrupting the elegance of a designer outfit with the addition of some tacky piece of costume jewellery) are New York 'in-jokes'. Carrie knows that her fellow New Yorkers will not mock her, or think she has made some sartorial *faux pas*; they understand her as a fashionable Manhattan woman 'playing' with, or 'twisting/ queering', the codes of fashion. The opening sequence of *Sex and the City: The Movie* shows Carrie in a summer dress adorned with her iconic style statement: a colossal, fabric corsage. As she walks past a group of other fashionable women they remark to Carrie how much they love her outfit: this acceptance of alternative fashion, this bending of the normative rules of sartorial elegance, can be read as a metaphor for the alternative expressions of sexuality at work in the show. Manhattan allows people to 'bend the rules of normativity' because its citizens are represented as sophisticated and non-judgemental. Samantha can be promiscuous without suffering the discrimination she might encounter elsewhere.

Fiona Handyside sees this acceptance in one of the running jokes of the series: the misrecognition of Carrie as a prostitute (2007: 414). Importantly, this mistake is only made by people who are *not* New Yorkers. For example, in the episode 'All or Nothing' (S.3, ep.10) a Japanese businessman, visiting New York, mistakes Carrie for a prostitute in the lobby of a hotel, while in 'The Power of Female Sex' (S.1, ep.5), a French architect leaves $1,000 on Carrie's pillow 'in return' for a one-night stand. Handyside suggests these sequences serve to highlight that 'sexual freedom can *only* be correctly "read" in Manhattan, by those who understand its workings' (414, our emphasis). In this respect, Handyside asserts that although 'the show clearly celebrates the ability of women to be financially and sexually independent, it places this new identity into a severely restricted arena. It is *only* in Manhattan that one's choices, and ultimately, identity, are not marginalized' (417, our emphasis).

The four characters rarely leave their beloved sanctuary of Manhattan, and on the occasions they do, their sexual poise seems to desert them. For example, in 'The Big Journey' (S.5, ep.7) Carrie and Samantha travel to San Francisco (where Carrie has a book launch) by cross-country train. The episode makes humorous intertextual references to the film *Some Like It Hot* (dir. Billy Wilder: 1959) and the comedy arises from the fact that the train is definitely not the glamorous experience that Carrie and Samantha had anticipated. Being removed from their precious Manhattan even invokes a physical change in both women: Carrie develops a monstrous zit on her cheek and spends most of the train journey doctoring the pimple, and Samantha's usual hunt for a hot guy is peculiarly unsuccessful. In one sequence, the women strut into the restaurant car where a group of 'eligible' bachelors are dining. As they sashay into the carriage, non-diegetic music plays a pastiche of stripper theme, thus their parade is both comic and rather tawdry. Similarly, their habitual fashion-sense seems to have deserted them – Samantha, usually attired in dresses reminiscent of 1930s Hollywood, is now wearing a stretchy, lycra dress, and Carrie, trying to hide her spot, has overdone the rouge, with the result that the huge circles of red smeared onto her cheeks are clown-like. Samantha orders some champagne and suggests one of the men may like to help her 'pop her cork'. The men stare in horrified disbelief at these unruly women, while Samantha is devastated that they don't respond to her with appropriate sexual interest. Although this sequence is primarily comedic, it also makes the point that outside the sanctuary of Manhattan, the women signify differently. On board this train, surrounded by provincial men and women, they look like 'sluts'.

So far this chapter has admired the representation of female heterosexuality in *Sex and the City*. The show represents the older, desiring woman as a sympathetic character rather than a figure of ridicule; it validates alternative sexual life-scripts beyond heteronormativity, but it makes it very clear that this is only possible with the class privilege that comes from being able to live in the centre of New York. However, the show is occasionally not so utopian in its representations. A key element in the show is its frequent focus on a sexual act many might find 'unnatural' or even 'disgusting'. Indeed, the series sometimes establishes a dichotomy of disgusting, 'unacceptable' sexuality contrasted with sanitized, acceptable sexuality. One of the most explicit examples occurs in the episode entitled 'Cock-a-Doodle-Doo!' (S.3, ep.18). In this episode Samantha Jones has just moved into her new downtown apartment but has become disenchanted by the surrounding neighbourhood, which is trendy by day but seedy by night. For a week, a group of pre-op transsexual prostitutes (or, as they're referred to at one point, 'chicks with dicks') have loitered outside Samantha's bedroom window, touting their trade. The noise of the prostitutes invades Samantha's bedroom and disturbs her concentration. One night Samantha is having sex when noise from outside disturbs her sexual rapture; she leaps out of bed and fills a bucket of water which she hurls out the window, soaking one of the prostitutes.

The sequence is very carefully coded to represent two different forms of sexuality – the attractive and the disgusting. The attractive is represented inside Samantha's apartment: softly lit and decorated in off-white colours, it is a clean and hygienic space. Samantha and her classically beautiful man are having sex in the most traditional way – the missionary position – while outside, beneath Samantha's elevated apartment, everything is dark, dingy and undoubtedly very dirty. (As the prostitutes are all black, there is an obvi-

92 Part II: Representations

ous racial element here too.) The three pre-op transsexuals are attired in cheap, synthetic clothes and, to emphasize this point, one of them even wears a polyester imitation of Samantha's luxury silk nightgown, suggesting that the sexuality expressed within Samantha's apartment is authentic while outside can only be a 'cheap' imitation. When Samantha throws the water over the transsexual trio, one of them becomes even more grotesque as her wig is washed off to reveal a bald head. Samantha, from her elevated position at the bedroom window, looks down on the freaks outside in the gutter and laughs. The sequence concludes with Samantha's gorgeous lover getting dressed, thus offering the further voyeuristic pleasure of his deliciously muscled body, and emphasizing his middle-class, white identity. This juxtaposition further creates a classed and raced distinction between normative, beautiful sexuality inside and the disgusting, aberrant sexuality outside. (Indeed, it is worth noting that even Samantha, the most sexually adventurous of the *SATC* quartet, was disgusted by the discourse of the prostitutes, one of whom apparently told a client to 'get that dick out of my ass before I shit on it'.)

The class discourse implicit in this sequence is further articulated by Samantha who, as she furiously fills up the bucket of water, rants that as a tax-paying citizen paying a huge amount of money for her apartment she shouldn't have to put up with this. In many ways, Samantha voices one of the most uncomfortable issues raised by *Sex and the City* – the relationship between socio-economic class and sexual identification. As *SATC* emphasizes throughout, Manhattan facilitates the characters' sexual lifestyles and identifications but they also require the socio-economic means to *afford* their lifestyles (see Negra, 2004: 22).

Nevertheless, we must not forget that the fight scene between Samantha and the prostitutes is dealt with in a light-hearted way and, importantly, no real harm befalls anyone. Indeed, the whole episode is largely screwball comedy and it ends happily with Samantha inviting the transsexual women to join Carrie, Miranda and Charlotte at a barbeque in the roof garden of her apartment. As Richardson notes, 'the party is unashamedly hedonistic, with an eclectic range of characters present, ranging from gay men to pre-op transsexuals. The scene offers a utopian image in which everyone, irrespective of sex, gender, sexuality race or class, is able to enjoy the beauty of a balmy Manhattan evening' (Richardson, 2006: 169). As the party develops into the usual mix of drink, dancing and comments on fashion (Carrie's iconic corsage becomes the object of fascination yet again) the camera pans across the rooftops of a dreamy Manhattan summer evening and Carrie remarks that she and her three friends have truly lovely lives. If *Sex and the City* poses any challenge to the representation of heteronormativity, it stresses that this is intrinsically linked to location. Perhaps our final words should belong to Carrie, who summarizes the show's agenda when she is asked, in one episode ('Out of the Frying Pan', S.6, ep.16), why everyone thinks living in

Manhattan is so wonderful. Smiling confidently and without the slightest hint of embarrassment for her simplistic reply, Carrie answers 'Because it is.'

Further Reading

Akass, K. and McCabe, J. (eds) (2004) *Reading Sex and the City* (London: I.B.Tauris).
Jermyn, D. (2009) *Sex and the City* (Detroit: Wayne State University Press).
Thornham, S. and Purvis, T. (2005) *Television Drama: Theories and Identities* (Hampshire: Palgrave Macmillan).

Representations of Heterosexuality 2

Chapter 7

Case Study: *Entourage*

This part has offered textual case studies exploring the relationships between sexualities and representation, reflecting the growth of academic interest in popular television's depictions of contemporary sexualities. In exploring the ways in which representations can often support normative ideals, media researchers have, quite properly, tended to focus on the treatment of marginalized or non-normative sexualities; in so doing they highlight the ways in which gender privilege – accorded to heterosexual men – is often hidden from view. By examining the ways in which marginalized 'others' are represented, the social constructions of masculinities and what it means to be a man are brought into view and challenged by analyses of queer and gay cultures. Even so, there is a paradox to investigations of the margins, whereby representations of heterosexual masculinity are overlooked as merely speaking to self-evident, privileged 'norms' which do not in themselves require interrogation.

In this chapter we look at the relations among heterosexual men through a focus on HBO's *Entourage*. First broadcast in 2004, *Entourage* was immediately successful, and continued for eight seasons until 2011. *Entourage* can be described as a 'bromance', as its narrative focuses on the theme of male friendship between a close-knit group of young men – Vince, E (Eric), Johnnie Drama and Turtle – living together in Los Angeles after relocating from their New York neighbourhood. Lifelong friends, their lives have become increasingly entwined following Vince's successful film career and his commission of his friends as manager (E), cook (Drama) and driver (Turtle) – his entourage. Alongside 'the boys' are a number of regular characters, most prominently Ari Gold (Vince's manager), Lloyd (Ari's gay assistant), Mrs Ari (Ari's wife), Barbara Miller (Ari's business partner) and an assortment of hangers-on and (real-life) film stars. Loosely based on the real-life experiences of Mark Wahlberg (one-time rapper, Calvin Klein model, and film star) and set in contemporary Hollywood, *Entourage* offers a glimpse into the celebrity lifestyle, where money, women and expensive toys are plentiful. *Entourage* constructs a close group of men whose relationships echo those we discussed between women in *Sex and the City*. As with Carrie and the girls, the entourage's friendships are based upon mutual support, where close ties to one another are more important than those with the opposite sex. But while that elevation of friendship is recognized as a positive element in *Entourage*, some writers have suggested that the celebration of the men's intimate ties are at the expense of women, creating a reactionary picture of women as expendable and one-dimensional characters only visible through their 'sexiness'. The show apparently does not offer the same kinds of resistance to heteronormative ideals that has seen *SATC* praised: in its representation of four young men 'living the life', *Entourage* isn't seen as validating alternative life choices that transgress ideological prescriptions, but often stands accused of celebrating normative attitudes precisely because the characters here are men and not women. *Entourage*'s depictions of free-wheeling, casual sex are not understood as a rejection of heteronormative family values, but just as lads being lads.

We want to consider whether or not *Entourage* merely offers a display of normative sexual aspirations focused on hegemonic masculine homosociality (and we'll examine each of those terms shortly). Are the relationships between the characters simply based on assumptions of normative heterosexuality and masculinity, or do they make an *exhibition* of those assumptions, and thus reveal and interrogate them? Is the text more complex, perhaps functioning as a commentary on twenty-first century masculinities and heterosexualities?

Entourage and its four main characters could be understood as a form of 'picaresque', which is one of the first genres of European novel originating in the seventeenth and eighteenth centuries. These novels centred on the adventures of a hero and his companions as they negotiate their paths from rags to riches. Certainly, Vince and the boys are outsiders in Hollywood: they come from the relatively mean streets of Queens, New York and attempt to make their way in the star system, encountering along the way numerous power players who enable or obstruct Vince's career. The picaresque novel is defined by its satirical and comic elements, with an emphasis on the hero's exposure of the hypocrisy and strategizing of other more powerful characters. In *Entourage*, the boys have to learn how to make deals, to choose the right film projects and keep on the right side of the Hollywood power-brokers – they use their wits, connections and Vince's burgeoning celebrity and good looks to make money, acquire expensive toys and, crucially, have sex with beautiful women. They are not always successful and, narratively (as in the picaresque), *Entourage* follows Vince's career through its various ups and downs.

A key concept is useful here: 'hegemonic masculinity' attempts to explain the power relationships between men and the broader social place of male power. Michael S. Kimmel writes that 'the hegemonic definition of manhood is a man *in* power, a man *with* power, and a man *of* power' (2010: 114). But to understand this more fully, we need to outline the wider concept of 'hegemony'. Hegemony is a concept related to analyses of class and seeks to explain the processes whereby dominant groups maintain their leadership by *winning* consent from other social groups, rather than by force or coercion. It is a means of understanding how and why, for example, the working classes support economic and market structures that rarely seem to benefit them, while they do seem to confer major advantages on the middle and upper classes. Such consent is not automatically achieved but has to be won through struggles and negotiation, particularly in the realms of discourse and representation. So, with regard to our interests in sexuality, heterosexuality as the dominant or 'norm' is not achieved by force or punishment. At least in the West, we no longer throw people in jail for not being heterosexual; rather, heterosexuality is maintained by the ways in which it is supported as a cultural *value* with material benefits. We cannot offer a detailed examination here, but we are drawing on Gramsci's (1971) conceptualization that hegemony is always an outcome of processes that fuse the social, political and economic ideas and practices promoted by the leading group. In this way, hegemony is always historical, and a way of viewing the world which is synthetic but not free-floating, and hegemonic ideas about what constitutes 'good' or 'healthy' sexuality are not simply a political ideal with no connection to social or economic imperatives. Hegemony is not just a way of thinking, it is a form of ideas and practices across all spheres of life which are also legitimated by the ideas and practices of the state. Thus, for example, the idea of 'healthy sexuality' is not just an ideal but a set of practices which are legitimated both discursively (in all those spaces and places where we are told to be healthy, for example sex education classes, agony aunt pages, doctors' surgeries) and practically (where benefits – tax breaks, access to childcare – are given to monogamous, married couples).

Similarly, hegemonic masculinity refers to the way in which certain ways of being male predominate and are valued above other ways of behaving in specific social formations. This links to an idea often cited in popular media commentaries – that we have seen (and are still in the grip of) a 'crisis of masculinity'. The 'crisis of masculinity' links sociological identifications of men's shifting role in culture to representations in television and cinema. For example, 1980s adventure movies with unusually musclebound heroes, such as *Rambo* (dir. Ted Kotcheff: 1982), were understood as reactionary responses to women's advances in education, employment and the 'masculine' world more generally. The 'crisis' is linked to the idea of the 'war of the sexes' – that males and females are always and continually in battle for the upper hand. The extent to which a crisis actually exists is disputed, but Heartfield (2002), for example, notes there are three distinctive emphases in the crisis theory. First is the characterizations of masculinity as 'intrinsically pathological' – as writers like Horrocks (1995) might note, masculine pride and men's refusal to acknowledge women's rights are actually part of the *problem* of masculinity. Within these analyses men are devoted to vanity, violence and criminality, and thus popular culture representations celebrate these values over and above more feminized values such as love, trust and intimacy. Second, other writers, such as Susan Faludi (2000), claim that men have been defeated by 'circumstances beyond their control', and the decline of traditionally masculine professions (such as manufacturing) and a 'feminization' of social space is responsible for male feelings of inadequacy, which are played out in representations that offer us nostalgic reflections on men's lost worlds (here we could cite *The Full Monty* (dir. Peter Cattaneo: 1997), or *Once were Warriors* (dir. Lee Tamahori: 1994)). Third, Heartfield identifies 'sceptical analyses … which reject the basic assumption that masculinity is in crisis, pointing to evidence that men continue to command disproportionate authority, wealth and power'. The idea of 'crisis' may be deployed by some politicians, for example, as a means of shoring up male power and insisting on a return to traditional roles for both men and women.

Hegemonic masculinity is valued for perceived attributes, including courage, physicality, logic, adventure, protectiveness, technical skills – you can surely add many others. These norms clearly rule out other forms of masculinity, and behaviours in men that are considered effeminate are rendered marginal or outside normative masculinity. It's not that there is only one way of being a man; rather, there are acceptable forms of masculinity and stigmatized or marginalized types of masculinity but these may vary across the spaces and places of culture. The importance of this theory is that it recognizes the ways in which barriers exist based on the designations of 'appropriate' and 'inappropriate' masculinities – and these labels are more complex than simply the recognition of gender differences between male and female. For example, while the notion that there is a simple continuity between biology and the social – that men have more power than women because they are physically stronger – is a powerful and ideological truism, men's grasp on power between themselves (and across the gender divide) may not be quite so solid. Class and race intersect with gender to produce further hierarchies in which certain groups of men may find themselves significantly disadvantaged. For example in white, middle-class, academic environments, men from black, working-class backgrounds may find themselves marginalized by those men and women who possess educational, race and class privilege. A working-class Asian man speaking with a thick northern accent can be marginalized within a university by his supposed 'deviance' from the 'socialized norms' of educated academics (whether male or female), so that the barriers to his success are based on the intersections between race, class and education as much as, or even in spite of, gender. Thinking about forms of hegemonic masculinity requires that we understand more than just the fact of gender and pay attention to the ways in which power circulates within particular spaces where class dynamics and other allegiances may be at play.

Thus, it is important to think about how particular institutions – education, politics, the Church, or the media, for example – maintain male dominance over women, and how, while most men may benefit from institutional barriers to women's full equality, the experiences of being male and the experiences of 'male power' may be differentially felt across and between people who conform to the bodily appearance of being male. In other words, in some situations it may not be enough to be male in order to have power, and a man will need to have other forms of capital (drawing on Bourdieu (1986): having gone to the 'right' school for example) to claim this ascendancy. Or, as Kimmel puts it, 'all masculinities are not created equal' (Kimmel, 1997).

Our case study here is *Entourage* and, because of its interests in women, fast cars and consumption, it would be easy to characterize the show as a celebration of masculine success. Yet it is not clear that Vince and the boys *are* actually examples of hegemonic masculinity, if this is defined by its access to power. At times, the boys have little or no power, and even in the midst of success they are rarely in control of their destinies – projects are cancelled on the whim of other more powerful men, money is often tight (and, where it is plentiful, is rarely secure), the boys' romantic relationships are fraught, and women often reject them (especially Drama and Turtle). Like the picaresque novel, the series is played for laughs, the highs and lows are heavily ironic and interactions between the boys and with other males, especially other male celebrities (the show features at least one famous guest playing a grotesque version of himself each episode), are most often characterized by jockeying for the upper hand. Indeed, at least in the early seasons, the adventures that befall the boys are usually the result of their failing to understand the rules of the Hollywood game.

While power in Hollywood seems to reside most 'naturally' with men, the plot's twists and turns highlight the ways in which the heads of studios, producers, directors and others are monstrous. Where we might assume that these professional men have achieved their place at the top of the tree through hard work, artistic ability, integrity and merit, the show offers us their petty, arbitrary, conniving, dishonest and vindictive actions. Sometimes, Vince gets a role because he manages to charm an important figure – for example, in 'The Script and the Sherpa' (S.1, ep.5), Vince secures a role in 'Queens Boulevard' because he is able to supply producer Scott Wick with some excellent marijuana. But in other episodes Vince loses out on various dream projects because he's failed to flatter someone's ego or has misread the mood of a meeting. Studio head Alan Gray so dislikes Vince that he buys up a script so that he can 'sit on it' just to spite him. Gray's determination to block Vince's career only comes to an end with his heart attack, following an argument with Ari ('ReDOMption', S.5, ep.6). The entourage boys' attempts to make deals often result in disaster, precisely because they're too young and inexperienced to play the Hollywood game according to its rules: E tries to auction off their dream project 'Medellin' to the highest bidder but it results in disaster, with the film finally sold for $1 because E has failed to fully comprehend who he was playing off against each other.

Of course, this kind of competitiveness is a recognizable and stereotypically 'masculine' trope. Media representations offer us multiple masculinities often engaged in forms of competition – comedies often draw on the antagonisms between men for their humour, and much critical work has explored how these representations might conform to or resist heteronormativity. In particular, comedies are seen to offer oppositional or resistant representations where an 'incompetent' or 'immature' man is shown failing to meet the dominant hegemonic masculine ideal while, at the same time, eventually succeeding in getting the girl, the job or whatever other goal he is pursuing. Often this man will have friends who sustain him through his various difficulties. The representation of close friendships between men is not new to television, but because the series overtly makes gender relationships, masculinity and male power its central themes, *Entourage* offers a particular examination of homosocial relationships between men. The term homosociality refers to non-sexual (platonic) relationships between heterosexual men. Homosociality between men has associated institutions and meanings that *can* serve hegemonic masculinity, but can also be used as a form of critique.

Television and cinema frequently offers us close male friendships played out in traditionally masculine ways. One example of this is *Band of Brothers* (HBO: 2001), which illustrates the bond which develops between men as a result of adversity. This is an example of homosocial friendship based on traditional values of bravery, fortitude and shared patriotic purpose. These portrayals can often include a distinct critique of class or of macho masculinity. More recently, homosociality seems to have become exclusively associated with 'laddishness' – for example the behaviours of young, heterosexual men at, say, a football match or on a night out. Similarly, we might recognize certain kinds of behaviours between adult men in a golf club or in a sports bar (both homosocial institutions, and often spaces from which women have been traditionally barred either by formal men-only rules or, more informally, by creating an atmosphere unwelcoming to women – no seating, pictures of naked women on the walls, single-sex toilets, etc.).

A conceptual understanding of homosociality provides us with a convincing theoretical explanation of – and many times also a case against – the dominance of particular cultural constructions of masculinity and, for feminists, an account of men's continued social and economic power over women. But at the same time, assumptions about how hegemonic, homosocial masculinity is articulated or played out by characters in popular culture have led to what is sometimes referred to as genre or textual essentialism: that the structure and form of a text determine its meaning. Hence, from this perspective, those texts featuring the exploits of a closely knit group of heterosexually identified men or boys whose point of view is privileged will *always* be essentially homophobic and sexist.

Thus, much research on homosociality focuses on its negative aspects – the idea of boys behaving badly. We don't want to deny those aspects, but it is also important to recognize that homosociality is complex and mutable, with positive aspects, as is masculinity itself. *Entourage* perhaps offers ways of thinking about popular culture representations as offering a broader and more complex range of feelings and modes of being heterosexual and male than might at first appear. In particular *Entourage* offers a version of homosocial friendships that conform to the relatively recent phenomenon of the 'bromance'. The term bromance is an abbreviation of the words brother (or bro) and romance, and labels a form of close, particularly emotional, bonding between male friends. In the 'off-screen' world, a number of celebrities are referred to as having bromantic relationships: in UK broadcasting, Ant and Dec's relationship is so close that it is often, jokingly, pronounced as an affair. So strong is their bond that, even though Ant is married, Dec lives next door. They not only work together as a single act (in award ceremonies they are nominated as a single performer), they socialize together, share the same interests (football and golf) and Dec even accompanied the newly wed Ant and his wife on honeymoon!

Newspaper reports on the phenomenon of the bromance cite changing life patterns for men:

> Experts say the prevalence of these friendships can in part be explained by the delay in major life milestones. Fifty years ago, a man could graduate from college, get a job and get married all within a couple of months. But today's men are drifting, as opposed to jumping, into the traditional notion of adulthood. (Bindley, 2008)

You can see in that analysis that there is a sense in which men in 'bromantic' relationships are understood as not meeting their *adult* obligations. This seeming lack of maturity, of not being properly adult, is a key element of the representations of the bromance in recent film and television, where we see 'man-child protagonists struggling to grow up' (Bartlett, 2010: 33). In the likes of *The Wedding Crashers* (dir. David Dobkin: 2005), *I Love You Man* (dir. John Hamburg: 2009) and TV's *Scrubs* (ABC: 2001–10), male characters appear to be locked in a kind of perpetual adolescence expressed through drug-taking, various kinds of horseplay, hanging out and prowling for girls. In *Entourage* we have a bromance ensemble with a variety of intimate duos – Turtle and Drama; E and Vince; Ari and Lloyd – and a broader 'gang' closeness where the entourage support each other. The boys are often at the mercy of forces they don't understand, but in their relationships with each other, they find forms of safety. The 'entourage' relationship is recognized as particularly important to the boys:

> VINCE: Turtle, how many relationships have I had?
> TURTLE: Huh?
> VINCE: Deep, real, meaningful relationships.
> TURTLE: Not counting us?

VINCE: Women.
TURTLE: I don't think any. ('The Big Bang', S.8, ep.6)

There is no doubt their relationships are very close but they are also boundaried and dependent upon quite complex dynamics – much of the tension of the series revolves around the ways in which other characters come in and disrupt the harmony of the four boys. Sometimes these disruptive forces are women – Vince's girlfriends have a particular tendency to mess things up – but just as often, the interloper is another man whose actions or simple presence disrupts the equilibrium of the entourage. For example, an old childhood friend, Dom, turns up uninvited in Season 3 and manages to upset Drama, Turtle and E with his appropriation of their roles as cook, driver and confidante. Furthermore, he has sex with hookers in the house, walks around naked, suggests visits to strip clubs at 10 am and generally fails to understand that while the boys are still 'guys from the hood', they have acquired other forms of cultural capital which means his physicality is out of place (there is a significant class element buried here too). It is Dom's muscling in on Vince which upsets the other guys: where E, Drama and Turtle are quite happy to take turns with each other in being Vince's most important partner, they react with jealousy when Dom takes over. The four of them are a stable network, a unit which operates well so long as everyone plays his part and any 'guests' are kept in their proper place. As Drama says when the guys vote to get rid of Dom, 'The Tribe has spoken!' In this humorous treatment of jealousy and emotional fall-out, *Entourage* echoes popular culture's more general denial and disavowal of the importance of emotion to men's lives. Crucially, and with implications both for the treatment of women and for that denial of feelings, there's the repudiation of any less than properly 'masculine' behaviours. Clearly, the boys love each other, and the term 'bromance' indicates a depth of emotion, but the relationships between them are stripped of any real hint of romantic love and eroticism by homophobic jibes/jokes, the constant discussion of women, and their recognition of each other's 'bro' status – their laddishness and up-for-it-ness – perhaps typified in Drama's statement, 'I'll chase puss with you, bro'. As Merl Storr observes, male homosociality depends upon homophobia:

> Homophobia is not just a contingent feature of homosocial institutions, but an essential part of both male homosociality and men's power. This is precisely because homosociality and homosexuality are dangerously close to each other – not because heterosexual men are all 'really' or 'repressed' homosexuals by preference, but because of the structure of homosociality. (2003: 43)

The idea that homosociality has a *structure* is an idea proposed by Eve Kosofsky Sedgwick, who argued that because male bonding is so intense, homosexuality is an ever present threat that must be channelled into the safe harbour of outright rejection. Robin Wood terms this the 'homophobic disclaimer' (2003: 261) – a gesture, image or language that is explicitly renunciatory to prevent potential gay appropriations of the intimacy between a narrative's male characters. In *Entourage* relationships we see this in the constant reiteration of the epithet 'bro', constant denunciations of 'bitchdom' and individual characters' celebrations of rampant heterosexuality.

Drama is the epitome of this man-child behaviour that typifies 'bro-ness': in the episode 'Day Fuckers', the boys make a bet to see whether E or Turtle can manage to pick up a girl and have meaningless sex. The episode reflects on what constitutes 'good' sexual conduct in the 'bro' world.

DRAMA: Yeah E, why you gotta look at every girl like a potential relationship?
E: Cos I don't want to spend my twilight years alone like you, Drama.
TURTLE: E loves falling in love.
VINCE: E is a nesting creature, what's the big deal?
DRAMA: Because it's not natural for a male, that the big deal.
E: I'm not a nesting creature.
DRAMA: Really. Name one girl you've ever had unemotional sex with?
[…]
DRAMA: Don't be mad E, it's not our fault you were born without the sport-fucking gene.
VINCE: Come on you guys, I can't just stand here and let you harass my boy. I know he can have unemotional sex, he just chooses not to. In fact, I'll bet he can get some before the both of you two.
DRAMA: Please, I'm a celebrity again, bro. We could get laid at a funeral.
E: And that would be unemotional for you or the dead girl?
DRAMA: Oh! Funny, E, but being a student of human nature and knowing a leopard can't change its spots I've come to accept you for what you are.
E: And what's that?
DRAMA: A pussy and such a pussy in fact that I bet Turtle could close a broad quicker.
[…]
E: I'm not searching out a girl just to fuck her.
DRAMA: Why not?
E: Because it's mean.
DRAMA: No, no, no. Mean is when I made Jess Maccini ride her bike home after I ass-fucked her… Trust me E, if you're able to find a girl who is willing to day-fuck you, she's using you as much as you're using her. It's 2007. Wake up, pussy!

Drama and Vince decide to make a bet – Vince backs E to bed a woman within 24 hours and Drama offers to coach Turtle to similar success. With $5,000 at stake, and not wanting to leave anything to chance, Drama leads Turtle to the one place 'where even a one-eyed leper can get laid': Craigslist. There they find a woman, Kelsey, looking for someone 'to fulfill all her fantasies'. Turtle and Drama turn up to meet her, and she's more attractive than they'd hoped, but Kelsey hands Turtle a dry cleaning ticket and tells him to meet her later. The dry cleaning turns out to be a pink rabbit suit: she's a furrophile. Drama seems to be incredibly knowledgeable about plushies, and plays on this to great comic effect, but Turtle isn't happy. He tries on the outfit, and finds himself the butt of the guys' jokes; it's clear that being made to dress up for sex is an emasculating experience for Turtle – even so, there is $5,000 at stake and Drama isn't about to let Turtle throw in the towel. Pulling up outside Kelsey's house:

DRAMA: I feel like I'm dropping my kid off to go trick-or-treating!
TURTLE: Can't do it, Drama!
DRAMA: Of course you can.
TURTLE: No, I can't. It's bad enough I got to wear this thing, but who knows what she's going to be wearing.
DRAMA: Who cares if she's dressed like Godzilla? Close your eyes, like you used to do when you banged that ugly chick … at high school.
TURTLE: You thought she was ugly?
DRAMA: Is that debatable?
[…]
Drama grabs the rabbit suit, shouting: 'Gimma the suit, Dick!'
TURTLE: Why, what are you going to do?
DRAMA: If I'm dropping 5 Gs, I'm at least gonna get me some pussy!

This is all played for comic effect and constructs similar hierarchies of normal/perverse sex we discussed in relation to *SATC*, where a sexual subculture is both mocked and embraced within a single episode. The plushie is a source of laughter during the episode, which serves to repudiate the pleasures of fur. But Drama does go in and have sex with Kelsey, and thus, at one level, plushies are brought into the fold of playful sex (this scene also confirms Drama's status as 'can-do' guy – he has no problem donning the suit in pursuit of orgasm). But there is a decidedly uncomfortable element here, and that lies in Drama substituting himself for Turtle without any negotiation with Kelsey – *her* desires, beyond the pink rabbit suit, don't seem to matter at all.

The episode is also particularly interesting because of the ways it highlights a number of themes within the bromantic trope, and 'laddish' homosociality more generally. Bromances often capture the delicate negotiation of a romantic relationship with a woman, and the balancing of that with the competing demands of friends. E's relationships, and his need to have more than 'just sex' with women, is a source of humour and irritation for the other guys who believe he should 'man up'. E is 'soft' – a pussy; he's also 'old-fashioned' – Drama tells him to 'wake up, it's 2007'. E typifies the sensitive or post-feminist man who populates chick-flicks, and in this scene he is contrasted with Drama who is surely the quintessential 'bro'. The insistent vulgarity of Drama's showing-off is key to the humour of the scenes above, but the contrasts between the characters and their differing ways of relating to women also create considerable dramatic and humorous tension. Even so, within the broader themes of the series, these disputes are not just about E or Drama as individuals: girlfriends who hang around for more than the three days the house rules allow begin to change the dynamics of the group and impact on every aspect of life. Thus women are a threat to the lifestyle and the entourage.

'Day Fuckers' illustrates some of the 'formal' features of homosociality: its forms of competitiveness, especially over female conquests, and the objectification of women, or treatment of women as only valued for their sexual appeal to men. But we ought to be clear that *Entourage* doesn't offer us Drama as a role model. Indeed, he is most often the butt of everyone's jokes, and the ridicule he endures serves to expose and deride his male chauvinism, and those macho traits which are objectionable to women. This doesn't mean he is a villain – Drama is funny and quite likeable, and gets some of the best lines in the series – but there is considerable disparity between Drama's perception of himself and the person we see on screen. Drama thinks he's a talented actor, but viewers see that he is, at best, mediocre; he espouses 'new age' thinking about diet, exercise and meditation, yet is constantly stressed and angry. His macho posturing about his physical prowess, celebrity and looks backfires constantly, setting him up for ridicule. Most importantly, Drama's inadequacies come out as he attempts to get 'pussy'; while Drama characterizes himself as a consummate lover of women and something of a sensitive guy, we see him rate women according to offensive criteria, his behaviour towards women is generally Neanderthal, and he frequently oversteps the line by touching women who don't want to be touched. Hence when Drama gets rebuffed by women, as happens frequently, it is a source of considerable humour for the other members of the entourage, and presumably for most audience members too. Drama offers a masculinity characterized as outmoded, insensitive, crass and unreflexive. By comparison, the other boys have warmth and a level of sensitivity. They are only occasionally portrayed as deliberately cruel, they don't actively seek to upset the women they have sex with, and indeed, they are often the ones who are chosen by women, rather than those doing the choosing. Female characters do come and go in the series and they are often presented as trophies, yet that doesn't mean they don't have important narrative roles.

The celebration of numerous liaisons comes to an end in one of Vince's few significant relationships. In Season 7, Vince meets porn star Sasha Grey (like Mandy Moore and Jamie Lynn Siegler, Grey plays a fictionalized version of herself). The narrative takes a number of dark turns as they embark on a relationship fuelled by drink and drugs. The other guys find the relationship with Sasha an opportunity to make a number of puerile observations about the promiscuity of the porn lifestyle, and there are many sneering remarks about her work, as well as opportunities for humour as different characters, meeting Sasha while out with Vince, realize where they have seen her previously. Vince takes these in his stride, falling out with E for being moralistic – when E says 'She has sex on camera', Vince replies, 'Every one of us in this town does on some level' ('Sniff Sniff Gang Bang', S.7, ep.8). But Vince's tolerance for Sasha's professional life comes to an end when she signs up for a five-man gang bang.

Vince's subsequent attempts to get her to give up the film in favour of a job on his latest project, 'Airwalker', are regarded by Sasha as attempts to control her, both emotionally and professionally. Interestingly, because of its placement within a series about an actor and his trials and tribulations, this narrative line acquires a particular significance. In a world where everyone is chasing the next role, making compromises about artistic integrity, and focused on 'the deal', Sasha's decisions are effectively normalized – her dilemmas are no different from Vince's. She appears as a *professional* – work in porn is just like acting.

In a later episode, Vince shows up on set and attempts to pick a fight with Sasha's ex.

VINCE: Are you fucking serious?
SASHA: I told you. Don't fucking tell me what to do.
VINCE: Like I'm crazy for trying to tell you not to do this.
SASHA: You knew what I did when I met you.
VINCE: Guys like him make me sick!
SASHA: Guys like you that go and fuck all sorts of girls just for the fun of it usually make me sick too. But I made an exception. I guess I fucked up. Go home Vince.
VINCE: If I leave now, I'm not coming back.
SASHA: Bye then.

In this and previous episodes, Sasha draws attention to the sexual double standard which judges her for the sex she has as *work*, while rewarding guys like Vince for their numerous partners. She makes obvious how the kinds of sex Vince engages in may be problematic: his sexual liaisons are often spontaneous, anonymous and short-term, but validated because they're not understood as a service. Vince is the one indulging in risky sex – he often has no idea who he is sleeping with. What is interesting about this liaison is the ways in which the consequences for Vince are not sexual, or physical: they are emotional. In that focus on his emotional fall-out from the affair, *Entourage* recognizes the ways in which romantic relationships can be important to men as well as being the source of much angst. For all his 'love and leave 'em' approach to sexual liaisons, Vince has no emotional resources to deal with his issues with Sasha. He admits to jealousy and, when cajoling doesn't work, he attempts to play tough, delivering ultimatums and threatening his rival. These stereotypically masculine behaviours scare her off. In this, of course, Vince is not alone. None of the guys are what we might call emotionally literate, and the long-term relationships with women they enjoy are seemingly only possible because of the work the women put in. But this representation also opens up an implicit critique of the pressures hegemonic masculinity places on men, and the emotional commitments they might seek to make. Ari and E, the two characters who *want* marriage, are constantly negotiating the parameters of their emotional relationships which are under threat from the tensions exerted by work and, as we've already discussed, the impossibilities of the hegemonic ideal. The Gold marriage is examined across the eight seasons: as the only constant female character in this male-centred drama, Mrs Ari is represented sympathetically, in that she puts up with Ari but is no doormat, her complaints about his inadequacies as a father and husband are narratively validated, and she frequently gets to come back on Ari in ways which highlight her power.

As Lee observes (drawing on Rosalind Gill's critique of post-feminist media culture), *Entourage* 'presents social notions of hegemonic masculinities in hyperbolic, humorous, and far-fetched ways' (2010: 184) as part of a wider rejection of social relations which place men as always and everywhere powerful. Lee argues that 'While *Entourage* ... sets out to entertain with ... humour and fantastical storylines, ... [it] subtly asks the audience to question the legitimacy of the norms of hegemonic masculinity' (ibid.). In Ari Gold, Lee sees a character who 'personifies the extremes of aggressive masculinity' (ibid.) and is in constant 'pursuit of masculinity' (Connell and Messerschmidt, 2005: 834), but whose antics, foul mouth and misogyny highlight his 'critical understanding of the constructed nature of hegemonic masculinity' (Lee, 2010: 187). For all Ari attempts to rule the roost, at home and at work, his relations with his wife, his daughter and his business partner illustrate the ways in which 'hegemonic masculinity has been historically constructed as the idealised norm, [but] it cannot always be embodied' (187). In his constant game-playing, deal-brokering and general bluster, Ari 'demonstrates the struggle and effort required to achieve hegemonic form' (189).

In our chapter on *Sex and the City* we pointed out the ways in which femininity was articulated to consumption and class, and in *Entourage* similar themes emerge. Unlike the women in *SATC* who are secure in their upper-middle class lifestyles, sashying around Manhattan seemingly without the everyday worries of bank balances and unpaid rent, the entourage have come from nothing and must work hard to participate in the playground of LA. They have to learn that the playground has rules: it is not enough to be guys on the make; they will have to 'kiss ass' and work constantly to maintain their grip on the celebrity lifestyle. There are many occasions where the boys are reminded that their place in Hollywood is not comfortable. In the first season, E is constantly mocked because his previous work experience was as a night manager of a pizza restaurant, and by Season 6 Turtle is visibly irritated by 50 Cent's drive-by comment, 'Yo Turtle! See you're out here in your Daddy's car!' ('One Car, Two Car, Red Car, Blue Car', S.6, ep.3). Drama suffers most: though not for want of trying, he rarely manages to find paid work, and his difficulties are compounded by his age, fading looks and receding hairline. Even so, because of their proximity to the celebrity Vince, Drama and Turtle have access to the most phenomenal opportunities for consumption. The boys rarely miss a chance to purchase the trappings of a fabulous lifestyle: in one episode, having been thwarted in their attempt to see 'Aquaman' at a cinema in the Valley, they go to a Ducati dealership where Vince orders four superbikes on a whim; news of a contract is celebrated by upgrading to a better house; the occasion of the 'Aquaman' premiere is marked by substantial purchases at Van Cleef & Arpels ('Aquamom', S.3, ep.1). In this fantasy world of consumerist possibilities, success and masculinity are complexly articulated through conspicuous consumption of luxury goods and high-end women.

Even if E, Turtle, Drama and Vince do not find their rise to fortune easy, the underlying theme of neighbourhood guys made good draws on the ideology of the 'American Dream' – that anyone, whatever their origins, can make a fortune in the USA. Jhally and Lewis suggest that

> [t]he American dream is not an innocent ideological notion. To sustain consent for a market economy constructed upon enormous disparities in income and wealth, it is necessary to persuade people not to question but to consume. People need to be convinced that, regardless of their circumstances, the system is fundamentally fair ... the American dream plays neatly into the hands of those promoting unfettered free market capitalism. However encouraging and hopeful the American dream may be, it sustains a right-wing political agenda. (1992: 74)

One of the ways in which this essentially right-wing agenda might surface in *Entourage* is, ironically, through the most hard-working character, Lloyd. Lloyd is also marginalized by his sexual orientation, and it is in this context that the 'American Dream' has significance for our discussion. Lloyd's relationship with Ari has been the focus of some critical attention. As we've already discussed, the series is full of homophobic disclaimers but in the relationship between Ari and Lloyd those disclaimers are absolutely centre-stage. There are too many instances to repeat here but these two exchanges will suffice to give an indication of the homophobic banter that Ari flings at Lloyd:

LLOYD: Are you hiding something from me Ari?
ARI: Only my cock and my asshole Lloyd. ('Gotta Look Up to Get Down', S.5, ep.7).

LLOYD: What's wrong?
ARI: Has so much cum squirted in those eyes you can't see what's right in front of your face? Amanda Daniels takes that job, Vince is fucked and I'm fucked. Which means we're all fucked. And we're fucked in the way you like to get fucked, not fucked in the way normal people like to get fucked. ('First Class Jerk', S.5, ep.8)

The insulting tenor of these conversations is undeniable, but any heteronormative reading is complicated by Lloyd's reactions. When Ari insults him, Lloyd doesn't behave as if he is, or ought to be, ashamed of his homosexuality. Lloyd doesn't trade insults with Ari, he often simply returns to doing his job as Ari continues to wave his arms and stomp around. In his calm toleration of Ari's insults and in remaining in his job and putting up with the abuse, Lloyd offers a strong gay identity, secure in its right to sexual pleasure centred on same-sex relationships. In this way the character undermines the definition of what is and isn't appropriate sexual behaviour for a man. However, there are ways in which Lloyd's sexuality is harnessed to the ideological project that is the American Dream: he is prepared to put up with the sexual slurs because he has ambitions:

LLOYD: I've worked 18 hours a day to save up the money to put myself through Stanford Business School. While I was there, I cleaned the cafeteria during the hours I wasn't studying and still graduated top of my class, only to take a job delivering mail to unappreciative overpaid little cocksuckers. Then to finally get the big promotion that would allow me to answer your phones and be both racially and sexually harassed for the next nine months. But I know the endgame ... and you Ari Gold, you are it. So stop your fucking whining, and go into your gorgeous three million dollar house, with your beautiful goddess wife and figure out how you're going to make both of our lives happen ... tomorrow!
ARI: That was a good speech, Lloyd. Yeah, if I was 25 and liked cock, we could be something. ('Exodus', S.2, ep.13)

Ultimately Lloyd gets his rewards – Ari eventually promotes him to Agent – but along the way perhaps we forget that institutionalized homophobia has real consequences for individuals, creating environments in which anyone who does not identify as straight may be subject to unfair and discriminatory treatment. Lloyd becomes a symbol of a social arrangement in which sexual discrimination is only a problem 'if you let it get to you'. As Jhally and Lewis argue in relation to racism and the eighties hit series *The Cosby Show* (NBC: 1984–92), the visibility of minorities in *positive* roles may well feed into decidedly illiberal ideas about opportunities and the reasons for failure; as they suggest, '*The Cosby Show*, by demonstrating the opportunity for African

Americans to be successful, implicates the majority of black people who have, by the Huxtable criterion, failed' (1992: 94). Similarly, Lloyd's success, his ability to make it in the heterosexist environment of Hollywood power-brokers, suggests that, in fact, the world is essentially fair, and that with hard work, determination and the right attitude anyone can reach the top. The implication is that should you fall by the wayside because you can't stand the homophobic banter, then that's your own problem. In this way, then, *Entourage* offers a version of gay identity which is both out and proud *and* denigrated. Lloyd's knuckling down in order to succeed in the workplace is partially mirrored in Drama's trials and tribulations – his macho bluster frequently results in him not getting the job he so desperately wants. Thus the pursuit of success requires that the livelier elements of gay subjectivity and old-fashioned masculinity be muted in order to play the game.

Like the other series we've discussed, *Entourage* is a complex representation, drawing on competing and intersecting discourses. The show provides us with an example that texts cannot be evaluated as either entirely positive or negative representations. It offers a very laddish conception of women as potential trappers of men, but it also highlights the problems such emotional immaturity can bring to its male characters. *Entourage* is not simply a celebration of masculine success over women, and although the show is about male bonding and friendship it is not a mere celebration of hegemonic masculine values. Like women, the male protagonists have little power in the corrupt public world of Hollywood where they struggle to be successful. Powerful men are corrupt, and not only women but also heterosexual men suffer under hegemonic masculine order. In these ways the show is a critique of hegemonic masculinity as an idealized norm.

Although *Entourage* allows us to explore representations of normative, heterosexual masculinity, it may not be considered groundbreaking in its depiction of a close-knit group of male friends in the way that other series discussed in this part, such as *The L Word*, frequently are. However, what our analysis has shown is that, rather than being dismissed as supportive of normative ideals, popular dramas such as *Entourage* require scrutiny if we are to understand the relationship between the politics of popular culture and sexuality. Indeed, to ignore such representations and to assume that representations of heterosexual masculinity remain unchallenging is tantamount to textual essentialism.

Further Reading

Feasey, R. (2008) *Masculinity and Popular Television* (Edinburgh: Edinburgh University Press).

Seidler, V.J. (2006) *Transforming Masculinities: Men, Culture, Bodies, Power, Sex and Love* (London and New York: Routledge).

Representations of Teenage Sexuality

Case Study: *Point Horror* and *Twilight*

Chapter 8

Newspapers and reality television programmes are currently fixated with teenage promiscuity. Recently the BBC factual series *Panorama* broadcast an episode entitled 'Too Much Too Young?' (15 January 2011), and BBC3 screened an inflammatory documentary on the perils of teenage oral sex entitled 'Is Oral Sex Bad for You?' (10 January 2011). The one-time head of the Mothers' Union, Reg Bailey, has been asked by the UK government's Children's Minister to carry out an investigation into the commercialization and sexualization of children, an exercise which follows hard on the heels of TV psychologist Dr Linda Papadopoulous' review for the Home Office, 'The Sexualisation of Young People'.

Child and adolescent sexualities are most often understood as a problem requiring intervention and regulation. This is not just the case in the UK, as there are similar concerns in Australia and the USA: the Australian Institute's 2006 report on 'Corporate Paedophilia' and the American Psychological Association's Task Force report on 'The Sexualization of Girls' (2007) have provided the models for UK versions. The fears about teenagers and their precocious sexual interests are a widespread feature of Western culture, with the blame for those interests being laid wherever teenagers seem to find amusement and pleasure. The magazines and books they read, the films and music videos they may watch – despite the classifications designed to keep them away – the music they listen to, the clothes they buy, the celebrities they admire, and, in particular, the pressure from other teens are all supposedly responsible for an 'unhealthy', 'unnatural' and 'premature' interest in sex.

From all this talk about young people it would seem that we should assume that teen popular culture is no longer (as was argued in the 1980s and 1990s) conservative in its depictions of sex. When Angela McRobbie (1991) looked at teenage magazines from the 1960s through to the mid-1980s, she found that they promoted a view of female sexuality as passive and dependent upon romantic love. Indeed, for many writers seeking to explore the gender politics of media aimed at teenage consumers, popular culture offered quite limiting messages about the need for girls to retain at least a semblance of sexual innocence until they found the right man. Since the 1990s there has been an increasingly and often explicitly sexual focus in features appearing in magazines aimed at young women, and it would be hard to deny that sexuality in its many forms has not been a commercial success in culture at large and specifically when presented to teenagers and young adults. We could cite all kinds of representations from girl-next-door Kylie Minogue's reinvention as a saucy minx in gold hot-pants to the sexual shenanigans and emotional fall-out which preoccupies Channel 4's drama *Skins* (Channel 4: 2007–11). Yet the picture is not as simple as increasing revelations of flesh and throwing-off of all moral constraints.

Linda McLoughlin's (2000) analysis of newspaper coverage of teen magazines and their contents revealed that journalists' concerns appear to centre on three main issues: (1) that the explicit nature of information in these magazines will result in the loss to young women of their innocence; (2) that to supply young women with sexual information will encourage them to rush out and put this into practice; and (3) that the 'bombardment' of sex information will put pressure on young women by making them feel that everyone is doing it, and that therefore they should, too (241). Interestingly, McLoughlin's assessment could be applied without modification to the more recent reports from Papadopoulous and both the American and Australian Psychological Association reports. Thus the panic about teens learning too much too young is not new.

Moreover, McLoughlin's in-depth study of the language of teen magazines found that while many magazines did include material focused on sex and sexuality, the explicitness of the information clearly depended on the target age range of the magazines. In other words, editors were extremely careful to pitch their discussions in such a way that they wouldn't alienate their actual readers, although that did not preclude upsetting teachers and parents. She also concluded that material aimed at the younger age range contained little which might be described as explicit. Where advice was given about sex the dominant message to the teen reader was to wait until a secure, romantic relationship was established.

If young women and sex are of such concern, what about young men? The debates, both recent and old, replicate the double standard regarding male and female sexuality. This assumes that adolescent boys' interest in sex is inevitable and, to an extent, natural, while in young women it is to be controlled for their own sake, and restrained in case it inflames young men. Young men are portrayed as being at the mercy of their own animalistic biology, and therefore the victims of young women's media-induced and presumably faked sexual interests. Young men's interests in pornography have increasingly become the subject of concern, particularly where some commentators cite children as young as 11 having access to porn via the web, but even so there remains a tendency to see such inquisitiveness as a healthy part of their growing up. Many parents are relieved to find hidden pornographic material in their son's bedroom (McLoughlin), though, of course, that might be different if the material were gay porn. What tends to unite the various worries and concerns about young people is a refusal to actually ask young people what *they* think they get out of popular culture's approaches to sex and how *they* think they might be influenced, if at all.

Those questions are beyond the scope of this chapter, but we would like to examine some popular texts consumed by teenage girls which have caused considerable controversy because of the sexual themes underpinning the stories they present to their young audiences. We will examine how those sexual themes both reflect cultural mores around developing sexuality and articulate particular problems that can be a part of teenage experience.

Teen magazines are not the only aspect of popular culture that has attracted concerns regarding the 'safety' of teenage girls and their media choices. The last two decades have seen repeated concerns about the ways in which teen horror novels have depicted sexuality. The book series *Point Horror*, first launched in February 1991, was subject to much criticism despite the fact none of the stories depict explicitly sexual activities. Published by Scholastic, *Point Horror* is something of a publishing phenomenon, with millions of books sold in Britain and up to three new titles appearing in the bookshops each month. The huge appeal of the series did not go unnoticed: its popularity received significant attention from parents, libraries, schools and the national press, to the extent that it was even suggested by Victoria Neumark, in her article 'The Attack of the Serial Thriller' (1996), that 'a moral panic concerning *Point Horror* now afflicts society'. According to the many literary reviews that appeared in newspapers during the mid-1990s, parents, teachers and educationalists considered *Point Horror* novels to be unsuitable reading for youngsters.

Such public discourses are interesting in that they express society's fears about how young people's reading material might affect their presumed sexual activity (we should note that as often as not, the expressed fears are about what kids *might* do, rather than what they *are* doing). However, in cultural studies, researchers are more interested in how sexuality is constructed and represented than in judging material as either suitable or unsuitable. In young people's literature, horror remains the most popular reading material for teenage girls today. In the rest of this chapter, we will examine the representation of teenage sexuality in the teen bestsellers *Point Horror* and *Twilight* using the psychoanalytic approaches outlined in Chapter 2. We are using the psychoanalytic approach here because Freud's emphasis on the transition from infantile to adult sexuality seems appropriate for examining the liminal spaces of the horror genre, but also because his ideas about the subconscious and repression are often so clearly articulated in horror's gothic and uncanny themes.

Nicholas Tucker (1992) argues that psychological theories have had crucial effects on children's literature, with many authors relying upon child psychology, particularly Freudian approaches, in their treatment of fictional characters. Referring to Freud, Italo Stevo argues that 'Freud is of more value to writers than to sick patients' while Emily Apter suggests that Freud wasn't just a psychoanalyst, he was also among the greatest fantasists (Apter, 1982).

Freud wrote specifically and extensively on the changing relationships that adolescents have to their parents in *Three Essays on the Theory of Sexuality* (1974). According to Freud (and recapping some of our discussion in Chapter 2) the onset of puberty is particularly disturbing to the personality because it reactivates conflicts and anxieties of the past but within the new context of what he termed the 'final sexual organization'. For Freud, the period of adolescence has the specific function of fixing heterosexuality through the young girl's giving up of desires for the father and turning to identification with the mother as castrated. This requires firstly a change to Oedipal objects, in that the teenager must finally give up Oedipal wishes; secondly, a change in relationships with peers; and finally, a change in attitude to the body so that the image of her body must now include her own sexually mature organs. He concluded, though, that for girls it is more difficult to deal with this separation since they are sexually more suppressed than boys within and by culture (Gross, 1996: 538).

> The development of the inhibitions of sexuality (shame, disgust, pity, etc.) takes place in girls earlier and in the face of less resistance than in boys; the tendency to sexual repression seems in general to be greater. (Freud, 1974: 85)

In the horror genre, Oedipal issues are often explored through the presence of a belittled mother and an absent father (think of Buffy and her inadequate mother in *Buffy the Vampire Slayer* (Fox: 1997–2003)). These are the themes we will focus on in this section.

The prominent convention in horror is to introduce, from the onset, a white, middle-class teenager who is entering the journey into adult sexuality and grappling with concerns such as friendships, family and independence. These issues are explored through the theme of isolation imbued in the genre. For example, from Scholastic's *Point Horror* series to *Buffy the Vampire Slayer* to *Twilight*, the central, female character is seen dealing with problems brought by her relocation to a new town following one parent's desertion of the family for a new relationship. The hero/heroine has lost her childhood friends through the move, rarely has siblings, but is also usually the product of a dysfunctional family and their behaviour is the result of previous trauma. Added to this is usually a supernatural element, and combinations of fear, revulsion and fascination for other outsiders such as vampires or werewolves, who have appetites they cannot control but who also offer excitements that ordinary mortals cannot. The lone hero/heroine has been abandoned by those who ought to protect them and has to navigate their way through trials and tribulations whilst developing skills of self-protection. The following is typical: the opening scenes of one of the most popular books from the *Point Horror* series *The Boyfriend* introduces central character Joanna as a deserted daughter suffering feelings of depression after her father leaves to live with his young lover.

> I was Daddy's girl. Of course, thought Joanna, her smile now completely gone, that didn't stop him from leaving. She hadn't even heard from him on her sixteenth birthday. (Stine, 1990: 1)

Not only has Dad abandoned her, but Mum turns out to be of little use. In *Point Horror* the mother is often portrayed from the daughter's viewpoint as a silly, weak or vain woman who is generally disparaged or scorned. In this, it is easy to see why these novels should be so popular amongst teenagers – they dramatize fairly typical teenage experiences of conflict (however minor) with parents. However, it is particularly interesting and clearly owes much to the notion of Freudian generational disputes that even though Joanna's depression is motivated by her anger at her father and his abandonment of the family, it is her mother who becomes the object of rejection – Joanna does not intend to become *like* her mother:

> There were lots of compliments from Dad, Joanna thought bitterly, walking away from the meeting place by the bookstore, crossing the aisleway, then stopping. I was Daddy's girl, 'a *real* Collier'.
> 'Daddy's little go-getter.' That's what Sherman Collier, Joanna's father, always called her. His highest compliment: 'Daddy's little go-getter. She'll never take no for an answer.' (Stine, 1990: 1)

Joanna persists in a kind of childish love for her father, resentful but at the same time reluctant to see him for the flawed human being he is. She is also reluctant to let go of her father's definitions of her:

> She straightened her blue sweater, the one her father had bought her because it matched her eyes so perfectly. It was getting a bit tight now. Why did she still insist on wearing it? (Stine, 1990: 6)

In this passage we see that Joanna is reluctant to accept the bodily changes that come with puberty (though at the same time, wearing a too-tight sweater demonstrates to others – especially Dad – that she is growing up) or indeed to accept the development of a new self-concept which isn't dependent on Dad's good opinion. Instead, we learn from the first page of *The Boyfriend* that Joanna yearns for her father's affection. As Freud said:

Representations of Teenage Sexuality 115

> There are those who never get over their parents' authority and have withdrawn their affection from them either very incompletely or not at all. They are mostly girls, who, to the delight of their parents, have persisted in all their childish love far beyond puberty. Girls with an exaggerated need for affection have an irresistible temptation to realize the ideal asexual love in their lives by holding fast throughout their lives to their infantile fondness, revived at puberty for their parents. (1974: 85)

Joanna is torn between love for her father and identification with her mother in her anger against him. In the *Point Horror* series the heroine's emotions towards her parents are complex – anger at the powerful father but also feelings of need for his continuing affection and attention even though she is often aware this cannot happen. Moreover, relations with the mother are even more fraught as the heroines feel resentment towards their mothers for allowing themselves to become victims. For mothers in these novels, ageing is a process that brings loss of beauty and thereby results in their loss of place as the father's object of desire, producing, in the heroine, feelings of revulsion towards Mum. The following opening scenes of two books illustrate the ways in which the mother in *Point Horror* is constructed as a figure to be ridiculed as the reader shares the main character's disapproving gaze:

> Her mousy little mother. She always looked so small and gunny inside the glamorous fur coat she wore everywhere with the collar pulled up almost over her head. It always made Joanna laugh – to herself of course. She couldn't blame her father for wanting a little more. (Stine, 1990: 3)

> [...] in her flowing fuschia-and-electric-blue dress that was just a little too snug on her plump body, her platinum hair piled high on her head. (Stine, 1990: 5)

In these ways the texts situate the heroine alongside the father, making the mother into an object that is both disparaged and marginal to the narrative. Mothers in *Point Horror* are depicted as powerless, and this gives rise to fears of the heroine's own sexual maturity, ageing and the fragmenting body. Joanna constantly looks in the mirror to affirm her beauty and this is articulated in contrast to her mother:

> She knew she was beautiful. Why should she force herself to have false modesty and pretend she didn't know, like some simpering young thing in one of those embarrassing Elvis movies Dex had forced her to watch on TV?
> She had the Collier good looks. That's what her father always told her – usually as a dig at her mother. She had high cheekbones, the perfect, straight nose, the clear blue eyes that always seemed to be opened wide,

the proud high forehead, and the straight sunlight-blonde hair, so smooth and straight that it looked beautiful even cut so stylishly short. (Stine, 1990: 3)

Even as Joanna is the centre of the narrative, and although readers are introduced to Joanna's depressed mental state in the opening chapters, more attention is given to describing her cruel and sexually transgressive behaviour than to explaining her unhappiness. In this way, the texts are hardly to be considered progressive in their gender and sexual politics. Joanna's 'crime', for which she is disproportionately punished in the narrative resolution, is that she breaks the discursive codes of romantic monogamy that insist that 'proper' female sexuality is confined to the context of sentimental love for one man. Instead, Joanna has two boyfriends, Dex and Shep, and cannot choose between them. When Dex discovers her disloyalty, he does not merely reject her but punishes her mercilessly. He pretends to die in an accident, and, terrified that she may be in trouble for driving her mother's car, Joanna runs away from the scene without reporting it. But Dex comes back from the 'dead' to punish Joanna for her behaviour in two-timing him. He pursues her, enters her bedroom at night, and terrifies the poor girl to the extent that she very nearly kills herself. At the end, it is finally revealed that Dex is not in fact dead; rather the accident had been a plan hatched between Dex and Joanna's friend Mary to punish her. So, although Joanna is an active agent and strong at the beginning, her power decreases, not only because she is the victim of a male figure of fear, but also because she is 'taught' socially acceptable behaviour in regard to adult relationships through the forced recognition of her own selfishness. 'I don't have a friend, a single friend. Maybe I never did. Because I never really knew how to care about any of them' (Stine, 1990: 164). Clearly there is a strong element of melodrama in these stories, but the idea that they might teach young women to be overly sexual is more than just an exaggeration – the narrative is resolved through punishment of the young woman who seeks to break sexual regulations.

Freud's influence on how adolescence has come to be understood cannot be underestimated – his ideas that normal adolescent development to adulthood is fraught with emotional turmoil and anxiety are widely accepted. But Freud saw this journey as inevitably leading to heterosexuality: as we have already argued, this 'normal' outcome of development renders other sexual practices and identities as 'abnormal' or 'perverse'. And in stories dramatizing the difficulties young people face in coming to sexual maturity, that Freudian influence can be keenly felt. As we discussed in Chapter 5 in relation to more adult representations, heterosexuality is often assumed; in teen popular culture there are few openly gay/lesbian characters and there is little on offer to a teenager looking for support and comfort allied to developing a lesbian/gay identity (although this is changing with dramas such as *Skins*, *Misfits* (E4: 2009–) and *Sugar Rush* (Channel 4: 2005–09)).

On the other hand, any discussion of the politics of representation needs to consider processes of constructing oppositional meanings. One way of considering oppositional meanings in relation to sexuality is illustrated by Alison Hennegan. In her essay 'On Becoming a Lesbian Reader', Hennegan discusses her relationship to novels, which, as an adolescent, opened up a space for her to produce her own oppositional, non-normative readings:

> Sometimes, I knew, books gave me something of that same ill-defined pleasure which I increasingly needed and sought. It wasn't easy to define at first, which made it difficult to seek it out, and made even stranger that sudden flash of recognition sparked by a particular book. (1988: 168)

Although the heroines in *Point Horror* are constructed as heterosexual, their descriptions of females who are objects of the heroine's gaze often have sexual implications:

> Constance was still facing Michael, drinking him in almost. Her lovely profile was outlined by the setting sun, and the perfection of her gave Althea shivers. (Cooney, 1992: 94)

In these novels, then, erotic descriptions constructed by another female open a space for a female reader to desire a female character. These are key pleasures in the horror novel, where the suspense and intrigue of the narrative relies upon nothing being what it seems. In this way the genre allows a space in which sexuality can become fluid and thrilling, especially in vampiric images:

> What a lovely neck she has, Althea thought. It really is swanlike; just the way a high-fashion model's should be. What soft white skin she has. (Cooney, 1992: 21)

Of course there are still limits to the potential of a non-normative interpretation for the lesbian reader. Although the heroine and the reader can desire other girls, they 'cannot, like them, be desired' (Hennegan, 1988: 168).

Even so, horror may well offer young readers particular pleasures centred on sexual feelings as well as the thrills of suspense and terror. Richard Dyer observed that the idea of the vampire lends itself to a sexual reading and is 'perhaps the highest symbolic representation of eroticism' (1993: 56). He argues that

> on the one hand, the point about sexual orientation is that it doesn't show, you can't tell who is and who isn't just by looking; but on the other hand, there is also a widespread discourse that there *are* tell-tale signs that someone is. The vampire myth reproduces this double view in its very structures of suspense. (Dyer, 1993: 58)

Precisely because the vampire takes an 'ordinary' human form, they can pass amongst humans. Early vampire fiction, says Dyer, expressed terror as well as the excitement of a forbidden sexuality, whereas more recent literature has tended to celebrate the possibilities presented by the vampire and his transgressive sexuality, as we can see in the relationship between Louis and Lestat in Anne Rice's *Interview with the Vampire* (1976). Dyer suggests that the horror genre relies on voyeurism, the privatized experience and exhibitionism:

> There is nothing inherently gay or lesbian in the ideas of privacy, voyeurism and exhibitionism. Yet homosexual desire, like other forbidden sexual desires, may well find expression, as a matter of necessity rather than exquisite choice, in privacy and voyeurism. The sense that being lesbian/gay is something one must keep to oneself certainly accords with an idea of the authenticity of private sexuality, but also it is something one had better keep private if one is not to lose family, friends and so on. Furtive looking may be the most one dare do. (Dyer, 1993: 57)

Although early vampire fiction stressed the ugliness of the un-dead man who preyed on innocents for their blood, since Bram Stoker's rendition of the myth, vampires have usually been considered handsome or beautiful, sophisticated and seductive. Their beauty may be only a façade but their attractiveness is intensely sexual. Their mode of destruction – the penetration of the skin by sharp canine teeth – is at once violent, tender and erotic.

Although they appear very different on the surface, the same fear found in *Point Horror* – of the pubescent girl who needs to be controlled – permeates *Twilight*, but as a vampire story there is a strong underlying eroticization of the male character, the sparkly, dangerous vampire. Written by Stephenie Meyer, *Twilight* (2005) and its sequels *New Moon* (2006), *Breaking Dawn* (2007) and *Eclipse* (2008) are international bestsellers that have made the transition to the screen with equal success. The story centres on Bella, a young woman who goes to live with her father (Charlie), in the town of Forkes, following her abandonment by her mother who has chosen to pursue her own adventures, travelling with her young lover. Isolated from her childhood friends and living with a father who hardly understands her, Bella is also beginning to come to terms with her own sexual desires. Bella's mother is not a 'good' mother, in that she refuses the self-abnegating role of self-sacrificing nurturer and demands her own life and pleasures. As first-person narrator, Bella offers her perspective on her mother's behaviour: although never sadistic or deliberately cruel, Bella's mother is so inept that she offers Bella little, if any, adult support or consolation. This 'failure' on the part of her mother leads Bella into a role reversal where she feels responsible and casts her mother as a childlike figure to be looked after.

For example, in an email telling of her safe arrival at Forkes, Bella reminds her mum that 'your blouse is at the dry cleaners – you were supposed to pick it up Friday' (29). Bella is amazingly stoic: '"My mom always says I was born thirty-five years old and that I get more middle-aged every year," I laughed, and then sighed. "Well, someone has to be the adult… My mother, she's very young for her age. I think Phil makes her feel younger"' (91). Rather than calling her father 'dad', Bella refers to him as Charlie, illustrating her perspective as his equal. He, too, is a victim of her mother's selfishness, but has also failed to mature: 'It was impossible, being in this house, not to realize that Charlie had never gotten over my mom. It made me uncomfortable' (10–11).

Thus, with two fairly ineffectual parents, Bella seeks romance: her favourite books are *Pride and Prejudice*, *Emma* and *Mansfield Park*, all novels written by Jane Austen. Interestingly, these are precisely the novels cited by critics of sexualized media as being 'better' than more contemporary fiction aimed at teenagers (Marshall, 2010). They are also romantic novels where girl meets boy and eventually the couple get their happy ending; they are also quite sharp in their observations of the ways in which class, money, family and gender are implicated in romance; and Bella's mother is just like at least one mother from a Jane Austen novel – Lady Bertram in *Mansfield Park*, whose vanity, childishness and selfishness means she fails to ensure the safety and chastity of her daughter. Lady Bertram lavishes love on the wrong object – her lapdog – and Bella's mother lavishes hers on her younger boyfriend. There is little to be admired in Bella's mother but this bears out gothic scholar P.A.M. Spacks' observations that 'the admirable daughters owe relatively little that we can see to their parents' (1981: 177). Indeed, in a reversal of roles, it is Bella who is self-sacrificial, pretending that she wants to live with her estranged father so that her mother can indulge herself. When her mother says, not very convincingly, that Bella can come home whenever she wants, Bella could see 'the sacrifice behind the eyes' and so lies and says that she wants to go (4).

In this context of abandonment and the need for someone to nurture her, Bella confronts issues of womanhood, emerging sexuality and intimacy for the first time. Although aged 17, presumably older than the reader (core readership is between 12 and 16) and unlike the experienced Joanna in *The Boyfriend*, Bella has never had a boyfriend or even been kissed. At school she meets the spellbinding Edward Cullen. In many ways Edward is typical of a Jane Austen hero like Mr Darcy: he is handsome, powerful, rich yet aloof. When they meet they are immediately attracted to one another but Edward responds to Bella angrily. It is not until Edward explains the reasons for his anger – that it is a mask for his love for her – that misunderstandings are worked through and the romance develops. And, although it may seem a contradiction in terms given the conventions of horror, *Twilight* is ultimately a romance.

Although Edward appears in Bella's bedroom every night, initially without her knowledge, and is clearly passionate in his desire for her, it is he who insists that they abstain from sexual intercourse until they are married:

> 'I'm tired of trying to stay away from you, Bella.' His eyes were gloriously intense as he uttered that last sentence, his voice smoldering. I couldn't remember how to breathe. 'Will you go with me to Seattle?' he asked, still intense.
> I couldn't speak yet, so I just nodded.
> He smiled briefly, and then his face became serious.
> 'You really *should* stay away from me,' he warned. 'I'll see you in class.' (72)

As with many vampire novels, vampirism and sexuality are entwined in *Twilight*. The mingling of blood and the sexual nature of the bite that brings living death have been explored as metaphors for sexual corruption. And in one scene it is clear that sex and becoming a vampire are one and the same thing. When Bella asks if they will ever be close, Edward replies 'I could kill you quite easily, Bella, simply by accident'. Edward's desire for blood is something he controls, and even if his particular desire for Bella's blood is almost overwhelming, he restrains himself. Edward is depicted as a boyfriend who cares enough to fight his own desires and delay Bella's sexual awakening. In response to her passion he urges sexual abstinence and restraint:

> 'You're ready now, then?' he asked.
> 'Um.' I gulped 'Yes?'
> He smiled, and inclined his head slowly until his cold lips brushed against the skin just under the corner of my jaw.
> 'Right now?' he whispered, his breath blowing cool on my neck. I shivered involuntarily.
> 'Yes,' I whispered, so my voice wouldn't have a chance to break. If he thought I was bluffing he was going to be disappointed. I'd already made this decision, I was sure. It didn't matter that my body was as rigid as a plank, my hands balled into fists, my breathing erratic.... (433)

Edward urges the long-lasting pleasures of romantic attachment rather than sexual lust, promising 'I *will* stay with you – isn't that enough?' (433). Much has been made of Stephenie Meyer's Mormon religion and therefore the idea that the abstinence message is tied up in a particular form of religious morality. For many, *Twilight* offers a very retrograde version of female sexuality and sexual desire. But it is the abstinence message that has really upset some critics:

> [T]he abstinence message – wrapped in the genre of abstinence porn – objectifies Bella in the same ways that 'real' porn might. The *Twilight* books conflate Bella's loss of virginity with the loss of other things, including her sense of self and her very life. Such a high-stakes treatment of abstinence reinforces the idea that Bella is powerless, an object, a fact that is highlighted when we get to the sex scenes in *Breaking Dawn*. (Seifert, 2008)

It is not just that critics like Seifert do not like the abstinence message, but that they see in it, and in the *Twilight* novels more generally, an attempt to regulate female sexuality and excuse male sexuality. As Foucault suggested, feminine bodies have been discursively produced as saturated in sexuality and therefore requiring constant surveillance, regulation and punishment. For Seifert this is a key element of *Twilight*'s narrative arc.

> Edward has taken on the role of protector of Bella's human blood and chastity, both of which, ironically, are always in peril when Edward is nearby. Bella is not in control of her body, as abstinence proponents would argue; she is absolutely dependent on Edward's ability to protect her life, her virginity, and her humanity. She is the object of his virtue, the means of his ability to prove his self-control. In other words, Bella is a secondary player in the drama of Edward's abstinence. (Seifert, 2008)

It could be concluded, therefore, that the conventions of popular teenage horror writing do little to challenge conservative discourses about regulation of sex and sexuality. The dominant discourses of romance prevail: that it is a heterosexual practice, that active sexuality is only given approval if it involves 'true' love, monogamy and the expectation of marriage, and that it is boyfriends who define and control the sexuality of the girls. Both *The Boyfriend* and *Twilight* construct Oedipal scenarios in their depiction of characters dealing with a parent's desertion and loss of friends. In *The Boyfriend* Joanna learns that her response to these Freudian difficulties was wholly inappropriate, whilst Bella, in *Twilight*, finds help through a young man who honourably insists that they abstain from sex until marriage. The significance of these texts is that, far from promoting promiscuity, both *Point Horror* and *Twilight* uphold conservative ways of thinking about female sexuality and appropriate ways of acting on feelings of desire. Both register teenage anxiety about changing relationships with parents and emerging sexuality whilst at the same time promoting the benefits of conforming to cultural constraints. In both instances it is teenage boys who restrain their girlfriends, control sexual advances and regulate female sexuality – Dex's punishment of Joanna's behaviour and Edward's protectiveness and refusal of sex beyond passionate kissing. We wonder how effective boys are as gatekeepers of sexual activity in the world outside representation – but that would be another story.

Further Reading

Harman, S. and Clayton, W. (eds) (2013) *Screening Twilight: Critical Approaches to a Cinematic Phenomenon* (London: I.B.Tauris).

Karlyn, K.R. (2011) *Unruly Girls, Unrepentant Mothers: Redefining Feminism on Screen* (Austin: University of Texas Press).

Radstone, S. (ed.) (1988) *Sweet Dreams: Sexuality, Gender and Popular Fiction* (London: Lawrence and Wishart).

Sexual Cultures

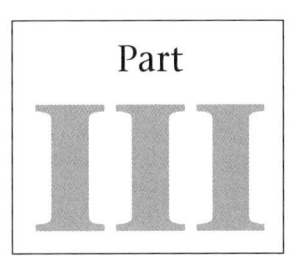

Part III

Introduction to Part III

In the previous part we considered contemporary media representations of sexuality, and in this part we move on to analyse specific practices. The chapters in this part will engage with the debates raised in the theories section in ways that complicate those theoretical perspectives, and question their universal applicability to the myriad practices of sex. While sex may be acknowledged as an important part of an individual's sense of self and thus understood as a matter of personal choice, we will consider how practices including masturbation, use of sex toys, sadomasochism, cybersex, subcultural sexual identifications and commercial sexual practices are intimately tied up in ideas of what counts as 'normal'. In the 1980s cultural anthropologist Gayle Rubin wrote a short but important paper about hierarchical approaches to sex, where 'proper' sex (heterosexual, married, procreative sex) is ranked at the top of the hierarchy and everything else goes underneath. But Rubin also wanted to capture some of the complications around sexuality. It isn't simply a matter of 'good' sex at the top and 'bad' at the bottom – even married heterosexuals can indulge in so-called 'bad' sex. To illustrate the complexities of attitudes to and definitions of sexuality, Rubin drew the 'charmed circle' (]Figure 1 near here[Figure 1). It consists of two circles, an inner and an outer, and various divisions within each. The closer to the centre of the inner circle one's practices fall, the more 'acceptable' or 'natural' they are understood to be. The outer circle encompasses the 'outer limits' of sexuality, where we find supposedly 'unacceptable' or 'unnatural' activities. We have already talked about the ways in which sex is defined as normative (see our discussion in Chapter 3), but what this circle allows us to see is that definitions of sex are a matter of degree, and that even the normative does not necessarily have a stable centre. Society is increasingly tolerant of 'alternative' sexualities – as we'll discuss in the following chapters, sex toys or a little bit of BDSM are recognized as appropriate ways of 'spicing up' one's sex life, especially for monogamous heterosexuals – but this can tip into 'unacceptable' behaviour if the practices are not contained within the bedroom or are filmed for distribution. Equally, sex between same-sex partners is increasingly 'acceptable', but often toleration only seems to extend to those whose sex lives remain 'private' and contained within marriage or a civil partnership.

The sexual does not exist separate from popular culture, national identity, politics and the social more generally. How we have sex, what we think about it, and our sexual pleasures and fears are closely tied to community, personal identity, forms of consumption, legislation and regulation – and in our focus

125

on practices these multiple sites come into view. Increasingly, sex is a matter of intense commercialization and individualization in most Western nations. New technologies and rising affluence have had an extraordinary impact on the ways we think and talk about sex, how we represent it and how we practise it. Print media, television, books and, more recently, the internet tell us how to improve our sex lives, get more or better sex, and keep on having sex even after marriage (funny how, despite its position as the only 'appropriate' outlet for sex, marriage is constantly referred to as the murderer of desire). We can now purchase the accessories for a 'good' sex life if not the actual sex itself. Sex is a leisure activity, a means of expressing oneself and immersing oneself in pleasure. Therapeutic eroticism is offered everywhere: good sex is *de rigueur*. Keeping the sexual flames alive in long-term relationships was the key theme of Channel 4's *The Sex Inspectors* (2004–06) and Channel 5's *How to Have Sex After Marriage* (2007–08), both reality-expert formats where couples were given the advice they needed to reignite their sexual passions. Television confessional shows from the US like *Jerry Springer* (NBC: 1991–) also focus on the different kinds of pleasures of sexual hedonism as well as the problems of playing with the boundaries of 'normative' sexual relations. Documentaries focus on the ways in which we acquire sexual knowledge – as in the *Sex Education vs Pornography Show* (Channel 4: 2009) – and their companion websites offer advice on a variety of topics from anatomy through to performance. As Jane Arthurs has observed, 'television discourses about sexuality are increasing not only in quantity but also in the range of moral and ideological positions from which events and issues are debated and evaluated' (2004: 2).

Sexual practices have also expanded to include forms of technologized interactions with like-minded individuals across the globe. One only needs an internet connection in order to hook up with someone somewhere who shares your sexual interests; most often we read about this in relation to the expansion of paedophile communities, but it is also true of less taboo eroticisms such as clothing fetishes and swinging. Socio-sexual identities have emerged including 'new femininities' characterized by 'sexual and social confidence, aspiration and career ambition' (Ticknell *et al.*, 2003: 47); homosexuality has shaken off the pathologized and medicalized definitions of the 'sad young man' (Dyer, 1993) to embrace gay pride and the pursuit of an open and pleasure-focused lifestyle; sexual minorities – gay, transsexual, transgendered and sadomasochistic – claim their spaces of visibility online and hence 'normalize' practices once considered outrageous.

As Feona Attwood remarks,

> what sex is about or for is changing. It is a cultural pursuit, an exercise of taste, a set of skills, a communicative practice, a performance, a form of self-care, and a type of leisure in which media are produced and consumed. (2010: 88)

Even as we recognize the ways in which our definitions of sex and our understanding of its role in our lives are changing, Rubin's charmed circle is still a useful conceptual tool. It is not a template for definitions of sex, but it does give us some sense of the ways in which definitions are fluid and political. As she observes:

> They are imbued with conflicts of interest and political maneuver, both deliberate and incidental. In that sense, sex is always political. But there are also historical periods in which sexuality is more sharply contested and more overtly politicized. In such periods, the domain of erotic life is, in effect, renegotiated. (Rubin, 2007: 143)

Even as we are more open about sex, there is still widespread unease about what sex can make us do. It is still considered a force to be contained for the good of the 'family', for women or particularly for children. Rubin suggests that we view sex as a kind of slippery slope: one false move and an individual can be outside the charmed circle in moments. This fear of sex as a destructive force is often evoked in calls for legislation against the internet, pornography, 'perverts' and others who indulge in 'bad' sex. Sex is a potent fear in that it is never just that certain individuals might want to 'defile' themselves, but that if some people stray outside, 'the barrier against scary sex will crumble and something unspeakable will skitter across' (Rubin, 2007: 152). As we'll discuss in the following chapters, worries about masturbation, BDSM and pornography are not just about particular individuals and what they get up to, they are worries about what might happen to society and culture. Thus part of what we would like you to take from the following is a sense of the ways in which 'acceptable' sexual practices are expanding, but also a recognition of how such expansions create their own sets of anxieties. This short part and the three chapters in it cannot cover all the different practices of sexuality in the early twenty-first century, nor indeed all the competing arguments about agency, freedom and identity that surface whenever analysis of a cultural practice is attempted. We offer some brief snapshots of contemporary practices but hopefully these will open up ways of thinking about other sexual activities, behaviours, practices and pleasures that you can carry over into your own studies and research.

Chapter 9

Sexualization, Commodifying Sex and the Mainstreaming of Masturbation

Experts estimate that more than 90% of men (Giddens, 1992: 16) and more than 80% of women (Hite, 2004: 463) masturbate regularly, thus it is one of the most everyday forms of sexual release and seemingly most 'natural'. Even so, the following problem sent to the Channel 4 Sex Education pages illustrates the ways in which this very personal pleasure is still a source of much anxiety and misinformation:

> Hi, I am 16 year old and I wanted to know that if masturbation had any adverse affects on a person's growth and development as I feel I have stopped growing in height since I was 15, and since then I have masturbated frequently. I wanted to know if I have stopped growing in height? (Channel 4 website)

As with many other sexual practices, masturbation occupies a contradictory space in Western culture. It is advocated as the safest sexual practice we can engage in, as there are no risks of sexually transmitted infections or unwanted pregnancies and, as Woody Allen put it, 'Don't knock masturbation: It's sex with someone I love' (*Annie Hall*: 1977). Apparently, it is also good for reducing stress, and promoting healthy self-esteem. Even so, there are many who see masturbation as a problematic practice leading to failure at school, inability to forge meaningful relationships and eventually addiction.

If we look to popular culture we see these contradictory understandings of masturbation played out. In an episode of the popular family sitcom *Roseanne* (ABC: 1988–97), the teenage character DJ (played by Michael Fishman) is discovered masturbating by his father (John Goodman) who then feels he must have a talk with his son. Dad is embarrassed by the discussion but wants to reassure DJ that it's okay to masturbate, and says 'The funny thing about this is that even though it's okay and everybody does it ... there's nothing wrong with it ... nobody ever talks about it' (S.6, ep.7: 1993). Masturbation is the subject of embarrassment, something to be done in secret. That capacity for shame is a key element in popular culture representations. In *There's Something About Mary* (dir. Farrelly Brothers: 1998), the character Ted (played by Ben Stiller) masturbates before his date with Mary so that he won't think about sex during the date. Masturbation is thus a form of hygiene, cleansing the mind of sexual thoughts, a means of disciplining the male sexual urge and rendering it safe: Ted's friend advises him that by getting rid of his immediate sexual excitement, he'll 'be thinking like a girl' during the date. But as well as 'cleaning the pipes', the scene also includes other euphemisms for masturbation including 'choking the chicken', 'spanking the monkey' and 'flogging the dolphin': all of which suggest the penis is a bit of a beast, a thing with a mind of its own – and that by dealing with its importuning horniness, the beast can be tamed.

Foucault wrote about masturbation as one of the key sites of prohibition *and* incitement to discourse. For Foucault, the pleasures of masturbation are actually produced by the attempts to prevent it. In the 'repressive hypothesis' Foucault shows how in the eighteenth and nineteenth centuries attempts were made to prevent boys masturbating and that this took a number of forms, so that questions of sex infused a whole range of seemingly unconnected areas of life including the building of schools:

> [T]he space for classes, the shape of the tables, the planning of the recreation lessons, the distribution of the dormitories (with or without partitions, with or without curtains), the rules for monitoring bedtime and sleep periods – all this referred, in the most prolix manner, to the sexuality of children. (1990a: 28)

So rather than repressing and silencing male children's sexuality, kids were drawn into a web of discourses which spoke about them and sometimes to them. What this meant was that rather than being silenced, the practices of masturbation were brought out into the open where they could be surveilled, endlessly discussed and policed. The teachers and parents who were so intent on repressing masturbation relied on it being practised in order to stop it: by condemning certain practices and forcing them into hiding, their discovery and examination becomes possible. This is a process which is intensely gratifying for everyone concerned: parents have the thrill of surveillance and discovery and children get the thrill of attracting attention and getting around the authority that wants to stop them enjoying themselves. Foucault offers a way of examining how particular pleasures are produced through negotiation with regulatory regimes: masturbation is not *just* pleasing yourself; its pleasures are also derived from the acknowledgement that others disapprove of what you're doing. But why are there the cultural, moral, social and medical injunctions against masturbation?

Drawing on religious teachings, medics used to think that masturbation was a 'bad' pleasure, and offered dire warnings about the effects of 'self-abuse' which ranged from madness to infertility. You won't find many people making those claims now, but there are still worries about masturbation as not 'real' sex that may well tell us more about our problems with pleasure than about what it means to masturbate. Many of our leisure pursuits focus on our bodies, or the putting aside of our rational minds. Our pleasures in fictions, drinking alcohol, taking drugs, sex, dancing and music revolve around trying to break away from our sense of self, doing something out of the ordinary. The attempts to regulate our hedonistic activities are often proposed for our own 'good' or for the good of 'society', which suggests there might be something intrinsically subversive in the pursuit of pleasure.

With masturbation, traces of those fears still remain, particularly in, for example, discussions of pornography, where objectors do not want to claim that masturbation is bad for you: instead they suggest that material which encourages masturbation has 'harmful effects', that it is sexist, degrading, exploitative and teaches men to view women as objects. Moreover, in the newspaper reports of internet porn addiction and the frequent appearance of problem page letters about men who no longer want to have sex with their partners because they are too busy enjoying sexually explicit websites, we find lots of claims that pornography is alienating, that it encourages 'solitary sex'. It is this element of doing it on one's own that supposedly leads to unrealistic expectations and 'unnatural' desires. One of the oldest complaints about pornography and the accompanying masturbation lie in the fact that it encourages a form of sex which is not tied to producing children, and is therefore wasteful and selfish. This economic argument about wastefulness has been around for a long time. As Thomas Laqueur writes, the arguments go that

> [s]emen, money and energy are all in short supply and are profligately expended at the wastrel's peril. Just as in the world of trade and commerce one must discipline one's use of scarce resources, so in the spermatic economy men need to save and to husband their precious bodily fluid... The economic realm maps nicely onto the corporeal one. (2003: 194–5)

Richard Dyer (2002) also suggests there is a link between the economic system and attitudes towards pleasure. He argues that our problems with pleasure stem from the body's problematic place in the capitalist system: under capitalism the body and its labours exist purely as the foundation of economic life. And it is not difficult to see why masturbation might be such a threat to the idea of the market – you don't need anyone else to do it, it's potentially a limitless pleasure, you can carry on as long as you like and it doesn't have to cost anything.

As we have already seen with the examples outlined above, masturbation is a potential cause of shame, especially for men, associated as it is with solitary and alienated experiences. As Mr Denton puts it in the BBC series *The League of Gentlemen* (1999–2002), 'In this house, we don't masturbate... It's not a very pleasant thing to do' (S.1, ep.1). And this formulation of masturbation as a not nice thing is confirmed in films as diverse as Almodóvar's *Matador* (1986) and *The Cell* (dir. Tarsem Singh: 2000), where self-pleasuring is part of a wider range of inadequacies and pathological issues typified by the main characters.

Thinking about sexual practices we can't avoid thinking about pleasure but often it gets displaced onto worries about deviancy, addiction and harm. As Paul Martin puts it in his recent book:

> Pleasure is a slippery beast. We know it when we feel it. Wanting more seems obvious. But what of the troubles it leads us into? ... What of that segue from pleasure to addiction – that dreaded slide from 'This is nice' to 'This is destroying me and I can't stop?' Secular and religious authorities have tried throughout history to control the main sources of human pleasure... They seem to have shared Plato's opinion that pleasure is the greatest incentive to evil. (2008: 1–2)

For Freudians our pleasures in recreational sex are ways of retrieving the erotic satisfactions we experienced as babies and getting back to a state of plenitude where we escape the restrictions imposed by society. In this sense, psychoanalytic perspectives on pleasure establish pleasure-seeking as an infantile desire to withdraw from social reality: a retreat into the pre-Oedipal, pre-linguistic world of plenitude, where differences and lack are erased. For Freud, masturbation was a lesser form of sexuality, and he claimed that men who masturbated risked not only reducing their sexual potency (1977), but also developing sexual neuroses.

Most of these arguments are intensely gendered, and it is *male* masturbation which is figured as the problem. From the founding treatise on the subject, *Onania, or the Heinous Sin of Self-Pollution and all its Frightful Consequences* (Anonymous, 1724), through the various disciplining techniques outlined by Foucault, to the jokes and comic scenes in popular culture, masturbating boys and men are the significant problem. Girls and women, on the other hand, were generally understood to have no interest in sex, let alone masturbation – and this conceptualization of female sexuality as entirely passive brings its own set of concerns. Yet in the past three decades we have seen the encouragement of female masturbation as a form of political and sexual liberation – women have been encouraged to engage in masturbation as a means of exploring their capacity for pleasure in pursuit of sexual fulfilment and through that a challenge to the sexual status quo. The masturbation projects of second-wave feminism suggested it was every

Sexualization, Commodifying Sex and the Mainstreaming of Masterbation

woman's responsibility to understand her own potential for pleasure; she ought to be able to achieve orgasm and she should certainly know how to achieve it for herself. If you read magazines like *Cosmopolitan* you will be very familiar with these ideas. Jane Juffer has called this the 'mainstreaming of masturbation' (1998). This growing visibility of women's sexual interests has become ever more marked and is the subject of quite furious debate. Women's expressions of sexual interests have become incredibly visible in the past two decades, and part of that visibility has been through the targeting of women as *consumers* interested in particular aspects of 'commoditized' sex, particularly in the growing market in sex toys.

In an early episode of *Sex and the City*, Carrie and the girls go on a shopping trip to buy a vibrator. Miranda shows the girls the *Rabbit*, a vibrator which claims to offer the ultimate orgasm.

MIRANDA: Ladies, I'd like you to meet *The Rabbit*.
CARRIE: 92 dollars?!
MIRANDA: Please? Think about the money we spend on shoes!
CHARLOTTE: Well, I have no intention of using that! I'm saving sex for someone I love.
MIRANDA: Fantastic! Is there a man in the picture?
(Carrie takes the rabbit out of the box)
CHARLOTTE: Look! Oh, it's so cute! Oh I thought it would be all scary and weird, but it isn't! It's pink, for girls! I love the little bunny! It has a little face! Like Peter Rabbit.
CARRIE: And it's even got a remote! I mean, how lazy do you have to be? ('The Turtle and the Hare', S.1, ep.9: 1998)

The scene is played for comic effect but Charlotte's comment that the vibrator is 'pink and for girls' demonstrates the ways in which retailers of sex toys for women have worked hard to distinguish their goods from the pornographic wares aimed at men. In the past couple of decades sex toys for women have been redesignated as a fashionable domestic appliance – they have been made in every shade of pink, purple and silver, from jelly to jewels, and been given cute faces and pretty names; they have also been designed to deliver the supposedly elusive female orgasm so efficiently that in this episode, Charlotte gets 'addicted' to her *Rabbit* and has to be rescued by her friends. Judging by sales figures alone (demand for the *Jelly* or *Rampant Rabbit* outstripped supply worldwide), women have been enthusiastically using the new designer toys in all shades of jelly, resin or glass – a clear indication of what Jane Juffer called the 'domestification' of sexual materials (the process by which 'outlaw' products such as pornography are 'tamed' by being reworked as *erotica* so that they can be brought into the home).

Toys like the *Rabbit* are part of an expanding discourse of female sexual self-discovery, which have helped to construct new sexual identities for women. Traditionally the *objects* of sex talk and sex production, women are now targeted as sexual *subjects* and consumers in their own right. Previously, sex toys were considered to be replacements for 'proper' sex, or therapeutic means of curing inability to orgasm rather than objects that provided particular pleasures of their own. They were most often called 'marital aids' and were recommended for those who were frigid, or who had difficulty achieving orgasm through normative heterosexual sex. (If you're interested in pursuing this further, there is a fascinating, although problematic, history of vibrators by Rachel Maines, *The Technology of Orgasm*, which describes how vibrators were used by doctors at the turn of the nineteenth century to cure women of hysterical symptoms.) Until quite recently vibrators looked ugly and were often made of tacky materials, so they might have produced orgasm but they weren't something you would want to admit to owning.

Now, though, the vibrator is something Miranda from *Sex and the City* can boast about, and like the speculum of the 1970s is

> an icon of women's claiming their bodies ... in the high tech 80s and 90s, and into the next century, women's symbol of independence and pleasure is the vibrator. (Loe quoted in McCaughey and French, 2001: 92)

During the 1970s heyday of second-wave feminism, some activists advocated women using a speculum – a piece of medical equipment – to examine their own vagina and cervix to learn about and from their own bodies, as part of a movement towards greater awareness of the ways in which the female body had been subjugated under patriarchy. Feminist as well as popular writings of the 1970s, 1980s and 1990s encouraged women to masturbate and explore their own sexual potential as key stages in achieving sexual freedom. So we can link the development of sexual goods for women to increasing discussion of specifically female sexuality that encouraged women to question and explore their own sexual interests separated from earlier models of heterosexual monogamy. Sex manuals addressed and continue to address women as 'liberated', urging them to move beyond passive receptivity and feelings of shame to a more active and pleasure-seeking involvement in physical relations (Betty Dodson's book *Liberating Masturbation: A Meditation on Self Love* published in 1974 was one of the first of this kind and is considered a feminist classic).

But there were and still are questions raised by this exploration. In particular, there are concerns that women's use of sex toys is just playing into the hands of men, maintaining gender divisions and encouraging women to commoditize their own private and intimate experiences. These arguments hark back to the 'sex wars' of the 1980s which centred on two themes – on the one hand, radical feminists argued that hetero-sex was a form of sexual enslavement of women to men's sexual desires, and that any and all sexual representations and sexual commodities contributed to that slavery. On the other, a less-organized set of voices called for acknowledgement of the conflicts, tensions and complexities of sexual pleasure – they wanted to acknowledge the difficulties of accessing an 'authentic' female sexuality outside representation, patriarchy and capitalism. As Vance pointed out, those arguments about hetero-sex completely refused the idea of women's autonomous desires, 'although theoretically acknowledged as possible in a utopian future, [female desire] remained an ethereal and remote presence' (1992: xix). This utopian ideal of a properly 'feminist' sexual practice requires the removal of all eroticization of power (though as discussed in Chapters 1 and 10, power and desire may not be so easily separated), not just in heterosexual relations where men were seen as wielding pleasure in order to ensure their grip on power over women, but also in lesbian relationships where gender equality was expected to 'undermine (or magically 'destabilize') power imbalance' (Gaines, 1995: 392). As Gaines observes:

> For feminism, egalitarian sex represents a sexual practice corresponding with a world free of domination and subordination, a world in which there are no tops and no bottoms. (1995: 391)

Thus there is an ideal of 'egalitarian sex' in feminism that tends to measure sexual activities for their 'correct' pleasures and require the rejection of 'incorrect' pleasures. For some feminists, lesbian sex was understood to be free of the taints of patriarchy (male power over women) because women were considered not capable of the kinds of objectification and power-games which were thought to characterize (heterosexual) male sexuality. But there is plenty of evidence that women do like 'incorrect' forms of sex – notably lesbian practices of sadomasochism which suggest that women can and do eroticize pain and power (see Califia, 1980; Gaines, 1995; Rich, 1981; Vance, 1992, for more discussion of these ideas).

Moreover, the 'lesbian dildo debates', as Findlay describes the arguments amongst academic and activist lesbians, highlighted the problems of using sex toys: while lesbian sex was presented as 'woman identified', the use of a phallic-shaped piece of plastic or latex posed real issues for observers and practitioners alike. Using sex toys, especially the dildo which looks like a penis, could be understood as merely replicating male sexual styles. One faction asked why did women want to '"portra[y]" themselves as equipped with penises?' (1992: 564). Their opponents argued that there was no direct reference between the dildo and the penis. Even so, designers began to think about the ways in which they could move away from 'simulation' models of sex toys to shapes more reflective of women's more 'natural' sexual interests:

> Lesbians [...] have marketed a series of dildos which, in an obvious attempt to break the association between a piece of silicon and a penis, are shaped like dolphins, ears of corn, and even the Goddess. This urge to steer away

> from realism stems from the fact that these feminist dildo suppliers and their customers are suspicious of conflating a representation with reality, especially in the case of a phallus. (Findlay, 1992: 566)

The phallic dildo was not just problematic for lesbians or feminist activists: many heterosexual women who wanted to experiment with toys were not happy with vibrators shaped like enormous penises and so, more recently, vibrators have been developed which also turn away from the overt 'phallicness' or genital focus of the more lifelike toy. A vocabulary of appropriate design has developed, summed up in the phrase 'by women, for women'. The rhetorical power of this can be seen in advertisements stressing women designers' inherent understanding of the needs and rhythms of female sexuality. For example:

> Since using a vibrator is as essential as brushing your teeth, we're always on the look out for this most important of all household items. Our current favourite is Candida Royalle's new *Ultime* – the latest in her line of vibrators called Natural Contours which are beautiful, high-tech, and ergonomically designed to fit the contours of a woman's body. What we really like about the *Ultime* is that it offers strong vibrations (as well as dual speeds) on both ends, allowing this innovative design to serve pleasure points ... well, all over the map. (Amazing how it locates the G-spot so effortlessly!) On top of it all, this beautifully designed vibrator is whisper-quiet. No one will think you are out mowing the lawn. (www.libidomag.com)

Descriptions like this draw on the authenticating narratives of female sexuality – the toy bears no resemblance to the penis, but instead is designed *for* the female body and its pleasure points. Its ergonomics ensure the maximization of pleasure without effort. The sex toy is an object to be enjoyed both for how it looks as well as what it delivers. In line with other aspects of the leisure economy which have shown an increased interest in design and taste cultures in all matters of contemporary life from home-styling through to travel, a major selling point of sex toy design is the signal of sophistication and experimentation. Toys have become a part of the educative process required by an era of 'reflexive selfhood' (Giddens, 1991). Toys, especially those sold in the upmarket erotic boutiques like *Coco de Mer*, *Gash* and *Sh!*, are no longer just for frustrated spinsters or married couples bored by years of unadventurous sex. Toys are now sold as items to enhance relationships, to play with, to encourage exploration and to facilitate the fantasies of people who are serious about sex. The last two decades have seen rapid growth in all kinds of toys for sexual arousal, play and pleasure, from sexy lingerie, nipple clamps and furry handcuffs to remote control vibrators, butt plugs, beads, jewel-encrusted whips and paddles – many of which are described in women's magazines and on daytime television as a set of fashion accessories for the sexually adventurous woman. If toys have become fashion items, women seem to want to purchase their playthings from stylish environments where sex is constructed as a leisure activity and a site of personal exploration.

Until the 1990s, if you wanted some choice about your vibrator or other sex toy, you needed to visit a licensed sex shop (still the only places in the UK where you can buy hardcore pornography, in particular 18R DVDs). For many, they were male-only spaces, and entering one of these shops could be seen as evidence of seedy sexual tastes and inadequacy. As a shopping experience, going into one of these sex shops could be rather furtive and secret, drawing attention to sex as a taboo. Although licensed sex shops are still around, they are often relegated to the outskirts of towns, and because of their blacked-out windows still seem a bit seedy. But there are now other retail environments that actively target women.

Ann Summers shops have been around in the UK since the late 1970s, so they are not a brand new phenomenon, but their shops were given a significant makeover during the late 1980s and early 1990s. *Ann Summers* stores provide what Jacqueline Gold (Chief Executive of *Ann Summers*) describes as 'an intimate, sexy and very girly boudoir' (Gold, 2007) feel for their customers. In the 1970s *Ann Summers* stores were licensed sex shops, and pretty down-at-heel, but when Gold took over the existing business from her father and uncle (British porn-publishers the Gold Brothers) she decided to stop selling pornography and to focus on women rather than on the traditional male customer. Gold developed a highly successful party plan business (where women sell goods to other women in their own homes, as with Avon and Tupperware) and then set about changing the existing *Ann Summers* stores to create a shopping environment that welcomed women and did not require the expensive licence. The basic definition of a sex shop is that the premises sell a 'significant number' of exclusively sex-related items, including pornography, but Gold focused on lingerie so that the revamped *Ann Summers*' stock came in below the percentage requiring a licence. The definition of what constitutes a 'significant' number of sex-related items is a confused element of the law that has seen a number of High Court challenges. Individual local authorities have different views – Westminster City Council assess it in terms of shelf space and storage, with 10% of total stock seen as 'significant', but in Croydon the level is in excess of 20% of either stock or value. In the London Borough of Lambeth the council attempted to set the standard at ten or more sex articles, but Lord Justice Mustill ruled in the High Court that the law surely meant 'more than a trifling' number (*Lambeth Borough Council* v. *Grewal*, 1985). The situation is further complicated by the fact that it is not always clear what constitutes a 'sex article'.

Ann Summers is now a household name, with more than 7,000 self-employed party planners hosting thousands of parties per week in the UK (Official Company Figures), as well as 130 shops in most high streets and shopping malls of the UK. From the outside the stores look like any other lingerie store and even inside, the display of vibrators, dildos, whips and handcuffs look less scary than they would in a licensed sex shop. As Jane Juffer puts it, a key element in marketing to women has 'involved the taming of a traditionally male genre ... and rewriting/reworking it within everyday routines' (1998: 5). This perspective is very neatly summed up in Jacqueline Gold's claim that

> [w]e're not really a sex shop, and we're more than a lingerie shop. What we've achieved is a very female-friendly environment where both men and women can be entirely comfortable. It's more of a naughty laugh than anything seedy, but it's also more fun than a normal lingerie store. It's become part of a normal shopping experience, women go out to shop in Croydon or Lakeside or wherever, and popping into *Ann Summers* is just part of a regular shopping trip. (Quoted in Addley, 2003: 2)

Not everyone has been happy about these changes: *Ann Summers'* intention to open a store in Tunbridge Wells was greeted with claims by the local vicar that the stores formed part of a wider cultural degradation of marriage, and local parents protested the opening of a shop in Perth. Their attempt to advertise jobs in Job Centres was challenged in the courts, though the company won that right in the High Court arguing that 'the company was engaged in a legitimate business in high streets and shopping centres up and down the country'. With gross sales of £110m and more than 1 million vibrators sold per year, *Ann Summers* has become the market leader (Perrone, 2002).

The developments in sex toy retailing are, then, the result of mixing a whole range of discourses that address women as sexual agents. The discourses of fashion, shopping and femininity are mixed with feminist ideas of agency and empowerment so that the woman who buys her own sex toy is constructed as a confident, desiring, active woman who knows what she wants (Attwood, 2007). For many academics, however, this is not as positive a development as the retailers and advertisers might insist. For example, Ros Gill suggests that cultural products claiming to 'empower' women may actually be forms of 'objectification in new and even more pernicious guise' (2003: 105). Merl Storr, whose book-length study *Latex & Lingerie* focuses on *Ann Summers* parties, is also critical of the ways in which women are addressed via a form of commodified feminism which is stripped of its politics so that sexual pleasure is only offered to women through their consumerism – they get to feel sexy because they buy the underwear – and that this is nothing more than '*feeling* empowered' (2003: 31) rather than actually being empowered. Both Storr and Gill worry that this 'empowerment' is simply another way of getting women to service men's sexual needs, and perhaps that is a reasonable conclusion when you consider some of *Ann Summers'* advertising. For example, the company's 2008 Valentine's Day TV campaign entitled 'Wood' certainly seemed more focused on ensuring male interest and pleasure than on women's sexual desire. In the ad, a number of scantily clad women hand men wooden gifts, and the advertisement ends with the strapline 'Give him wood this Valentine's Day', foregrounding male sexual arousal. However, another reading could focus on the ad humorously attempting to balance female sexuality as both 'desiring and being desirable' (Storr, 2003: 92) and addressing women's sexual interests through discourses of fashion, design, fun and self-expression.

It is in the testing and development of a female-centred marketing style that *Ann Summers* has been an important innovator. The company's parties are not just places where women sell each other sex toys, but they also offer the opportunity to talk about sexual practices and pleasures, from masturbation to partnered sex with toys. McCaughey and French (2001) argue that *Ann Summers* has contributed to the expansion of women's expectations of orgasm, pleasure and empowerment. Women sharing, talking with and selling sex aids to other women has rendered the sex toy 'safe' and brought masturbation into the public sphere in ways which do not reference the horror of self-abuse or shame which we discussed earlier. Even so, masturbation remains something of a conundrum: it is an urge men and women share, yet our understandings of it follow gendered lines with assumptions of 'difference' constantly referenced in popular culture. One of the ways in which it is problematized is through the links to capitalism and business. While authors like Juffer stress the ways in which certain forms of commodification have tamed the taboo about sex toys and rendered them safe, others claim that commodification is a significant problem for culture at large – nowhere more than in the current debates about the sexualization of culture.

The various aspects of sexualization – through the individuation of personal choice and the idea of 'pleasuring oneself' – have the appearance of positive moves towards sexual liberation but have also fuelled fears about the de-personalization of sexuality and its increasing commercialization. Many commentators agree that something new is happening in our presentations, expectations and experiences of sexuality, and that culture is characterized by 'public nakedness, voyeurism and sexualised looking ... permitted, indeed encouraged, as never before' (McNair, 2002: ix). While they agree on that point, they are not agreed as to how this should be interpreted or whether or not the effects of this 'sexual revelation and exhibitionism' (ibid.) will prove harmful. For some commentators sexualization is commodifying what ought to be private, intimate experiences (Hitchens, 2002); for others, who draw on and develop earlier feminist critiques of sexual representations, women's bodies are being re-packaged and re-sexualized within a fake empowerment politics which is stripped of any sense of community and entirely dependent upon the idea of individual 'choice' (Gill, 2009; Levy, 2005). Yet others see a more positive outcome – the possible 'democratisation of desire' (McNair, 2002: 11) and 'a more pluralistic sexual culture' (ibid.). This chapter couldn't assess each of these positions in detail, or decide which is most plausible. However, we have established that our understandings of intimate and sexual relations are changing as we engage with the diverse presentations of sexuality in all forms of culture, and increasingly embrace 'public intimacy' (McNair, 2002: 98) as it is mediated and commodified. As Bernstein observes,

> [there is] a shift from a relational to a recreational model of sexual behaviour, a reconfiguration of erotic life in which the pursuit of sexual intimacy is not hindered but facilitated by its location in the marketplace. (2007: 397)

Further Reading

Juffer, J. (1998) *At Home with Pornography: Women, Sex and Everyday Life* (New York: New York University Press).
McNair, B. (2002) *Striptease Culture* (London: Routledge).

Sadomasochism: Definitions and Legislation

Chapter

10

Because it eroticizes power and sensation, sadomasochism is often misrepresented as eroticizing violence. When *News of the World* journalists discovered that Formula 1 boss Max Mosley made regular visits to dominatrices they revelled in the detail of a supposed Nazi orgy, and claimed that Mosley was 'beaten until he bled' (*The Sun*, 2008: 13). Far from being a 'Carry On Spanking'-style caper, it was claimed the orgy had been 'a truly grotesque and depraved episode' (Warby, 2008: 5). The Mosley story was a journalist's dream, but so too were the high-profile deaths of the British MP Stephen Milligan and musician Michael Hutchence, who are both believed to have died whilst engaging in autoerotic asphyxiation (although the official cause of death recorded for Hutchence was suicide). The reporting of all three cases highlights the ways in which preferences for non-normative forms of sexual pleasure are often misunderstood and criticized by those who do not share those predilections. Foucault's perspective on this is interesting:

> If you are not like everyone else then you are abnormal, if you are abnormal then you are sick. These three categories, not being like everybody else, not being normal and being sick are in fact very different but have been reduced to the same thing. (2004: 95)

Sadomasochism occupies a very problematic space in culture and in theories of sexuality. For many observers it is a 'perverse' and 'dangerous' practice requiring legal and medical intervention. For its practitioners, it is a complex sexual expression drawing on sexual dissidence, pleasure, escapism, transcendence and the refusal of normative genital sexuality, allowing for safer sex explorations of the lived body and its transformative potentials (Beckman, 2001). In our chapter on Foucault we have already discussed the importance of *naming* to the production of sexual identities, and in this chapter we want to explore some of the ways in which sexual behaviours experienced as alternative and queer have been problematized. Our discussion of the manifestations of sadomasochism cannot be comprehensive, and it is important to recognize that a book such as this cannot offer a definitive exploration of the meanings, experiences and identifications of sadomasochism as a set of practices. There is always the risk in looking at specific sexual subcultures of engaging voyeuristically or moralistically with practices we do not actually engage in ourselves. You should be aware as you read this chapter that we offer an examination of the place of sadomasochism in culture and not an anthropological study of its practitioners.

The American Psychiatric Association continues to list sadism and masochism among the paraphilias, which are practices considered to arise from psychiatric disorder and which result in sexual pleasure from 'abnormal' objects/activities. In its Manual of Mental Disorders, the APA describes Sexual Masochism as 'sexual urges, fantasies or behaviors involving the act (real not simulated) of being humiliated, beaten, bound or otherwise made to suffer' (DSM-IV). Meanwhile Sexual Sadism is defined as 'sexual urges, fantasies or behaviors involving acts (real, not simulated) in which the psychological or physical suffering (including humiliation) of the victim is sexually exciting to the person' (DSM-IV).

The terms sadist and masochist were first coined in the Victorian era and drew their inspiration from two writers – the Marquis de Sade and Leopold Sacher-Masoch. De Sade was a French aristocrat, revolutionary, philosopher, author and libertine whose fiction included themes of sexualized violence and force. Sacher-Masoch was the author of the erotic novel *Venus in Furs* (1870) in which a man, Severin, requests his lover treat him as her slave. It is not clear that contemporary practices of sadomasochism have any direct relationship to the writings of either of these authors (particularly de Sade's). There are many different interpretations of de Sade's work, and some suggest his writings are explorations of the very real social and political changes occurring in his social milieu in eighteenth-century France: that he was writing about the break between the *ancien regime* (a political and social system in which power resides with the aristocracy) and the revolution which brought a new politics of equality. Others suggest that his work is a critique, expressed via the descriptions of sadistic priests violating maidservants, of the parasitic power of Church and aristocracy. Other analyses demonstrate de Sade's pleasures in activities that did not recognize victims' pain – that de Sade personally sought pleasure in *forcing* someone to take part in acts against their will – and pointing to the ways de Sade's protagonists in the novel *Juliette* are

> amused by ... tears, excited by ... distress, irritated by ... capers, inflamed by ... writhings. (de Sade, 1968: 287)

It is precisely their victims' *unwillingness* to engage in sexual activities that creates the excitement of the libertines; 'any enjoyment is weakened when shared' (de Sade: 22); the libertines like to rape. Thus, for many people, using the term 'sadist' for those people who like to mete out 'punishments' or sensations to *consensual* partners brings with it too many negative associations of cruelty and excess. The true sadist wants to inflict pain on an unwilling victim, whereas the sadomasochist looks for a reciprocal and staged performance of sensual suffering.

The identification and delineation of the sexual identity 'masochist' comes from the science of the nineteenth century, in particular from the works of Richard von Krafft-Ebing in his *Psychopathia Sexualis, with Especial Reference to Contrary Sexual Instinct: A Medico-Legal Study*, published in 1892. In it he describes masochism as

> a congenital sexual perversion, constitutes a functional sign of degeneration in (almost exclusively) hereditary taint; and this clinical deduction is confirmed in my cases of masochism and sadism. (Krafft-Ebing, 1892: 147)

Thus for Krafft-Ebing, as a man of his time, sexual deviance was a moral condition, related to hereditary features and part of a range of sexual neuroses characterized by inappropriate sexual excitation, that is, sexual arousal not tied to the proper object (a member of the opposite sex) and activity (penetration). The only treatment recommended for this diagnosis was abstinence. Krafft-Ebing did not see sadism and masochism as complementary, with the masochist refusing their tormentor any pleasure in their interaction. As a contemporary of Krafft-Ebing, Sigmund Freud also regarded masochism as a problem, although in the 'Three Essays' he linked it absolutely to sadism:

> Sadism and masochism occupy a special position among the perversions, since the contrast between activity and passivity which lies behind them is among the universal characteristics of sexual life. (Freud, 1974: 87)

Interestingly, in that quote Freud does not see sadism and masochism as merely 'perverse', he also sees them as closely linked to the formation of *all* sexuality. In their extreme play on activity and passivity, the eroticization of power is an intensification of the pleasures of gender difference that Freud saw in all, even the most 'normal', heterosexual relations.

One of the particular problems in thinking about sadomasochism is its history as *pathology* and its particular place in many of the writings about sexuality, representations and practices. In particular, sadomasochism has a very problematic place in arguments about pornography. And here we are going to make a foray into a set of complex arguments about representations, which may have very little relationship to the ways in which sadomasochism is experienced.

Andrea Dworkin's work on pornography provides a framework for thinking about representations as a form of documentary evidence of actual sexual practices and the state of relationships between men and women not confined to just the sexual sphere. Her radical feminist approach argues male sexuality is premised on power, the domination and subordination of women. She is not the only writer to take this approach but she is perhaps the most influential. She saw pornography as a kind of handbook to male sexuality:

> The strains of male power are embodied in pornography's form and content, in economic control of and distribution of wealth within the industry, in the picture or story as thing, in the photographer or writer as aggressor, in the critic or intellectual who through naming assigns value, in the actual use of models, in the application of the material in what is called real life (which women are commanded to regard as distinct from fantasy). (1981: 24–5)

Thus for anti-porn writers, sadomasochism cannot be understood as a 'radical' form of sexuality, but simply another form of traditional sexual practice where men dominate women and women pretend to enjoy it. Dworkin wrote that

> [f]or Sade, libertinage was the cruel use of others for one's sexual pleasure. Sade's libertinage demanded slavery; sexual despotism misnamed 'freedom' is [his] more enduring legacy. (1981: 92)

Women's embrace of sadomasochism (whether heterosexual or lesbian) also poses a significant problem for feminisms of various political persuasions. Melissa Farley argues that

> [t]he political values of sadism are blatantly antifeminist, totalitarian and right-wing. Sadomasochism is business as usual; power relations as usual; race, gender and class as usual. Sadomasochism is one ritual version of dominance and submission. Sadomasochism is not a creative deviation from normal heterosexual behavior. It is the defining quality of the power relationship between women and men. Sadism is the logical extension of behavior that arises out of male power. (1993: 21)

In these accounts, sadomasochism may well be linked to what Farley here terms 'normal' sexuality through the eroticization of power, but it is clearly not in itself 'normal' (see our earlier discussion of the differences between normal and normative). For many commentators, sadomasochism is figured as a perversion, as not 'normal', but we would suggest that sadomasochism as a subculture can be seen as offering the possibility of non-normative sexual pleasures which cannot be reduced to either a reproductive imperative or a genital model of sexual activities. In order to understand that radical potential we need to move beyond the traditional conceptions of sadomasochism as 'perverted'. Understanding sadomasochism as a modern-day sexual practice is difficult because it has been named after practices that have a very particular construction which doesn't correspond to what contemporary practitioners believe they are doing. Arguments for the pleasures of sadomasochism stress the consensual nature of the practice, and reject the pathologizing impulses of psychoanalytic and psychiatric accounts. In so doing, they reject the idea that sadomasochism is fundamentally based upon patriarchal power structures. As Foucault argues, social structures of power are institutionalized and rigid whereas the sexual practice of sadomasochism remains a 'fluid' relation – 'an acting out of power structures by a strategic game that is able to give sexual pleasure or bodily pleasure' (Gallagher and Wilson, 1984: 30). The practices of humiliation, bondage and excess are *techniques* for accessing and understanding the potentials of bodily sensation. This refocusing refuses the insistence on pain as the defining characteristic of sadomasochism and insists on prioritizing the sexual *affects* of its practices. Furthermore, if the key achievements of sadomasochistic practices are *sensation* and *affect* there is no necessary correlation between its practices and the eroticization of gender difference that characterizes normative sexuality. A flagellation scene, for example, does not require partners of different genders to be successful – a woman can give and receive pleasurable sensations to another female, and this also does not mean that the two women need identify as lesbian to give and take such satisfaction.

For the rest of this chapter we are going to refer to contemporary sadomasochist sexuality as SM, and distinguish between its roles by using Dom (dominant) and Sub (submissive) in order to differentiate between the historical analysis of sadism as a pathological pleasure in brutality and the idea of consensual sexual play which characterizes contemporary SM. SMers say that their sexual pleasures are based on play, on the eroticization of difference within consensual parameters and with an emphasis on communication between Dom and Sub. For this reason, Brewis and Linstead suggest that modern-day SM is a form of pastiche, and a simulacrum of sadism and masochism (2000: 141). In this they are supported by Foucault's suggestions that power is a strategic game, with rules that can be transgressed via play in ways that are pleasurable and potentially ethical:

> Power is not evil. Power is games of strategy... For example, let us take sexual or amorous relationships: to wield power over the other in a sort of open-ended strategic game where the situation may be reversed is not evil; it's part of love, of passion and sexual pleasure.... (Foucault, 1997: 298)

For an SM scene to be successful, Dom and Sub need to be aware of the other's interests in the scene; the Dom must be aware that control over the Sub is only possible through the Sub's willing and enthusiastic submission. This also means that the Sub must trust the Dom to keep them safe (psychologically and physically). Through the twists and turns of power and consent, pleasure and pain, its practitioners argue, SM allows for the potential breaching of individual boundaries and the possibility of experimenting with the physical and psychological limits of 'normative' sexual pleasure.

While we use the umbrella term SM, in fact the 'scene' or 'lifestyle' is made up of a variety of identities under the larger title BDSM, a compound acronym drawn from the terms bondage and discipline (B&D, B/D, or BD), dominance and submission (D&s, D/s, or Ds), and sadism and masochism (S&M, S/M, or SM). As with any other subculture, the umbrella title covers a range of diverse identifications. BDSM is not necessarily a lifestyle or routine that *requires* pain for satisfaction. What is required is an acknowledgement of the erotic potentials of the binary relationship of dominant and submissive. This can mean that pain can have a role to play – as may 'ordinary' sexual intercourse – in the pleasurable activities of the lifestyle but it is not necessarily a central concern. Some people are interested in genital torture, needle play, blood play or even some seemingly more 'extreme' practices such as erotic asphyxiation, but these activities do not necessarily form a part of the repertoires of all those individuals who would identify as part of the BDSM community. You should also be aware that there is no necessarily gendered dimension to BDSM; although much psychiatric theory, especially when condemning these activities, might like to assign the roles of active/Dom to males or passive/Sub to females, many BDSM practitioners play with these gendered roles, so that even where someone generally identifies as a dominant or a submissive they can also 'switch' or be 'omniviant' (a compound of omni, meaning all, and deviant): enjoying both a dominant and a submissive side in their behaviours.

As the beginning of this chapter indicated, there is intense media interest in BDSM, especially those cases where play has gone wrong, even resulting in death. It is possible to think of BDSM as not just a despised sexual form but also a besieged one. Its practices are open to condemnation by various commentators from the moralist to the medic, and of course it is not difficult to see why, when some activities seem so counter-intuitive to the cultural norms of sexuality – in particular, the practices of consensual erotic murder pacts, or autassassinophilia and erotophonophilia (see John Money's (1986) discussion of these). When these cases have come to light, practitioners have been keen to distance BDSM from the extremes. For example, in the aftermath of the highly publicized case of American Sharon Lopatka, who co-planned her own killing for erotic pleasure with Robert Glass, a man she met in an internet chat room, an SM spokeswoman, Nancy Ava Miller, stated: 'I don't know what they were doing, but it wasn't S&M. The fundamental rule of the S&M community is to keep interaction "safe, sane and consensual"' (cited in Jackson, 1996).

Safe, sane and consensual (SSC) is a phrase used by many BDSMers to describe themselves, their activities and their philosophy (discussed in depth in Langdridge and Barker (2008)). For those subscribing to SSC, all BDSM practitioners should identify and prevent risks to health before engaging in an activity, and they should ensure that they undertake any activities in a sane and sensible way. Moreover, they should ensure that all parties give full consent (even as they will need to acknowledge, in the UK at least, that this does not necessarily make their activities lawful). Of course, SSC is not just a philosophy, it is also a definition: it creates BDSM as a singular sexual practice, recognizing a single community with shared goals and interests. As well as the subjective problems in the definitions of SSC – how safe is safe enough? who defines 'sane'? – SSC rules out as many kinds of behaviour as it rules in, creating acceptable and unacceptable BDSM activity. One of the practices it makes unacceptable is the one which resulted in the deaths of Stephen Milligan and Michael Hutchence with which we opened this chapter: erotic asphyxiation (also known as asphyxiophilia, hypoxyphilia, breath play or breath control play). In these cases, consent does not seem to be an issue because Milligan and Hutchence had no partners with them, but clearly the implication of SSC is that they were not engaging in 'safe' activity.

Many BDSMers do not believe SSC is an accurate term for their chosen activities; they prefer to use the term Risk Aware Consensual Kink (RACK), which they feel more nearly encapsulates the responsibilities of practitioners to be well-informed about the risks involved in an activity before giving consent. This means that practice may encompass activities others might deem to be unsafe. The idea is that so long as all parties are aware of the risks involved and have consented to take that risk, there is no unsafe practice even if it might be one potentially resulting in illegal injury. That the law might consider a practice unsafe would not necessarily mean it is unsafe for the informed, risk aware BDSMer.

It is perhaps this highly conscious mode of sexual engagement that truly sets BDSMers apart from more 'ordinary' sexual actors. In its focus on agreement and contractual play, BDSM offers new ways of understanding the body and its pleasures, many of which don't focus on the traditional pleasure zones of genitals, breasts and lips. Instead practitioners eroticize other sensations. An example might be rope binding, in which one person takes pleasure in the activity and skill of binding another, in the disposition of another's body in aesthetically pleasing ways, in using ropes and other paraphernalia to render them helpless; while the person being bound takes pleasure in the sensations of passivity, the feelings of being constrained, the sensation of rope being tied around their body, and the excitements of being worked on by an expert. Thus the body comes alive in new ways that can have sexual dimensions, but are not focused on straightforwardly orgasmic potentials. Certainly this is something that Foucault found in his own experiences of same-sex leather SM.

Towards the end of his life, Foucault felt that SM offered possibilities to construct alternative forms of community and relationality which, by playing with power, would get around the regulatory and normative relations of knowledge and power. SM role-play offered the opportunity for dramatizing power, for recognizing it as a game with the potential to be productive as well as repressive. The reversals of dominant and submissive in SM role-play, and its focus on different pleasure centres of the body, give the possibility of reconfiguring bodily pleasures. If, for example, culture and normative conceptions of female sexuality construct women as needing tenderness, stroking and kissing from an 'active' male partner, the SM woman who ties up her partner may find other ways of experiencing sexual excitement and satisfaction.

Moreover, many argue that SM allows for the exploration of limit experiences – pushing oneself (or being pushed) to the extremes of sensation – offering the potential for surprise, shock and getting beyond what is generally assumed to be pleasurable, so that sexual identity is disrupted rather than confirmed (Bouchard and Simon, 1998). David Halperin argues that some practices such as fisting can '[decenter] the subject and [disarticulate] the psychic and bodily integrity of the self to which a sexual identity has become attached' (1995: 97). Thus some forms of SM can be understood as a radical political practice whose acts on and through the body disrupt rather than confirm identity. Foucault also suggested that

> the practice of S/M is the creation of pleasure, and there is an identity with that creation. And that's why S/M is really a subculture. It's a process of invention. (Quoted in Gallagher and Wilson, 1984: 29)

This conceptualization of SM as a creative process focused on experience of pleasure is different to that proposed by psychoanalysis which sees identity as something that is discovered alongside one's 'true desires'. SM allows for a process of invention rather than discovery. Even so, as Halperin and others have suggested, SM can produce 'new forms of discipline' and construct 'even more insidious processes of normalisation' (Halperin, 1995: 112). The mantras of SSC can have this effect, creating boundaries, and refusing the possibilities of constant invention and re-invention. As Lisa Downing has suggested:

> In censoring the risky pleasures of EA (erotic asphyxiation) from its field of inclusion, in seeking to codify it in the very terms of the mental health and safety discourses used to vilify SM itself, the community does not respond but merely accepts and echoes the 'opponent's manoeuvre', parroting it back. (2008)

BDSM is then caught in something of a bind – how should the community respond to attacks on its rights to expression? There is no doubt that when the law seeks to limit certain forms of sexual expression, it does so by casting doubt on the sanity of its practitioners. To illustrate this more fully, let's look at how BDSM was caught up in the calls for legislation against 'extreme pornography' which culminated in the passing of Part 5 of the 26th Criminal Justice and Immigration Act in 2008.

The law, which came into force in January 2009, criminalizes the possession of images which are both 'extreme' and 'pornographic' and which

> portray, in an explicit and realistic way, any of the following—
> (a) an act which threatens a person's life,
> (b) an act which results, or is likely to result, in serious injury to a person's anus, breasts or genitals,
> (c) an act which involves sexual interference with a human corpse, or
> (d) a person performing an act of intercourse or oral sex with an animal (whether dead or alive), and a reasonable person looking at the image would think that any such person or animal was real. (Criminal Justice and Immigration Act, 2008)

Written in the seemingly rational language of the state, you might think that there's nothing very wrong with this new law. But take another look: certain sexual practices such as fisting might well result, or be likely to result, in serious injury to a person's anus; equally, nipple piercing carried out as a part of an SM scene could also be considered an injury – as indeed was the case with the Spanner prosecutions in 1990, in which sixteen men were arrested on charges, including assault, for their participation in consensual BDSM activities. This law criminalizes the possession of *images* depicting these practices. As the Spanner Trust (a BDSM rights advocacy group) argued:

> Part of this 'protection of morals' is a blatant attempt to clamp down on the BDSM community. In spite of bland assurances during the consultation process that the proposals were not intended to target anyone in particular, the actual bill drops this pretence, and explicitly refers to the Spanner trial (R v. Brown and Others) as an example of activities that are illegal in themselves and will now become illegal to film or photograph. (http://sm-feminist.blogspot.com/2007/07/shout-out-to-anyone-uk-based.html)

The law came about as a result of a campaign launched after the sad death of Jane Longhurst, a teacher asphyxiated by Graham Coutts in 2003 in what he claimed was a sex game gone wrong. During his trial the prosecution described Coutts' habitual use of pornographic internet sites featuring sexual violence, which led to the victim's mother, Liz Longhurst, calling for a ban on extreme pornography, getting together a petition of 50,000 signatures and the support of two Members of Parliament. As the campaign grew, moral campaign groups and newspapers joined in claiming that the murder was a symptom of our fascination with kinky sex and the availability of websites which 'normalized' Coutts' perverted view of sexual pleasures.

Among the sites specifically named in the media coverage was Necrobabes, a website offering a variety of sexual fantasies of murder (Necrobabes features women; a companion site Necrodudes features men). In the media these sites were portrayed as strange – what 'normal' person could have sexual interests in dead bodies even if these were performed for camera? Claims were made about other representations of forms of sex which involved hurting people, and which involved props, weapons and paraphernalia. All of these reports stressed the horrors on offer and refused to acknowledge the images and stories were representations of fantasies. Campaigners for the new law suggested that existing law wasn't able to cope with the specific threats posed by the availability of 'extreme' materials online. Home Office Minister Vernon Coaker made it very clear that

> [s]uch material has no place in our society, but the advent of the internet has meant that this material is more easily available and means existing controls are being bypassed – we must move to tackle this. (Quoted in 'Cracking Down', 2006)

Similar arguments about the 'unnaturalness' of certain kinds of desire and their representations were made during the consultation process for the legislation, with Coaker claiming that 'The vast majority of people find these forms of violent and extreme pornography deeply abhorrent' (quoted in *Daily Mail*, 2006). The police commented that the law should go even further than what was being proposed:

> In our opinion acts of coprophilia (excrement, urination) within pornograph [sic] are examples of the total degradation of the person subject of such acts. It is our view that such acts are enjoyed by sadists. Likewise acts of belonephilia (needles fetish), agonophilia (pseudo rape) and other forms of extreme violence are also enjoyed by sadist [sic] and those persons with sadistic tendencies. Such tendencies would skew the mindset of the viewer of such material to believe that this is the norm. As such we feel it should not be tolerated. (Detective Inspector Winton quoted in Petley, 2009)

These recommendations for further inclusions were not taken up, but it was clear that the government also believed something must be done. However, the proposals did not go unchallenged. As well as academics and individuals who questioned the evidence that internet imagery caused sexual murder, a diverse group of activists including Feminists Against Censorship, the Spanner Trust, SM Dykes and the Libertarian Alliance responded to the proposed law under the umbrella name of Backlash. Backlash campaigned against the law on a number of fronts: that it was an unnecessary attack on personal freedoms, that it gave the police powers they would misuse, that the law itself was badly formulated, subjective, and probably went counter to European directives on human rights. In particular, for the interests of this chapter, they felt that it criminalized a whole swathe of previously law-abiding citizens by outlawing consensual, non-abusive activities just because the 'majority' don't understand or like them.

The debates about 'extreme pornography' which accompanied the passing of the Criminal Justice and Immigration Act highlight cultural anxieties about representations and sexual activities which foreground the physicality of the body, especially when those activities play with power, control and consent and emphasize extreme states of being. It is precisely those elements that Foucault and others have suggested might make BDSM a radical form of sexual expression. In so doing, the construction of BDSM as evidence of pathology or perverted sexuality was to the fore. Proponents of the law were drawing a line between what was considered acceptable kinkiness and unacceptable deviance.

Interestingly, the iconography of 'kinky sex' has become more visible in advertising and sex advice: SM has become visible in popular culture, from cinematic representations such as *9½ Weeks* (dir. Adrian Lyne: 1986), *Blue Velvet* (dir. David Lynch: 1986), *Crash* (dir. David Cronenberg: 1996), *Quills* (dir. Philip Kaufman: 2000) and *Romance* (dir. Catherine Breillat: 1999), *Secretary* (dir. Steven Shainberg: 2002); through advertising such as Tony Kaye's Dunlop advert *Tested for the Unexpected* (1993), the Keep Britain Tidy *Don't Be A Gimp!* (2006) and the Mini Metro online ad campaign *Dominate Winter* (2006); to fashion spreads in *Elle* and *Vogue* and, on television, the recurring character, Lady Heather, in *Crime Scene Investigation: Las Vegas*. This list is obviously not exhaustive, and you can probably add many examples of your own, but it demonstrates that, in popular culture at least, there is a fascination with BDSM – its clothing, its supposed perversity, and its presumed ability to reveal something very real about our inner selves.

We can see this as part of the so-called 'sexualization of culture', where some images and practices previously associated with porn and obscenity become re-classified as chic, cool or unremarkable while others are reimagined as entirely taboo. The representations of BDSM in popular culture are rendered safe because of their reliance on humour and stereotypes, but the actual practices of BDSMers, which are underpinned by a philosophy and ethos of invention, continue to be demonized. Linda Williams has suggested that the categorization of obscenity is being remade: if obscenity was once defined as 'an extreme explicitness of representation' (Williams, 1992: 233) it is now imagined in relation to perversity. She goes on to argue that in the US the prosecution of sex crimes has 'moved away from the notion of explicit sex and towards the targeting of scapegoat-able "deviants"' (Williams, 2004b: 166). Sexual representations and villainous others 'take their place as convenient objects of blame' for a variety of social ills (Williams, 2004b: 170). A similar process can be seen in the UK, where concerns about violence are displaced onto consensual sex practices such as BDSM, onto the figure of 'a homosexual sadomasochist stalking defenceless children' (Williams, 2004b: 170), and onto extreme porn.

The campaign against extreme porn is not, then, just a matter of concern to a few individuals who want to preserve their sexual interests and practices; it is important to all of us, as it collapses a whole range of anxieties about the growing sexualization and mediatization of society, about a broader turn to the 'extreme' across a range of cultural forms, and about an appetite for graphic spectacles of the body (Lockwood, 2009). These graphic spectacles are not just confined to porn, but are found in scenes of 'opening up' the body in television drama and documentary such as the *Crime Scene Investigation* franchises (CBS) and *BodyShock* (Channel 4: 2001–), and the representations of torture and terror in fictional and factual media. All of these images are interested in extreme states – sexual and non-sexual – and the strong reactions they evoke. Across these media formats, the body's responsiveness, its unruliness and its vulnerabilities are explored – and in turn, as Lockwood observes, these 'body genres' present and provoke sensation and affect in their viewers. What is problematic in relation to BDSM is that these arguments against extreme images import various discursive formations of panic, and a refusal to recognize how these media forms might speak to a variety of experiences, feelings, intentions and motives that are not primarily driven by mental illness (for more discussion of the Criminal Justice and Immigration Act, see Attwood and Smith (2010)). The moves to regulate against extreme pornography online have to be understood as part of a wider set of constraints on sexual expression, in which, on the one hand, sex in any form is depicted as dangerous, and on the other, more 'acceptable' kinds of sexual activity are normalized, while more challenging forms are demonized and criminalized. Representations of BDSM, and the practices of BDSM themselves, can be understood as 'dramatizations' of sexual feeling. BDSM practices allow for the exploration of what many might consider extreme feelings: of shame, excitement, humiliation, surrender, coercion, powerlessness and power. But with their emphasis on 'rules', consent and role-playing, these are clearly experienced within a boundaried environment that may make such explorations political as well as personal.

What can we conclude from our discussion? BDSM encompasses a range of sexual practices that are deeply troubling to conservative forces in our culture. Practices not dependent upon normative genital contact can be understood to open up new possibilities for sexual expression. By its focus on sensation as the primary locus of pleasure, BDSM offers the potential for separating gender roles from biological and essentialist imperatives. It can demonstrate there is no need to think of sexual pleasure as being inherently tied to heterosexual or homosexual norms, or even mutuality (where two people come together in an 'equal' relationship). In the debates we have discussed here and the continuing arguments over what is safe and sane in the sexual realm, BDSM offers students of sexuality the opportunity to explore the ways in which what counts as 'sex' is *always* cultural.

Further Reading

Beckmann, A. (2009) *The Social Construction of Sexuality and Perversion: Deconstructing Sadomasochism* (London: Palgrave Macmillan).

Langdridge, D. and Barker, M. (eds) (2007) *Safe, Sane and Consensual: Contemporary Perspectives on Sadomasochism* (London: Palgrave Macmillan).

Neumahr, S. (2011) *Playing on the Edge: Sadomasochism, Risk, and Intimacy* (Bloomington: University of Indiana Press).

Online Sexual Practices

Chapter 11

The relationship between sex and technology is a subject of fascination. With the rise of the internet and its transformation of the possibilities of sexual pleasure, creation of online sexual communities, new forms of sex work and its proliferation of pornographies, debate has raged as to the meanings of sex in the contemporary age, and the changes which might follow the supposedly unlimited sexual expressions and unfettered access that the internet makes possible. This chapter will engage with some of those debates, examining areas of online sexual representations, considering their politics and practices, and their relationships to questions of identification and desire beyond the confines of the physical body. We will begin by looking at some of the mainstream pornographic productions online but then turn to more alternative production and the possibilities new technologies offer for their own forms of sexual practice – cybersex – as well as the possibilities opened up to 'new communities' which exploit the connectivity of the internet to move beyond the limitations of physical place.

We are starting with an exploration of online pornography. This is partly to clear this out of view: pornography has begun to be seen as a significant problem in modern culture, and the role of the internet in the spread and distribution of pornography has been debated, with claims of its intrusiveness and potential for causing 'addiction' and the undermining of 'healthy' sexuality and relationships. We can only scratch the surface here, but at the end of the chapter there is a list of further reading where you can find more detailed discussion.

The many histories of pornography tell how representational technologies have been used to create and transmit images of sexuality and sexual practices. Many argue that creators of sexually explicit imagery not only exploited the possibilities of print, photography, film, video and new media to circulate images depicting sexual acts, but they actually drove the changes in those technologies (Johnson, 1996; Perdue, 2002). For example, pornography is often cited as the reason for the popularizing of VHS over the Betamax format in the 1980s' battle for home video playback. Lane's history of 'Obscene

Profits' details the growth of a new economic sector, showing how production of sexually explicit imagery grew during the last six decades 'from a largely underground enterprise into a multibillion-dollar industry' (2001: xv). That growth was possible not just because developments in photography and film enabled the capture of naked bodies on film, but because the domestification of new technologies via the VCR changed the sites of consumption from the cinema to the home. Most importantly, new technologies have blurred the divisions between production and consumption: digital cameras and web publishing mean that individuals can now produce, upload and share their own images with a worldwide audience. It is important to note that histories of pornography are not limited to a discussion of increasing visibility (Williams, 1989) or the revealing of more and more flesh (an idea which underpins the claims that pornography is getting more and more explicit or extreme) or a focus on the exponential growth of the financial rewards of pornography. Recent scholarship addresses the fact that modes of production, distribution and reception have also changed (Jenkins, 2007). As a result so have our attitudes and expectations about sex, sexuality and their relationships to our bodies and identities. It is no longer the case that the porn viewer is conceptualized as a sad, lonely individual. Porn consumption has, for many, become respectable (Maddison, 2004).

First, let's look at a few statistics (though they are far from the whole story).

Every second $3,075.64 is being spent on pornography.
Every second 28,258 internet users are viewing pornography.
The pornography industry has larger revenues than Microsoft, Google, Amazon, eBay, Yahoo, Apple and Netflix combined.
2006 Worldwide Pornography Revenues were $97.06 billion.
42.7% of internet users view pornography.
4.2 million websites contain pornography (12% of the total number of websites).
Average age of a child's first exposure to pornography is 11.
90% of children ages 8–16 have viewed pornography online.
40 million U.S. adults regularly visit pornography websites.
10% of adults admit to an internet sexual addiction
20% of men say they access pornography at work.
1 in 3 visitors to porn websites are women
The 35- to 44-year-old age group consumes the most pornography in the United States (26%) and 18–24-year-olds purchase the least (14%). (Ropelato, 2006)

Those statistics are highly contested – especially the revenues. For example, in 2001 the *New York Times* suggested that a low estimate of total revenue for the porn business (including porn networks, pay-per-view movies on cable and satellite, websites, in-room hotel movies, sex toys, phone sex and porn magazines) was $10 billion (Forrester Research). In the same year, however, business magazine *Forbes* gave a figure of no more than $3.9 billion. Even so, it is clear that pornography is a big business and large companies such as Playboy and Vivid are making profits. However, within the larger formation that is the 'porn industry', there are many small producers, amateurs, independent sites and bloggers whose individual revenues (if they make money at all) are very modest. It is not just in terms of revenue that the numbers might be problematic – consider the last in our list above: people between 18 and 24 years old purchase the least amount of pornography but, given that lots of online pornography is available for free, we haven't learned much about viewing habits from that statistic. The same is true of the stats about kids under 18 viewing porn – 90% of them have seen online porn, but we have no idea from the statistics what *kinds* of pornography they may have seen (people's definitions of porn vary enormously; for some it's nude bodies, for others it's hardcore sex), nor do those stats give any indication of where they saw it, how they saw it and whether or not they liked it, hated it or were just plain puzzled by it. Thus the statistics give a broad brushstroke picture, but conceal as much as they illuminate. What is clear is that pornography is, as Linda Williams asserts, 'a fully recognizable fixture of popular culture' requiring 'better understanding' (Williams, 2004a: 1).

Online pornographies come in all varieties. In this section we look at some varieties of online representations. There are plenty of big players online, one of which is Vivid Entertainment Group, the world's largest porn production company. Formed in 1984, the company produces videos with high production values and a coterie of contract stars – The Vivid Girls – including Briana Banks and Jenna Jameson. Many of the Vivid films have won awards, including their remakes of 1970s classic porn movies such as *The New Devil in Miss Jones* (2005) and *Debbie Does Dallas ... Again* (2007). The company produces more than sixty titles per year but, as with most porn products, these are not only sold as the complete package (the feature-length film); they are cut up, repackaged and re-marketed across various distribution channels – as short scenes on pay-per-view TV or websites, as compilation DVDs, as teaser promos, and using stills for print and online distribution. As well as pioneering HD content and online distribution, Vivid does not limit itself to one form of content. Alongside its mainstream productions, the company offers alt porn (we'll talk about this later), gay porn, celebrity sex tapes and a range of education videos.

Vivid is interesting because, with its emphasis on high production values, full-length and feature movies, named directors, contract stars, attractive website and corporate licensing across products as diverse as condoms and snowboards, the company is an example of the new breed of porn companies which aspire to a *business* identity in the mould of Hollywood or other big media production companies. This new business profile is something that Biasin and Zecca discuss as 'an articulated *branding strategy*' (2009: 135) where companies seek to promote themselves as offering a blend of authenticity, innovation, quality and specialism. Branding in pornography, as in any other area of corporate production, works on a number of levels: as a 'reputation signal' – offering, for example, reliability, trustworthiness, choice; also as a carrier of symbolic meaning – brands achieve iconic status and offer a point of identification. In the case of Vivid, the name and logo profess to guarantee a certain level of quality.

The company message is carried further than the video store or website. The faces of the Vivid girls adorn billboards across the States, there's a reality TV programme *Vivid Valley* (World of Wonder: 2001) and a range of erotic books and comics sold in high street bookshops. As well as the branding possibilities of the stars employed by Vivid, the company has made some astute recruitment in terms of directors, including employing a feminist 'sexpert', Tristan Taormino, to front their education videos. At an awards ceremony Taormino was introduced with the following tribute:

> In an industry with an incredibly high turnover rate, it is remarkable when someone can sustain a ten-year career while simultaneously continuing to stay true to her intentions and expand the scope and impact of feminist porn. A trailblazer makes way for others to follow and opens up new opportunities for people attempting to forge their own path through similar avenues. In feminist pornography, one name evokes an understanding of art, of advocacy, of education and of quality – Tristan Taormino. (VividStudioInsider, n.d.)

We could regard this as no more than a bit of industry adulation, but Taormino and her status as a 'feminist trailblazer' enables the company to position their educational output, at least, within a progressive sexual politics (Juffer, 1998: 123) that avoids any taint of exploitation. Moreover, their remakes of classic movies draw on the legitimacy of traditional filmic conventions such as a complex narrative, character development and innovation – making reference to the golden age of pornographic production (Paasonen and Saarenmaa, 2007) while offering the improvements of contemporary porn performance in order to establish Vivid as an authentic producer of pornographic *art*. Vivid recently celebrated its twenty-fifth anniversary and is reputed to make in excess of $100 million profits per year although, more recently, it admitted to a 35% drop in DVD sales. In its mix of professional standards with an alt sensibility, the company looks set to remain a leading player.

Alt or indie porn is, as Cramer and Home suggest, 'the pornography of this decade, if not of the whole century… Websites like Suicidegirls.com, Cleansheets.com, ThatStrangeGirl.com and FatalBeauty.com combine the punk styling of their models with visual punk aesthetics and do-it-yourself punk attitude' (2007: 164). The punk styling is clearly an important visible signal of alt porn's difference from mainstream pornography production, but alt producers would suggest that there is more to their alt-ness than simply punky hairstyles and tattoos. As Scott Owens of EroticBPM puts it:

> When it comes to ideas I am always trying to think of ways to do something better than what the standard is. I am always thinking of how I can stimulate the community in new ways and provide a fun environment for models and members. (Quoted in Joyce, 2010)

Owens stresses that the BPM models are not just doing a job: 'what you see is a very real expression of the sexuality of each individual' (Joyce, 2010). Alt porn is, then, not just a production but an *expression*. It promotes itself as a form of collaboration rather than the commercial exploitation of women for men's pleasure and profit.

For academics such as Katrien Jacobs, alt porn offers a 'democratisation of pornography', and her book *Netporn* (2007) explores this in some detail, arguing that artists, subcultural groups and amateurs have seized pornographic expression as a means of articulating more fluid, identity-morphing sexualities. In these 'everyday' acts of resistance to mainstream sexual representations, women are, she argues, able to express their own versions of sexual pleasure and desire as part of a new 'gift-giving' economy which is not subject to the same masturbatory and commercial imperatives as mainstream porn. While common sense suggests that pornography has a singular purpose, new porn studies (such as Jacobs', Smith's (2007b) and Attwood's (2010)) suggest that engagements with pornography are more complex, relating as much to forms of community and exploration of new modes of being as they are about simply 'getting off'. Jacobs sees these newer forms of porn production as important to future sexual identities, claiming that 'amateur porn exchange and digital networking will guide the performance of our sex lives for many more decades to come' (2007: 78).

While Jacobs' account highlights the importance of the web-based technologies and the sexual behaviours/representations they have enabled, her discussion relies on an understanding of a de-materialized online world which doesn't necessarily take into account the substance of the critiques of pornography and the conditions in which it is produced. Jacobs is, perhaps, easily accused of naively celebrating the opportunities for self-expression provided by the web and of maintaining a too simplistic boundary between commercial (bad) and non-commercial (good) pornography. That boundary is not so clear when one begins to examine the ways in which the amateur and corporate (such as Vivid) forms of pornography (as with any other form of commerce on the net) are becoming increasingly blurred.

Before discussing that blurring, let us take a look at some of the alt porn sites. Some, such as beautifulagony.com, draw on earlier art/porn crossovers and feature videos of people's faces during orgasm in direct homage to New York artist Andy Warhol's 1964 *Blow Job*, a thirty-five minute silent film of a man's face as he receives fellatio (female artist k r buxey is also an influence here with her (2002) homage to Warhol entitled *Requiem*). Sites such as these offer imaginative erotic content which seems to explicitly challenge claims that pornography is always an abusive form. Where feminists accused pornography of exploiting female sexuality for profit and male pleasure, alt sites stress their (at least) proto-feminist ethic of women-friendliness and exploration of non-normative sexual interests. For example, Suicidegirls.com claims it is 'a community that celebrates alternative beauty and alternative culture from all over the world', offering an alternative to the airbrushed and heteronormative productions of 'industrial pornography'. With models whose bodies do not necessarily conform to standards of ideal beauty, these sites present potentially subversive imaging of gendered codes of sexuality and a challenge to the traditional gender relations thought to underpin mainstream pornography. As Feona Attwood (2010) points out, the term 'alt' encompasses a very broad range including fetishes, age play (role-play in which one or more partners imagine themselves as older or younger than they actually are), queer, trans and kink (an umbrella term for practices such as spanking, bondage, tickling, etc. – see our discussion in Chapter 10) but they share interests in the sexual exhibition of 'real people' in sex-positive ways. The *authenticity* of these 'real people' is expressed via the biographies that accompany photo-shoots, giving details of their interests outside the sexual sphere, as well as the ways in which each feels that sexuality (as a cultural ideal/practice) and as a personally felt expression of self is something to be celebrated – a form of self-representation denied to models in traditional centrefold interview.

When Suicidegirls was launched in 2001 much was made of its feminist politics and the fact that its women were not *just* models but also key players in the site's production. Suicidegirls was promoted as 'a community of girls, where girls could express their sexuality' (Fulton, 2005). Key to its successful presentation as a 'feminist' site was founder Miss Suicide's emphasis on the site's ethos of *real* women exploring sexual possibilities in an environment which actively espoused female empowerment and where all the significant employees were female. The claims to offer an alternative production model as well as unconventional aesthetics and a new ethic of subcultural erotica were tested when, in 2005, around forty models left the community amongst claims that '[Suicidegirls is] exploitational to women, and abusive, because it lures women in with a marketing scheme that purports feminism, when in actuality the sole owner of the company is an active misogynist' (Fulton, 2005). The revelation that the site was at least part-owned by a man, Sean Suhl, threatened the mythology of the site's woman-friendly production ethos (Dotinga, 2005; Hills, 2006).

The furore around the 'web-out' highlights one of the significant problems in our current conceptions of pornographic production which tend, against poststructuralist theories of the 'death of the author' (Barthes, 1977; Foucault,

1969), to stress producers' intentions as the key determinants of meaning in a text. Barthes criticized literary criticism that relies on the uncovering of the author's identity – for example their political views, religion, ethnicity or gender – to explain the meaning of a particular work. When it comes to pornography, there is still a tendency to talk in terms of pornography's intentions to objectify women as a direct result of it being produced by men – although it needs to be acknowledged that such discussions rarely actually address the detail of production except to identify the bogeyman figure of the 'pornographer' (for a discussion of this and an alternative account see Smith (2007b)). The story about Suicidegirls with its allegations of a bullying, neoconservative CEO and abusive work environment, while fitting that particular script, also highlights the problems inherent in more recent discussions which have sought to emphasize the potential radicalism of women's involvement in creating sexually explicit materials. Is it really the case that by the mere fact of women being involved in the production of pornography at all levels from performance through creative input to profit-sharing, that pornography becomes radicalized? Certainly, the knowledge that women are heading up production companies and involved in creative work within sexually explicit media complicates the picture of the male perpetrator and female victim which characterized older debates about pornography. But that still raises, for some commentators, fundamental questions about how those representations speak to and reflect the material realities of gender in late capitalist culture.

Echoing earlier concerns that transgression is always understood as radical (and here we could say that in a culture which often denigrates women as sluts, women speaking openly about their sexual desires *can be* transgressive), in accounts such as Jacobs' which tend to value transgression for its own sake, focusing on the 'unorthodox bodies' and 'disorderly tastes and desires' (2007: 180) that the web has made visible, there is a seeming refusal to acknowledge the ways in which these minority practices may not seriously challenge the hegemonic and commercial model of 'extreme visibility' (Williams, 1989) of the female body as an object of desire. Cramer and Home argue that far from being an alternative model, alt porn

> pretends to be different from the industry, but works with the same business model. Just as punk and indie pop saved the music industry in the 1980s and 1990s, indie porn will save the porn industry of today. It is the research and development arm of the porn industry. An industry that otherwise would go bankrupt because everyone freely shares its products on the Internet. (2007: 165)

This pessimistic account could be substantiated by looking at how Vivid and other large companies have turned to alt representations as a means of broadening their appeal. However, as Attwood has argued, alt porn, with its emphasis on collaboration, self-expression, art and activism, offers new forms of porn professionalism underpinned by a 'refusal of moralistic assumptions that sex should be private, that commercial sex is simply "wrong" or always damaging, that sex workers are inevitably alienated, exploited, or dehumanized by their work' (2010: 102). Alt porn indicates that the ways in which producers and consumers relate to representations of sexual interests and practices may well be undergoing significant change, an element we hope will become clearer in our discussion of user-generated pornographies.

With the advent of the internet, customers do not have to leave the comfort of their own homes to access pornography, and they can now also make their own using Tube sites such as XTube.com, RedTube.com and yuvutu.com. Just like YouTube, these sites allow users to view films but, most importantly for our discussion here, also to post videos of themselves, to create profiles and to communicate with other users. When viewers register for the sites, they categorize themselves as male or female and interested in films featuring males/females or both. The sites allow for searches via a number of filters – for those who have particular interests, films are archived according to 'tags' such as 'blowjob' or 'anal', via bodily features such as 'large ass' or 'blonde' as well as a variety of other categorizations such as 'Asian', 'Mom' or 'Babysitter'. Users who want to upload their own films are given lots of advice about ensuring that their films get clicked on/viewed – uploaded films are tagged to enable searches and clearly the more tags one places on one's video the more likely it is to be found within the hundreds of thousands of videos now available on individual Tube sites.

The sites enable the interactivity and participation that has come to characterize Web 2.0. Web 2.0 is supposed to have dissolved the line between author and reader, producer and consumer, subverting the one-way communication of earlier media forms where the few created content for the entertainment of the many. The internet offers platforms for *participation* rather than publishing, enabling interactivity rather than passive consumption and inverting traditional patterns of content and consumption. By facilitating amateur productions, sites such as XTube offer a kind of 'democratization of desire' (McNair, 2002) Just as with the alt porn we discussed earlier, particular claims for 'authenticity' are being made by the Tube sites:

> There are absolutely no professional models, paid actresses or any kind of fake people here. No 'porn stars' with fake boobs and silicone lips – it is all about girlfriends and wives and couples. (Redclouds)

It is in this 'truthfulness' that we might find particular aesthetic differences from 'industrial' pornography, though you will have noted that the focus here is still on women to be looked at. Van Doorn explores the aesthetic and narrative claims of 'realness' and 'authenticity' in videos on YouPorn and combines this with an analysis of their presentation of gender. He cautions against any overly optimistic acceptance of the Tube sites' claims to 'a privileged relationship to "reality"' (2010: 425) and suggests that there may be politically regressive elements to YouPorn's presentations. Indeed van Doorn argues that while these amateur films might offer non-normative bodies engaged in unusual sexual connections, there is, nonetheless,

> widespread adoption of a normative 'pornoscript' structur[ing] the possible ways in which sexual pleasure is visualized in the 'amateur' videos on YouPorn ... [and which] perpetuate an essentialist (and sometimes sexist) gender ideology. (2010: 427)

This highlights a particular problem which has dogged studies of pornography and particularly newer academic investigations into the forms and meanings of sexually explicit materials. Too often exploration of the pornographic becomes a search for evidence of either 'harm' – for example politically regressive gender ideologies – or liberation – for example the transgression of gender stereotypes. Given the hegemony of feminist arguments of porn's harm and objectification of women, it is hardly surprising that discussions of pornography are frequently couched in these dichotomous terms, but they don't seem to get us very far. In this next section, we want to explore an argument which looks at the content of Tube site videos, to ask *why* some people want to post videos of themselves in possibly their most intimate moments, for others to view.

In her seminal study *Hard Core*, Linda Williams argued that pornography operates with 'the principle of maximum visibility' (1989: 48); not only does it record sex for camera but it also tries to show the 'truth' of sexual desire and pleasure, taking us up close to the action and capturing the moment of orgasm: male ejaculation (the money-shot) and the 'confessions' of the female body. Because the female orgasm is so elusive and can be easily faked, Williams suggested that modern pornography attempts to narrativize the truth of the orgasm via its capture of the *progress* of sexual congress from initiation through to climax. Thus, for Williams, the dynamic at work for the producer is to reveal as much as possible, whereas, for the consumer, it is to get to see as much as possible. These dynamics speak to fundamentally voyeuristic pleasures.

In home-made or amateur videos these dynamics may be changing. In his discussion of the Tube site XTube, Evangelos Tziallas suggests that

> the conventional methods of sexual presentation which dominate the commercial narrative pornographic industry [are challenged]. Videos here can start mid-way through oral sex and end *without* orgasm, or even if orgasm occurs, the fetishistic and narrative connotations of the 'cum shot' are negated by the orgasm occurring internally or at such a distance from the camera as to make it *invisible*. (2010)

The short scenes offered on Tube sites – some only sixty seconds long – owe more, Tziallas argues, to forms of surveillance (covert recordings or CCTV) than to cinematic traditions of production. Hence, amateur videos uploaded to these sites make a virtue of their amateurism – the grainy, shaky, hand-held camerawork, the inadequacies of the soundtrack, lighting and settings and the lack of clear visibility of the bodies filmed in motion. Rather than see these films as deficient attempts to copy professional production, Tziallas argues that they create their own aesthetics 'whereby surveillance moves beyond its technology into a "way of seeing"', promising particular pleasures of the authentic and enabling further sets of pleasures focused on the notion of self-surveillance – offering up oneself to the camera and the site user to be viewed but also, importantly, to be judged and rated. While we could see this as a negative form of disciplinary practice (as Foucault might argue) or simply another form of voyeurism (as per Freud), Tziallas suggests these sites offer a contemporary and complex articulation between the fact of being surveilled and new forms of exhibitionist delight enabling 'self-exploration through self-surveillance': we are no longer concerned with being caught in the act, but rather we wish to be visible, to be seen even in those moments which have been traditionally conceived as intensely private. This brings into focus one area of porn studies which is remarkably thin – *who* appears in these films and why? Although Tziallas can't answer this definitively, he makes an interesting case that surveillance has its own pleasures that may well reverse the idea that the filmed body is being offered for the pleasure of others – it may, in fact, be taking its own pleasures from performing to be watched:

> Surveillance culture has reversed and fetishized visibility and so the power and pleasure lies with those who are being watched. When performers look into the camera, they are not looking at the one they are performing on, but rather into the *future* gaze of the distant spectator. (Tziallas, 2010)

More than this, Tziallas suggests that those who film themselves are engaging in forms of auto-ethnography, a staging of the self which has elements of the confessional, and a transformation of subjectivity into performance. Though Tziallas doesn't want to make any extravagant claims for what this might mean, he suggests 'a desire to put one's body, one's self, and most importantly, one's desires on display for public consumption' complicates the conception of sexual display as a pathologic exhibitionism (as Freudians might suggest). A purely textual account of pornography – at least of user-generated porn – cannot get at the ways in which the patterns of production, distribution and consumption are changing.

Alongside pornography, cybersex is arguably one of the great modern 'problems'. Type in the term 'cybersex addiction' and millions of webpages are found detailing the signs of addiction, the causes, results and therapies. Add in the potent fears of pornographic representations and the internet's capacity for distribution ignoring geographical and legislative boundaries and we find the notion of cybersexual encounters problematized daily. Of course, some people do experience significant problems in their personal lives and their relationships perhaps caused by their interests in cybersex, but the talk of 'addiction' leads us into particular ways of thinking about those problems and from there to 'protecting' individuals from ideas, images and practices which supposedly operate on us like 'drugs'. There is no necessary connection between pornography and cybersex but they are often lumped together in order to make a strong case for regarding the internet as a dangerous force which allows de-personalized and dangerously anonymous sex. But perhaps there are other ways of thinking about the possibilities for sexual interaction now available.

Behaviours online seriously complicate our notion of what constitutes sexual practice: in a book like this, which focuses on sex as an object of critical thinking, it is all too easy to avoid the particularly embodied nature of sexual activity – the 'wet, odoriferous, and teeming with biological organisms' (Waskul et al., 2000: 375) nature of 'corporeal sexual encounters' (ibid.) – and yet it is precisely those elements which create the specific problems of sexual practices – unwanted pregnancy, disease transmission and embarrassment. Cybersex – a curiously out-of-body sexual practice – might seem to avoid the specific embodiednesses of sexual practices, but only if we focus on sex as a practice of co-presentness, as a set of acts which require bodily interaction between two or more people.

The dictionary definition of cybersex is sexual arousal or activity through communication via computer. A vast array of activities come under this umbrella term, with more likely to be added as the internet expands. The following are all instances of cybersex, though some of them overlap: sex messaging (where individuals send each other messages describing a sexual experience), sex play (where two or more people together author, via messaging, a sexual interaction), role-playing (often in virtual worlds where avatars are used to act out a sexual interaction), webcaming (real-time video interactions between one or more partners), and hooking up (where people use the internet to find partners for physical world sexual liaisons). Of course, these activities bleed into the myriad opportunities for arousal, interaction and masturbation provided by online pornography and other kinds of commercial sex sites, such as xxxpanded.com or livesex.com. Cybersex is facilitated by the easy accessibility, affordability and anonymity of the web – so long as you have an internet connection you can engage in cybersex. Even so, what particularly interests us here are the possibilities the internet has opened up for new forms of community based around sexual interests, which attempt to break down the barriers of geographical distance as well as the boundaries imposed by social and moral concerns about what constitutes 'proper' sexual behaviour. To illustrate this further, we'll close with a brief discussion of sexual 'community' online.

Dogging websites are an interesting phenomenon because they straddle the divide between on- and offline selves. Dogging is an offline (i.e. real world) practice combining 'public sex, voyeurism and exhibitionism, "swinging", group sex and partner swapping' (Bell, 2006: 388) and which takes place in car parks, beauty spots and other secluded public spaces. It can be thought of as a particularly British pastime but is also practised around the world. It is also a feature of online spaces – there are sites dedicated to images and videos of dogging activities, but also community sites which suggest this is a thriving sexual subculture. On the community sites, members can find out about local, national and international dogging sites, arrange meetings, swap experiences/images and information and communicate with other doggers.

As with other forms of participatory sexual expression online, authenticity and 'amateurism' are important. Site owners post their credentials – for example, 'We are a genuine swinging couple from the North West' – and mix discussion of dogging or swinging practices with text and pictures about their home lives, their work, and family. Thus, the websites conform to what Barcan has termed 'a broad postmodern taste for "authentica"' (2004: 145–6). They may also be instances of what Attwood has described as new forms of sexual self-representation facilitating 'taste cultures' where 'sex is the focus of participatory cultures and where commerce and community are combined' (2007: 442). Trust and responsibility are also important in these 'sex communities' (Jacobs, 2007): as well as the sharing of online fantasies, experiences and pictures, questions of responsibility to oneself and one's partner(s) in practices offline are discussed. For example, Mel (of melanies-uk-swingers.com) gives the following advice on her site for planning, enjoying and leaving a dogging meet:

> Talk about it – If it's your first time dogging, then you need to talk about what you're looking to get out of it. It's easy for a partner to get confused about how far to go. Talk to each other, decide what you're both comfortable doing, the last thing you want is to overstep your partner's boundaries. ... Ending it – A simple thank you to all the males that watched or took part in the fun is all that's needed. Everyone will get the idea and say their goodbyes. (Dogging Advice)

Moreover, interestingly and drawing attention to the ways in which the internet is 'part of' rather than 'apart from' everyday life (Miller and Slater, 2001), another key consideration expressed on the community sites is responsibility to members of the wider public. In our research for this chapter we found that all the dogging community sites are very aware of the negative publicity their particular practices have garnered in the popular press. There have been tales of celebrities caught in the act, and even an on-duty policeman found neglecting his duty (from the *Daily Record* (2006), 'halfway through, the randy copper received a police radio call – but told colleagues: "I'm busy at the moment. I'll get back to you in 20 minutes'"). The press also reports on the dangers of sexual infection for those engaging in dogging, as well as numerous scandalized articles about the breach of public space and the mess left by doggers. For example, Rev. Rob Wykes, of Crewe Christian Concern, was outraged by dogging:

> All right-minded adults recognise that sexual activity is about intimacy, privacy and sensitivity and not something that should be carried out in a public park which is there for family enjoyment.
> What gives these people the right to do whatever they want in a public place? They have completely forgotten their responsibility to the wider community. (Roberts, 2004)

Hence, many community sites exhort their members to

> [a]lways dispose of your 'dogging kit' safely and properly. Areas that are left full of used condoms and other items will soon get closed down by the authorities. If you wouldn't want your kids to find it, don't leave it.' (All About Dogging)

The mundane good sense of this advice emphasizes the ways in which dogging is not just a sexual practice but also a complex negotiation of the public/private divide and of online/offline presence. Contrary to the idea that the web is some entirely separate place from the 'real' world, dogging community sites indicate a more complex oscillation between the possibilities of immersion in a virtual or fantasy space where 'anything goes' and the 'real world' realities of engaging in activities that other people would seek to censor or prevent. It demonstrates the ways in which community protocols and mores are established online in relation to wider social prohibitions and possible regulation of a community's practices, and how these might impact on offline activities.

So to conclude, alongside the watching of pornography, the web has offered parallel opportunities for self-presentation, construction of communities and publicizing of practices. Online sexual practices offer interesting opportunities for thinking about the ways in which the web complicates the idea of the differences between production and consumption. The internet, with its plethora of self-produced porn and online spaces for sexual play and interaction, has done away with the strict boundary between producer and consumer and, as part of that boundary breaking, may well be enabling new forms of sexual subjectivity.

Further Reading

Attwood, F. (ed.) (2010) *Porn.com: Making Sense of Online Pornography* (New York: Peter Lang Publishing).

Paasonen, S. (2011) *Carnal Resonance: Affect and Online Pornography* (Cambridge, MA: MIT Press).

Waskul, D. (2003) *Self-Games and Body Play: Personhood in Online Chat and Cybersex* (New York: Peter Lang).

Conclusion

We hope that this book has opened up a series of issues for you about sex, sexuality, sexual identities and the media representations that draw upon this most complex of human interests. We've tried to explore some of the key concepts in sexuality studies to help stimulate your own ideas, to help you think through the cultural politics of sex, its representations and practices. Key to our approach is an awareness that sexuality is much more than simply a matter of biology or a fixed essence. As experiences, identities and practices, sex is not as clear-cut as might at first appear. Our intention has been to get you to think about the ways in which sex is defined, described and depicted in popular media, and how those definitions are central to ways in which sex is made to signify culturally and politically. Those definitions have impacts on the ways in which we might experience our own selves as sexual.

We've argued that sex is a product of discourses: of the ways in which we talk about who does what with whom and why. As with any cultural phenomenon, the critical approaches to sex are not fixed – we have tried to show you that there are productive dialogues and exchanges around sexuality, that definitions and ideas are important to think about and to debate. Of course, this means that if we no longer talk of sex as a fixed essence, you can be left with the unsettling sensation that hours of reading and researching have not produced any definitive answers about what sex is. But take heart: studying sexuality is not about searching for certainties! We hope we've shown you that sexuality studies enables us to think about sex as historically contingent, as changed by political, economic and cultural developments and also having its own impact on those areas of life. We have tried to stay away from the 'moral panics' versions of sexuality but these are a backdrop to the discussions we've offered, and it is important to recognize that sex is so intensely personal, and at the same particularly public, that it can be the cause of much angst. We've discussed theoretical approaches to sexuality and sexual identities, we've offered some explorations of the semiotics of representations of sex and their meanings, but it is important to recognize that sex involves acts, personal histories, as well as being a matter of representation. We are moving into new spaces of representation, where sex becomes ever more fragmented and differently experienced; yet at the same time, the same questions, same worries are being articulated – what should be represented, how might this be good or bad for young people, what is healthy sexual development, who does the representing and why, what are the histories of these representations and what do we know of their impressions on viewers?

These questions are constantly rehearsed and they are deeply political. Debates across the various disciplines which examine sexuality are riven by conceptual and methodological disputes, but this makes sex, sexuality and their representations in the media one of the most vital and exciting areas of study. We hope we've given you some inspiration here for pursuing your own investigations.

Bibliography

Addley, E. (2003) 'Toys are Us', *The Guardian*, 16 January: 2.
Akass, K. and McCabe, J. (eds) (2004) *Reading Sex and the City* (New York and London: I.B.Tauris).
—— (eds) (2006) *Reading the L Word: Outing Contemporary Television* (New York and London: I.B.Tauris).
All About Dogging, www.doggingcentral.co.uk, accessed 19 January 2008.
Allen, D. (1995) 'Homosexuality and Narrative', *Modern Fiction Studies*, Vol. 41, No. 3–4: 609–34.
Almaguer, T. (1991) 'Chicano Men: A Cartography of Homosexual Identity and Behaviour', *Differences: A Journal of Feminist Cultural Studies*, Vol. 3, No. 2: 75–100.
American Psychological Association (2010) *Report of the APA Task Force on the Sexualization of Girls*, available at www.apa.org/pi/women/programs/girls/report-full.pdf, accessed 21 March 2010.
Ang, I. (1985) *Watching Dallas: Soap Opera and the Melodramatic Imagination* (London: Methuen).
Anonymous (1724) *Onania, or the Heinous Sin of Self-Pollution and all its Frightful Consequences*, available at http://english.byu.edu/facultysyllabi/KLawrence/ONANIA.pdf.
Apter, E. (1982) *Fantasy Literature: An Approach to Reality* (Bloomington: Indiana University Press).
Aries, P. (1962) *Centuries of Childhood* (New York: Vintage Books).
Arthurs, J. (2004) *Television and Sexuality: Regulation and the Politics of Taste* (Maidenhead: Open University Press).
Attwood, F. (2005) 'Fashion and Passion: Marketing Sex to Women', *Sexualities*, Vol. 8, No. 4: 392–406.
—— (2006) 'Sexed Up: Theorizing the Sexualization of Culture', *Sexualities*, Vol. 9, No. 1: 78–9.
—— (2007) 'No Money Shot? Commerce, Pornography and New Sex Taste Cultures', *Sexualities*, Vol. 10, No. 4: 441–56
—— (2010) '"Younger, Paler, Decidedly Less Straight": The New Porn Professionals', in Attwood, F. (ed.) *Porn.com: Making Sense of Online Pornography* (New York: Peter Lang Publishing).
Attwood, F. and Smith, C. (2010) 'Extreme Concern: Regulating "Dangerous Pictures" in the United Kingdom', *Journal of Law and Society*, Vol. 37, No. 1, March: 171–88.
Austin, J. (1962) *How to Do Things with Words* (Oxford: Clarendon Press).
Australian Institute (2006) *Corporate Paedophilia: Sexualisation of Children in Australia* (authors E. Rush and A. La Nauze), available at https://www.tai.org.au/documents/dp_fulltext/DP90.pdf, accessed 21 March 2010.
Bacon-Smith, C. (1992) *Enterprising Women: Television Fandom and the Creation of Popular Myth* (Pittsburgh: University of Pennsylvania Press).

Barcan, R. (2000) 'Home on the Rage: Nudity, Celebrity and Ordinariness in the Home Girls/Blokes Pages', *Continuum: Journal of Media and Cultural Studies*, Vol. 14, No. 2: 145–6.
—— (2004) *Nudity: A Cultural Anatomy* (New York: Berg).
Barthes, R. (1968) *Elements of Semiology* (New York: Hill and Wang).
—— (1977) 'Death of the Author', *Image, Music, Text* (1998) (New York: Noon Day Press).
Bartlett, M. (2010) 'The Art of (B)romance: "I Love You Too"', *Metro Magazine: Media & Education Magazine*, No. 165: 32–7.
Battles, K. and Hilton-Morrow, W. (2002) 'Gay Characters in Conventional Spaces: *Will and Grace* and the Situation Comedy Genre', *Critical Studies in Media Communication*, Vol. 19, No. 1: 87–105.
BBC Online (2005) 'Gay Weddings Become Law in UK', 5 December, available at http://news.bbc.co.uk/1/hi/uk/4493094.stm, accessed 5 December 2010.
Beckman, A. (2001) 'Deconstructing Myths: The Social Construction of "Sadomasochism" versus "Subjugated Knowledges" of Practitioners of Consensual SM', *Journal of Criminal Justice and Popular Culture*, Vol. 8, No. 2: 66–95.
Bell, D. (2006) 'Bodies, Technologies, Spaces: On "Dogging"', *Sexualities*, Vol. 9, No. 4: 387–407.
Bell, D. and Binnie, J. (2000) *The Sexual Citizen: Queer Politics and Beyond* (Cambridge: Polity Press).
Berger, J. (1972) *Ways of Seeing* (London: Penguin).
Bergmann, M. (1994) 'The Female Oedipal Complex', in Mendell, D. (ed.) *Body and Self: Exploration of Early Female Development* (USA: Jason Aronson Inc. Publishers).
Bernstein, E. (2007) *Temporarily Yours: Intimacy, Authenticity, and the Commerce of Sex* (Chicago: University of Chicago Press).
Biasin, E. and Zecca, F. (2009) 'Contemporary Audiovisual Pornography: Branding Strategy and Gonzo Film Style', *Cinema & Cie: International Film Studies Journal*, Vol. 9, No. 12.
Bindley, K. (2008) 'Bromances aren't Uncommon as Guys Delay Marriage', *Seattle Times*, 7 April, available at http://seattletimes.nwsource.com/html/living/2004328748_bromance07.html, accessed 25 September 2011.
Blair, T. (2006) 'Our Nation's Future', 5 September, available at www.number-10.gov.uk/output/Page10037.asp, accessed 27 September 2008.
Bordo, S. (1999) *The Male Body: A New Look at Men in Public and in Private* (New York: Farrar, Straus & Giroux).
Bouchard, D.F. and Simon, S. (trans.) (1998) 'Foucault, A Preface to Trangression', in Faubion, J. (ed.) *Michel Foucault: Essential Works 1954–1984, Vol. 2, Aesthetics* (Harmondsworth: Penguin).
Bourdieu, P. (1986) *Distinction: A Social Critique of the Judgment of Taste* (trans. R. Nice) (London: Routledge).
Boynton, P. (2004) 'Real Life: My Mum is My Dad', *British Medical Journal*, Vol. 329, 7 August, www.bmj.com/content/329/7461/355.1.full.pdf, accessed 1 November 2011.
Brasfield, R. (2006) 'Rereading *Sex and the City*: Exposing the Hegemonic Feminist Narrative', *Journal of Popular Film and Television*, Vol. 34, No. 3: 130–9.
Bray, A. (1988) *Homosexuality in Renaissance England* (London: Gay Men's Press).
Brewis, J. and Linstead, S. (2000) *Sex, Work and Sex Work* (London: Routledge).

Briggs, M. (2009) *Television, Audiences and Everyday Life* (Milton Keynes: Open University Press).

Bruzzi, S. and Church Gibson, P. (2004) '"Fashion is the Fifth Character": Fashion, Costume and Character in *Sex and the City*', in Akass, K. and McCabe, J. (eds) *Reading Sex and the City* (New York and London: I.B.Tauris).

Buckland, F. (2002) *Impossible Dance: Club Culture and Queer World-Making* (Connecticut: Wesleyan University Press).

Butler, J. (1993) *Bodies that Matter: On the Discursive Limits of 'Sex'* (London and New York: Routledge).

—— (1999) *Gender Trouble: Feminism and the Subversion of Identity*, 2nd edition (London and New York: Routledge).

Califia, P. (1980) *Sapphistry* (Tallahassee: Naiad Press).

—— (1992) 'The Limits of the S/M Relationship', *Outlook*, Winter: 16–21.

—— (1997) 'Identity Sedition and Pornography', in Queen, C. and Schimel, L. (eds) *PoMoSexuals: Challenging Assumptions about Gender and Sexuality* (San Francisco: Cleis Press).

Campbell, J. (2000) *Arguing with the Phallus: Feminist, Queer, and Postcolonial Theory: A Psychoanalytic Contribution* (London: Zed Books).

Castiglia, C. and Reed, C. (2004) '"Ah, Yes, I remember it well": Memory and Queer Culture in *Will and Grace*', *Cultural Critique*, Vol. 56: 158–88.

Champagne, C. (2004) 'Gaywatch: *The L Word*', first published on gay.com, available at http://thelword2004.tripod.com/index/id8.html, accessed 1 November 2011.

Channel 4, Sex Education Website, http://sexperienceuk.channel4.com/education/about/male-anatomy, accessed 1 March 2011.

Chauncey, G. (1994) *Gay New York: Gender, Urban Culture and the Making of the Gay Male World 1890–1940* (New York: Basic Books).

Chodorow, N. (1999) *The Reproduction of Mothering: Psychoanalysis and the Sociology of Gender* (Berkeley: University of California Press).

Clover, C. (1992) *Men, Women, and Chainsaws: Gender in the Modern Horror Film* (New York: Princeton University Press).

Connell, R.W. and Messerschmidt, J.W. (2005) 'Hegemonic Masculinity: Rethinking the Concept', *Gender and Society*, Vol. 19, No. 6: 829–59.

'Cracking Down on Violent Pornography' (2006) www.homeoffice.gov.uk/about-us/news/violent-porn-outlawed, 30 August, accessed 31 March 2009.

Cramer, F. and Home, S. (2007) 'Pornographic Coding', in Jacobs, K. *et al.* (eds) *C'Lick Me: A Netporn Studies Reader* (Amsterdam: Institute of Network Cultures).

Cramer, J.M. (2007) 'Discourses of Sexual Morality in *Sex and the City* and *Queer as Folk*', *Journal of Popular Culture*, Vol. 40, No. 3: 409–32.

Criminal Justice and Immigration Act 2008 (c4) Part 5, available at www.opsi.gov.uk/acts/acts2008/ukpga_20080004_en_9, accessed 13 March 2009.

Daily Mail (2006) 'Victory for Victim's Mum in Crackdown on Web Sex Violence', 30 August.

Daily Record (2006) 'PC Lumber is Sacked for Dogging on Duty; Cop in Threesome told Colleagues: I'm Busy', 15 September: 33.

Davis, G. (2009) *Queer as Folk* (London: BFI).

Delamater, J.D. and Shibley Hyde, J. (1998) 'Essentialism vs Social Constructionism in the Study of Human Sexuality', *The Journal of Sex Research*, Vol. 35, No. 1: 10–18.

Dogging Advice, www.melanies-uk-swingers.com/php/pages/advice/advice-dogging.php, accessed 19 January 2008.

Dolan, J. (2005) 'Fans of Lesbians on TV: The L Word's Generations', *Flow*, http://flowtv.org/2005/04/fans-of-lesbians-on-tv-the-l-words-generations/, accessed 1 November 2011.

Dollimore, J. (2001) *Sex, Literature and Censorship* (Cambridge: Polity Press).

van Doorn, N. (2010) 'Keeping it Real: User-Generated Pornography, Gender Reification, and Visual Pleasure', *Convergence: The International Journal of Research into New Media Technologies*, Vol. 16, No. 4, November: 411–30.

Dotinga, R. (2005) 'Suicide Girls Gone AWOL', *Wired*, 28 September, available at www.wired.com/culture/lifestyle/news/2005/09/69006, accessed 21 March 2011.

Douglas, M. (1966) *Purity and Danger: An Analysis of Concepts of Pollution and Taboo* (London: Routledge & Kegan Paul).

Dovey, J. (2000) *Freakshow: First Person Media and Factual Television* (London: Pluto).

Downing, L. (2008) 'Beyond Safety: Erotic Asphyxiation and the Limits of SM Discourse', in Langdridge, D. and Barker, M. (eds) *Safe, Sane and Consensual: Contemporary Perspectives on Sadomasochism* (London: Palgrave Macmillan).

Dreisinger, B. (2000) 'The Queen in Shining Armour: Safe Eroticism and the Gay Friend', *Journal of Popular Film and Television*, Vol. 28, No. 1: 3–11.

Dreyfus, P. and Rabinow, H. (1982) *Michel Foucault, Beyond Structuralism and Hermeneutics* (Chicago: University of Chicago Press).

Dworkin, A. (1981) *Pornography: Men Possessing Women* (London: Women's Press).

Dyer, R. (1988) 'Children of the Night: Vampirism as Homosexuality', in Radstone, S. (ed.) *Sweet Dreams: Sexuality, Gender and Popular Fiction* (London: Lawrence and Wishart).

—— (1993) *The Matter of Images* (London and New York: Routledge).

—— (2002) *Only Entertainment*, 2nd edition (London and New York: Routledge).

Eichner, M. (2009) 'Feminism, Queer Theory, and Sexual Citizenship', in Grossman, J. and McClain, L. (eds) *Gender Equality: Dimensions of Women's Equal Citizenship* (Cambridge: UNC Legal Studies).

Elias, N. (1969) *The Civilizing Process Vol. I: The History of Manners* (Oxford: Blackwell).

—— (1982) *The Civilizing Process Vol. II: State Formation and Civilization* (Oxford: Blackwell).

Faludi, S. (2000) *Stiffed: The Betrayal of Modern Man* (London: Vintage).

Farley, M. (1993) 'Ten Lies About Sadomasochism', originally published in *Sinister Wisdom*, No. 50, Summer/Fall: 29–37, available at www.mediawatch.com/wordpress/?p=21, accessed 21 July 2009.

Fausto-Sterling, A. (1985) *Myths of Gender: Biological Theories about Men and Women* (New York: Basic Books).

Ferris, P. (1994) *Sex and the British: A Twentieth Century History* (London: Mandarin).

Findlay, H. (1992) 'Freud's "Fetishism" and the Lesbian Dildo Debates', *Feminist Studies*, Vol. 18, No. 3: 563–80.

Fiske, J. (1999) *Television Culture* (London: Routledge).

Forest, B. (1995) 'West Hollywood as Symbol: The Significance of Place in the Construction of a Gay Identity', *Environment and Planning D: Society and Space*, Vol. 13, No. 2: 133–57.

Foucault, M. (1969) 'What is an Author?', in Harari, J.V. (ed.) (1979) *Textual Strategies: Perspectives in Post-Structuralist Criticism* (Ithaca: Cornell University Press).

—— (1977) *Discipline and Punish: The Birth of the Prison* (London: Allen Lane).
—— (1988) *Technologies of the Self: A Seminar with Michel Foucault* (Amherst, MA: University of Massachusetts Press).
—— [1976] (1990a) *The History of Sexuality Vol. I: The Will to Knowledge* (London: Penguin).
—— [1984] (1990b) *The History of Sexuality Vol. III: The Care of the Self* (London: Penguin).
—— (1992) *The History of Sexuality Vol. II: The Use of Pleasure* (London: Penguin).
—— (1997) 'The Ethics of the Concern for Self as a Practice of Freedom' (trans. R. Hurley and others), in Rabinow, P. (ed.) *Michel Foucault: Ethics, Subjectivity and Truth: The Essential Works of Michel Foucault 1954–1984, Vol. 1* (London: Penguin Press).
—— 1975] (2004) 'Je suis un artificier', in Droit, R.-P. (ed.) *Michel Foucault, entretiens* (Paris: Odile Jacob).
Freud, S. [1905] (1974) 'Three Essays on the Theory of Sexuality', in Strachey, J. (ed.) *The Standard Edition of the Complete Psychological Works of Sigmund Freud, Vol. 7* (London: Hogarth Press).
—— [1905] (1977) *On Sexuality*, Penguin Freud Library, 7 (trans. J. Strachey) (London: Penguin).
—— (1995) 'Three Essays on the Theory of Sexuality (An Excerpt)', in Fitzpatrick Handy, M.A. (ed.) *Essential Papers on Masochism* (New York: New York University Press).
Fulton, D. (2005) 'SuicideGirls Revolt', *The Portland Phoenix*, www.portlandphoenix.com/features/other_stories/documents/05018238.asp, accessed 21 April 2010.
Gaines, J. (1995) 'Feminist Heterosexuality and its Politically Incorrect Pleasures', *Critical Inquiry*, Vol. 21, No. 2: 382–410.
Gallagher, B. and Wilson, A. (1984) 'Michel Foucault, An Interview: Sex, Power and the Politics of Identity', *The Advocate*, No. 400, 7 August.
Garber, E. and Paleo, L. (1990) *Uranian Worlds: A Guide to Alternative Sexuality in Science Fiction, Fantasy, and Horror* (Boston: G.K. Hall).
Gerhard, J. (2005) '*Sex and the City*: Carrie Bradshaw's Queer Postfeminism', *Feminist Media Studies*, Vol. 5, No. 1: 37–49.
Giddens, A. (1991) *Modernity and Self Identity: Self and Society in the Late Modern Age* (Stanford: Stanford University Press).
—— (1992) *The Transformation of Intimacy* (Oxford: Polity Press).
Gill, R. (2003) 'From Sexual Objectification to Sexual Subjectification: The Resexualisation of Women's Bodies in the Media', *Feminist Media Studies*, Vol. 3, No. 1: 99–106.
—— (2007) 'Postfeminist Media Culture. Elements of a Sensibility', *European Journal of Cultural Studies*, Vol. 10, No. 2: 147–66.
(2009) 'Supersexualize Me! Advertising and the "Midriffs"', in Attwood, F. (ed.) *Mainstreaming Sex: The Sexualisation of Western Culture* (New York: I.B.Tauris).
Gold, J. (2007) 'How to Build a Brand like Ann Summers', available at www.newbusiness.co.uk/how-build-brand-ann-summers, accessed 21 March 2011.
Gramsci, A. (1971) *Selections from the Prison Notebooks of Antonio Gramsci* (New York: International Publishers).
Green, J. (1998) *All Dressed Up: The Sixties and the Counter-Culture* (London: Jonathan Cape).
Gross, R. (1996) *Psychology: Science of Mind and Behaviour* (London: Hodder and Stoughton).

Hall, S. (1992) 'The Question of Cultural Identity', in Hall, S. and McGrew, T. (eds) *Modernity and its Futures* (Cambridge: Polity Press).
Halperin, D. (1990) *One Hundred Years of Homosexuality and Other Essays on Greek Love* (London and New York: Routledge).
—— (1995) *Saint Foucault: Towards a Gay Hagiography* (Oxford: Oxford University Press).
Handyside, F. (2007) 'It's Either Fake or Foreign: The Cityscape in *Sex and the City*', *Continuum: Journal of Media and Cultural Studies*, Vol. 21, No. 3: 405–18.
Hankin, K. (2002) *The Girls in the Back Room: Looking at the Lesbian Bar* (Minneapolis: University of Minnesota Press).
Hansen, M. (1986) 'Pleasure, Ambivalence, Identification: Valentino and Female Spectatorship', *Cinema Journal*, Vol. 25, No. 4: 6–32.
Hayward, S. (2006) *Cinema Studies: The Key Concepts* (London and New York: Routledge).
Heartfield, J. (2002) 'There is no Masculinity Crisis', *Genders* 35, available at www.genders.org/g35/g35_heartfield.html, accessed 21 March 2011.
Hennegan, A. (1988) 'On Becoming a Lesbian Reader', in Radstone, S. (ed.) *Sweet Dreams: Sexuality, Gender and Popular Fiction* (London: Lawrence and Wishart).
Herdt, G. (1994) *Guardians of the Flutes Vol. 1* (Chicago: University of Chicago Press).
Higson, A. (2003) *English Heritage, English Cinema: Costume Drama since 1980* (Oxford: Oxford University Press).
Hills, R. (2006) 'Anatomy of an Ethical Porn Site', *YEN*, available at http://rachelhills.wordpress.com/2010/08/02/anatomy-of-an-ethical-porn-site/, accessed 21 March 2011.
Hitchens, P. (2002) 'The Failure of Sex Education', in Lee, E. (ed.) *Teenage Sex: What Should Schools Teach Children?* (London: Hodder and Stoughton): 23–35.
Hite, S. (2004) *The Hite Report: A Nationwide Study of Female Sexuality* (New York: Seven Stories Publishing).
Holland, J., Ramazanoglu, C., Scott, S., Sharpe, S. and Thomson, R. (1992) 'Young Women and the Negotiation of Safer Sex', in Aggleton, P., Davies, P. and Hart, G. (eds) *Aids: Rights, Risk and Reason* (London: The Falmer Press).
Horrocks, R. (1995) *Male Myths and Icons: Masculinity in Popular Culture* (London: Macmillan).
Jackson, J. (1996) 'Murder She Wrote. Cyperpunk Archives', 12 November, www.joabj.com/CityPaper/murder.html.
Jacobs, K. (2004) 'The New Media Schooling of the Amateur Pornographer: Negotiating Contracts and Singing Orgasm', in Fox, B. (ed.) 'Rethinking the Amateur: Acts of Media Production in the Digital Age', *Spectator*, Vol. 24, No. 1, Spring: 17–29.
—— (2007) *Netporn: DIY Web Culture and Sexual Politics* (New York: Rowman & Littlefield).
Jagose, A. (1996) *Queer Theory: An Introduction* (New York: New York University Press).
Jeffreys, S. (1993) *The Lesbian Heresy* (Marrikville, NSW: Southwood Press).
Jenkins, H. (1992) *Textual Poachers: Television Fans and Participatory Culture* (New York: Routledge).
—— (2007) 'Porn 2.0', http://henryjenkins.org/2007/10/porn_20.html, accessed 20 April 2010.
Jermyn, D. (2009) *Sex and the City* (Detroit: Wayne State University Press).
Jhally, S. (1995) *Dream Worlds II: Desire, Sex and Power in Music Videos* (Media Education Foundation).

Jhally, S. and Lewis, J. (1992) *Enlightened Racism: 'The Cosby Show', Audiences and the Myth of the American Dream* (Boulder: Westview Press).

Johnson, P. (1996) 'Pornography Drives Technology: Why Not to Censor the Internet', *Federal Communications Law Journal*, Vol. 49, No. 1, www.law.indiana.edu.fclj/pubs/v49/no1/johnson.html, accessed 20 April 2010.

Joyce, G. (2010) 'Interview with Scott Owen of EroticBPM', *Pop My Cherry: Sexuality and Popular Culture*, http://popmycherryreview.com/columns/interview-with-scott-owens-of-eroticbpm/, accessed 22 May 2010.

Juffer, J. (1998) *At Home with Pornography: Women, Sex and Everyday Life* (New York: New York University Press).

Keller, J.R. (2002) *Queer (Un)Friendly Film and Television* (Jefferson, NC: McFarland and Company).

Kimmel, M.S. (1997) 'Integrating Men into the Curriculum', *Duke Journal of Gender Law & Policy*, Vol. 4, No. 1, 181–95.

—— (2010) 'Masculinity as Homophobia', in Kimmel, M.S. and Ferber, A.L. (eds) *Privilege: A Reader* (Boulder: Westview Press): 107–31.

Kitzinger, C. (1996) 'Social Constructionism: Implications for Gay and Lesbian Psychology', in D'Augelli, A. and Patterson, C. (eds) *Lesbian, Gay, and Bisexual Identities over the Lifespan: Psychological Perspectives* (Oxford: Oxford University Press).

Knowles, J. (2004) 'Material Girls: Location and Economics in Chicklit Fiction, or, How Singletons Finance their Jimmy Choo Collections', in *Chicklit*, Special Issue of *Diegesis: Journal of the Association for Research in Popular Fictions*, No. 8, Winter: 37–42.

König, A. (2004) 'Sex and the City: A Fashion-Editor's Dream', in Akass, K. and McCabe, J. (eds) *Reading Sex and the City* (New York and London: I.B.Tauris).

Krafft-Ebing, R. von (1892) *Psychopathia Sexualis, with Especial Reference to Contrary Sexual Instinct: A Medico-Legal Study*.

Krochmal, S.N. (2005) '*L Word* Tour of West Hollywood', available at www.butch-femme.com/showthread.php?13048-Quotes-URL-s-Links-And-References-by-older-Femmes-Butches-Ftms-Mtfs-Queer-Etc/page33, accessed 17 July 2012.

Krut-Landau, R. (2007) 'The New XXX: Of, By, and For the People', *The Johns Hopkins Newsletter*, http://media.www.jhunewsletter.com/media/storage/paper932/news/2007/03/29/Features/The-New.Xxx.Of.By.And.For.The.People-2815221.shtml, accessed 21 April 2010.

Lacan, J. (2001) *Ecrits: A Selection* (London: Routledge Classics).

Lane, F.S. (2001) *Obscene Profits: The Entrepreneurs of Pornography in the Cyber Age* (London: Routledge).

Langdridge, D. and Barker, M. (eds) (2008) *Safe, Sane and Consensual: Contemporary Perspectives on Sadomasochism* (London: Palgrave Macmillan).

Laqueur, T. (2003) *Solitary Sex: A Cultural History of Masturbation* (New York: Zone Books).

Lee, N. (2010) '"Let's Hug It Out, Bitch!" The Negotiation of Hegemony and Homosociality Through Speech in HBO's *Entourage*', *Culture, Society and Masculinities*, Vol. 2, No. 2: 181–98.

Levy, A. (2005) *Female Chauvinist Pigs: Women and the Rise of Raunch Culture* (London: Simon & Schuster).

Littlejohn, R. (2011) 'The Daleks are Doing What, Darling?' *Daily Mail*, 1 September, www.dailymail.co.uk/debate/article-2031514/Danny-Cohen-says-BBC1-cater-older-viewers-The-Daleks-doing-darling.html#ixzz1XfYo1cxe, accessed 9 September 2011.

Lockwood, D. (2009) 'All Stripped Down: The Spectacle of "Torture Porn"', *Popular Communication*, Vol. 7, No. 1: 40–8.
Macdonald, M. (1995) *Representing Women: Myths of Femininity in the Popular Media* (London: Edward Arnold).
Maddison, S. (2004) 'From Porno-Topia to Total Information Awareness, or What Forces Really Govern Access to Porn?', *New Formations*, No. 52: 35–57.
—— (2010) 'Online Obscenity and Myths of Freedom: Dangerous Images, Child Porn and Neoliberalism', in Attwood, F. (ed.) *Porn.com: Making Sense of Online Pornography* (New York: Peter Lang Publishing).
Maines, R. (1999) *The Technology of Orgasm: 'Hysteria', the Vibrator and Women's Sexual Satisfaction* (Baltimore and London: Johns Hopkins University Press).
Marcuse, H. (1987) *Eros and Civilization*, 2nd edition (London: Routledge).
Marshall, P. (2010) 'Teenage Boys Watching Hours of Internet Pornography Every Week are Treating their Girlfriends Like Sex Objects', *Daily Mail*, 8 March.
Martin, P. (2008) *Sex, Drugs and Chocolate: The Science of Pleasure* (London: Fourth Estate).
McCarthy, A. (2003) 'Must See Queer TV: History and the Serial Form in *Ellen*', in Jancovich, M. (ed.) *Quality Popular Television* (London: BFI).
McCaughey, M. and French, C. (2001) 'Women's Sex-Toy Parties: Technology, Orgasm and Commodification', *Sexuality and Culture*, Vol. 5, No. 3: 77–96.
McKee, A., Albury, K., Dunne, M., Grieshaber, S., Hartley, J., Lumby, C. and Mathews, B. (2010) 'Healthy Sexual Development: A Multidisciplinary Framework for Research', *International Journal of Sexual Health*, Vol. 22, No. 1: 14–19.
McLoughlin, L. (2000) 'Boys are Us!: The Commodification of Sex in Teenage Magazines', in Hallam, J. and Moody, N. (eds) *Consuming for Pleasure* (Liverpool: Liverpool John Moores Press).
McNair, B. (1996) *Mediated Sex: Pornography and Postmodern Culture* (London: Arnold).
—— (2002) *Striptease Culture: Sex, Media and the Democratisation of Desire* (London and New York: Routledge).
McRobbie, A. (1991) *Feminism and Youth Culture: From Jackie to Just-17* (London: Macmillan).
—— (1996) 'More!: New Sexualities in Girls and Women's Magazines', in Curran, J., Morley, D. and Walkerdine, V. (eds) *Cultural Studies and Communication* (London: Arnold).
Medhurst, A. (1997) 'Introduction', in Medhurst, A. and Munt, S.R. (eds) *Lesbian and Gay Studies: A Critical Introduction* (London: Cassell).
Meltzer, F. (1988) 'Introduction: Partitive Plays, Pipe Dreams', in Meltzer, F. (ed.) *The Trial(s) of Psychoanalysis* (Chicago and London: University of Chicago Press).
Merck, M. (2004) 'Sexuality in the City', in Akass, K. and McCabe, J. (eds) *Reading Sex and the City* (London: I.B.Tauris).
Mikes, G. (1958) *How to Be an Alien: A Handbook for Beginners and Advanced Pupils* (London: Penguin).
Miller, D. and Slater, D. (2001) *The Internet: An Ethnographic Approach* (Oxford: Berg).
Mitchell, D. (2005) 'Producing Containment: The Rhetorical Construction of Difference in *Will and Grace*', *Journal of Popular Culture*, Vol. 38, No. 6: 1050–68.
Modleski, T. (1982) *Loving with a Vengeance: Mass-Produced Fantasies for Women* (Connecticut: The Shoe String Press).
Mohan, D. (2003) 'Miriam is a Reality TV Too Far', *The Sun*, 1 November.

Money, J. (1986) *Lovemaps: Clinical Concepts of Sexual/Erotic Health and Pathology, Paraphilia and Gender Transposition in Childhood, Adolescence and Maturity* (New York: Prometheus).

Moore, C. (2007) 'Having it all Ways: The Tourist, Traveler, and the Local in *The L Word*', *Cinema Journal*, Vol. 46, No. 4: 3–22.

Moran, J. (2001) 'Childhood Sexuality and Education: The Case of Section 28', *Sexualities*, Vol. 4, No. 1: 73–89.

Moran, L.J. (1996) *The Homosexual(ity) of Law* (London: Routledge).

Mort, F. (1987) *Dangerous Sexualities: Medico-Moral Politics in England since 1830* (London: Routledge).

Mulvey, L. (1975) 'Visual Pleasure and Narrative Cinema', *Screen*, Vol. 16, No. 3: 6–18.

—— (1981) 'Afterthoughts on "Visual Pleasure and Narrative Cinema" inspired by *Duel in the Sun*', in Thornham, S. (ed.) (1999) *Feminist Film Theory: A Reader* (Edinburgh: Edinburgh University Press).

Munt, S.R. (2000) 'Shame/Pride Dichotomies in *Queer as Folk*', *Textual Practice*, Vol. 14, No. 3: 531–45.

—— (2008) *Queer Attachments: The Cultural Politics of Shame* (Farnham: Ashgate Press).

Neale, S. (2003) 'Questions of Genre', in Grant, B.K. (ed.) *Film Genre Reader III* (Austin: University of Texas Press).

Negra, D. (2004) 'Quality Postfeminism?: Sex and the Single Girl on HBO', *Genders*, No. 39, www.genders.org/g39/g39_negra.html, accessed 12 July 2010.

Neumark, V. (1996) 'The Attack of the Serial Thriller', *The Guardian*, 23 February.

Paasonen, S. and Saarenmaa, L. (2007) 'The Golden Age of Porn: History and Nostalgia in Cinema', in Paasonen, S., Nikunen, K. and Saarenmaa, L. (eds) *Pornification: Sex and Sexuality in Media Culture* (Oxford: Berg).

Paul, P. (2005) *Pornified: How Pornography is Transforming Our Lives, Our Relationships and Our Families* (New York: Times Books).

Perdue, L. (2002) *EroticaBiz: How Sex Shaped the Internet* (New York: Writers Club Press).

Perkins, T.E. (1979) 'Rethinking Stereotypes', in Barrett, M. *et al.* (eds) *Ideology and Cultural Production* (London: Croom Helm).

Perrone, J. (2002) 'Ann Summers', *The Guardian*, 22 January, www.guardian.co.uk/Print/0,3858,4340689,00.html, accessed 23 June 2003.

Petley, J. (2009) 'Pornography, Panopticism and the Post-Social Democratic State', *Sociology Compass*, Vol. 3, No. 3: 417–32.

Plummer, K. (1995) *Telling Sexual Stories: Power, Change and Social Worlds* (London: Routledge).

Prince, S. (1996) 'Psychoanalytic Film Theory and the Problem of the Missing Spectator', in Bordwell, D. and Carroll, N. (eds) *Post Theory: Reconstructing Film Studies* (Madison: University of Wisconsin Press).

Pronger, B. (1990) *The Arena of Masculinity: Sports, Homosexuality, and the Meaning of Sex* (London: Gay Men's Press).

Proulx, A. (1997) 'Brokeback Mountain' short story in *The New Yorker*, 13 October.

Quimby, K. (2005) '*Will and Grace*: Negotiating (Gay) Marriage on Prime-Time Television', *Journal of Popular Culture*, Vol. 38, No. 4: 713–31.

Radner, H. (1995) *Shopping Around: Feminine Culture and the Pursuit of Pleasure* (London: Routledge).

Radway, J. (1984) *Reading the Romance* (Chapel Hill: University of North Carolina Press).

Bibliography

Reed, J. (2005) 'Ellen DeGeneres: Public Lesbian Number One', *Feminist Media Studies*, Vol. 5, No. 1: 23–36.

Retter, Y. (1997) 'Lesbian Spaces in Los Angeles 1970–1990', in Ingram, G.B., Bouthillette, A. and Retter, Y. (eds) *Queers in Space: Communities, Public Places, Sites of Resistance* (Washington: Bay Press).

Rich, B.R. (1981) 'Feminism and Sexuality in the 1980s', *Heresies*, No. 12.

Richards, H. (2003) '*Sex and the City*: A Visible Flaneuse for the Post-modern Era?', *Continuum: Journal of Media and Cultural Studies*, Vol. 17, No. 2: 147–57.

Richardson, N. (2006) 'As Kamp as Bree: The Politics of Camp Reconsidered by *Desperate Housewives*', *Feminist Media Studies*, Vol. 6, No. 2: 157–74.

—— (2009) 'Effeminophobia, Misogyny and Queer Friendship: The Cultural Themes of Channel 4's *Playing it Straight*', *Sexualities*, Vol. 12, No. 4: 525–44.

Roberts, J. (2004) 'Park's Sex Shame', *Crewe Chronicle*, 17 March, available at http://iccheshireonline.icnetwork.co.uk/0100news/0100regionalnews/content_objectid=14061799_method=full_siteid=50020_headline=-Park-s-sex-shame-name_page.html, accessed 13 August 2006.

Ropelato, J. (2006) 'Internet Porn Statistics', *Top Ten Reviews* available at http://internet-filter-review.toptenreviews.com/internet-pornography-statistics.html, accessed 3 May 2010.

Rubin, G. [1984] (2007) 'Thinking Sex: Notes for a Radical Theory of the Politics of Sexuality', in Aggleton, P. (ed.) *Culture, Society and Sexuality: A Reader*, 2nd edition (London: Routledge).

Russo, V. (1987) *The Celluloid Closet: Homosexuality in the Movies (revised edition)* (New York: HarperCollins).

de Sade, Marquis (1966) *The 120 Days of Sodom and Other Writings* (trans. A. Wainhouse and R. Seaver) (New York: Grove Press).

—— (1968) *Juliette* (trans. A. Wainhouse) (New York: Grove Press).

Sandbrook, D. (2007) *White Heat: A History of Britain in the Swinging Sixties* (London: Abacus).

Sauer, A. (n.d.) 'How is Porn Penetrating the Mainstream Market?', *Brand Channel*, www.brandchannel.com/features_effect.asp?pf_id=199, accessed 21 May 2010.

Sedgwick, E.K. (1990) *Epistemology of the Closet* (Berkeley: University of California Press).

—— (1991) 'Jane Austen and the Masturbating Girl', *Critical Inquiry*, Vol. 17, No. 4, Summer: 818–37.

—— (1993) *Tendencies* (New York: Duke University Press).

—— (1998) 'A Dialogue on Love', *Critical Inquiry*, Vol. 24, No. 2, Winter: 611–31.

—— (2006) 'Foreword: The Letter L', in Akass, K. and McCabe, J. (eds) *Reading the L Word: Outing Contemporary Television* (New York and London: I.B.Tauris).

Seifert, C. (2008) 'Bite Me! (or Don't): Stephenie Meyer's Vampire-Infested Twilight Series has Created a New YA Genre: Abstinence Porn', *Bitch*, http://bitchmagazine.org/article/bite-me-or-don't, accessed 1 November 2011.

Shugart, H.A. (2003) 'Reinventing Privilege: The New (Gay) Man in Contemporary Popular Media', *Critical Studies in Media Communication*, Vol. 20, No. 1: 67–91.

Siegel, L. (1998) 'The Gay Science: Queer Theory, Literature, and the Sexualisation of Everything', *The New Republic*, 9 November.

Simon, B. and Blass, R.B. (1992) 'The Development and Vicissitudes of Freud's Ideas on the Oedipus Complex', in *The Cambridge Companion to Freud* (Cambridge: Cambridge University Press).

Sinfield, A. (1994a) *Cultural Politics: Queer Readings* (London: Routledge).
—— (1994b) *The Wilde Century: Oscar Wilde, Effeminacy and the Queer Moment* (London: Cassell).
Skinner, B.F. (1964) 'Education in 1984', *New Scientist*, 21 May: 484.
Smith, C. (1996) 'What is this Thing Called Queer?', in Morten, D. (ed.) *The Material Queer: A LesBiGay Cultural Studies Reader* (Boulder: Westview Press).
Smith, C. (2007a) 'Designed for Pleasure: Style, Indulgence and Accessorized Sex', *European Journal of Cultural Studies*, Vol. 10, No. 2: 167–84.
—— (2007b) *One for the Girls! The Pleasures and Practices of Reading Women's Porn* (Bristol: Intellect).
Spacks, P.A.M. (1981) *The Adolescent Idea: Myths of Youth and the Adult Imagination* (New York: Basic Books).
Spargo, T. (1999) *Foucault and Queer Theory* (Cambridge: Icon Books Ltd).
Stern, S.E. and Handel, A.D. (2001) 'Sexuality and Mass Media: The Historical Context of Psychology's Reactions to Sexuality on the Internet', *Journal of Sex Research*, Vol. 38, No. 4: 283–91.
Storey, J. (2001) *Cultural Theory and Popular Culture*, 3rd edition (Harlow: Prentice Hall).
Storr, M. (2003) *Latex & Lingerie* (Oxford: Berg Publishers).
Sullivan, N. (2003) *A Critical Introduction to Queer Theory* (Edinburgh: Edinburgh University Press).
Sweet, M. (2002) *Inventing the Victorians* (London: Faber & Faber).
Sweney, M. (2008) 'Heinz "Men Kissing" Ad: US Christian Group urged Firm to Pull Commercial', *The Guardian*, 1 July, www.guardian.co.uk/media/2008/jul/01/advertising.usa, accessed 1 November 2011.
Tatchell, P. (2005) 'Civil Partnerships are Divorced from Reality', *The Guardian*, 19 December, available at www.guardian.co.uk/world/2005/dec/19/gayrights.planningyourwedding, accessed 5 December 2010.
Taylor, G. and Ussher, J. (2001) 'Making Sense of S & M: A Discourse Analytic Account', *Sexualities*, Vol. 4, No. 3: 293–314.
The Sun, 10 July 2008: 13.
Thompson, D. (2004) 'Calling all Fag Hags: From Identity Politics to Identification Politics', *Social Semiotics*, Vol. 14, No. 1: 37–48.
Thornham, S. and Purvis, T. (2005) *Television Drama: Theories and Identities* (Hampshire: Palgrave Macmillan).
Ticknell, E., Chambers, D., Van Loon, J. and Hudson, N. (2003) 'Begging for It: "New Femininities", Social Agency, and Moral Discourse in Contemporary Teenage and Men's Magazines', *Feminist Media Studies*, Vol. 3, No. 1: 47–63.
Tropp, L. (2006) '"Faking a Sonogram": Representations of Motherhood on *Sex and the City*', *Journal of Popular Culture*, Vol. 39, No. 5, 861–77.
Tucker, N. (1992) 'Good Friends or Just Acquaintances? The Relationship between Child Psychology and Children's Literature', in Hunt, P (ed.) *Literature for Children* (London: Routledge).
Tziallas, E. (2010) 'XTube and "Tagging": Surveillance, Amateur Sex and the Archive', paper to *Porn Studies: Economies, Politics, Discoursivities of Contemporary Pornographic Audiovisual*, part of the *VIII Magis – International Film Studies Spring School*, Gorizia, Italy, 19–24 March.
Vance, C.S. (ed.) (1992) *Pleasure and Danger: Exploring Female Sexuality* (London: Pandora).

Vanesco, J. (2004) 'The Good Word about *The L Word*', *Independent Gay Forum*, http://igfculturewatch.com/2004/01/28/the-good-word-about-the-l-word/, accessed 1 November 2011.

VividStudioInsider (n.d.) Available at http://vivid.com/news/2010-04-16/vivid-studio-insider, accessed 21 May 2010.

Warby, M. (2008) Counsel for the Defence, cited in 'No Truth in Nazi Orgy Claim, Mosley QC says', *The Guardian*, 15 July: 5.

Warn, S. (2006) 'Introduction', in Akass, K. and McCabe, J. (eds) *Reading the L Word: Outing Contemporary Television* (New York and London: I.B.Tauris).

Warner, M. (1993) 'Introduction', in Warner, M. (ed.) *Fear of a Queer Planet: Queer Politics and Social Theory* (Minneapolis: University of Minnesota Press).

Waskul, D. (2003) *Self-Games and Body Play: Personhood in Online Chat and Cybersex* (New York: Peter Lang).

Waskul, D. *et al.* (2000) 'Cybersex: Outercourse and the Enselfment of the Body', *Symbolic Interaction*, Vol. 23, No. 4: 375–97.

Watney, S. (1982) 'Hollywood's Homosexual World', *Screen*, Vol. 23, No. 3–4, September–October: 107–21.

Weeks, J. (2007) *The World We Have Won* (London: Routledge).

Wells, S. (2004) *Looking for Sex in Shakespeare* (Cambridge: Cambridge University Press).

Werndly, A. (2000a) 'Reading the Romance in Point Horror', in Hallam, J. and Moody, N. (eds) *Consuming for Pleasure* (Liverpool: Liverpool John Moores Press).

—— (2000b) 'The Isolated Teenager Convention in Point Horror', *Diegesis: Journal of the Association for Research in Popular Fiction*, No. 6, Spring: 39–45.

Williams, L. (1989) *Hard Core: Power, Pleasure and the 'Frenzy of the Visible'* (London: Pandora).

—— (1992) 'Pornographies On/Scene, or Diff'rent Strokes for Diff'rent Folks', in Segal, L. and McIntosh, M. (eds) *Sex Exposed: Sexuality and the Pornography Debate* (London: Virago).

—— (2004a) 'Porn Studies: Proliferating Pornographies On/Scene: An Introduction', in Williams, L. (ed.) *Porn Studies* (Durham: Duke University Press).

—— (2004b) 'Second Thoughts on Hard Core: American Obscenity and the Scapegoating of Deviancy', in Church Gibson, P. (ed.) *More Dirty Looks* (London: BFI).

Wittig, M. (1992) *The Straight Mind* (Boston: Beacon Press).

Wolfenden Report (1957) *Report of the Committee on Homosexual Offences and Prostitution* (London: HMSO) Cmnd 247.

Wood, H. (2009) *Talking with Television: Women, Talk Shows, and Modern Self-Reflexivity* (Illinois: University of Illinois Press).

Wood, R. (2003) *Hollywood from Vietnam to Reagan* (New York: Columbia University Press).

Woolf, V. [1929] (1984) *A Room of One's Own* (New York: Harcourt Brace & Co.).

Media and Fiction

Media

27 Dresses, Dir. Anne Fletcher, USA: 2008.
9½ Weeks, Dir. Adrian Lyne, USA: 1986.
Annie Hall, Dir. Woody Allen, USA: 1977.
Band of Gold, Granada, UK: 1995–97.
Big Brother, Channel 4, UK: 2000–10.
Black Narcissus, Dir. Michael Powell and Emeric Pressburger, UK: 1947.
Blow Job, Dir. Andy Warhol, USA: 1963.
Blue Velvet, Dir. David Lynch, USA: 1986.
BodyShock, Channel 4, UK: 2001– .
Boys Beware, Dir. Sid Davis, USA: 1961.
Bridesmaids, Dir. Paul Feig, USA: 2011.
Bridget Jones Diary, Dir. Sharon Maguire, UK: 2001.
Brokeback Mountain, Dir. Ang Lee, USA: 2005.
Buffy the Vampire Slayer, Fox TV, USA: 1997–2003.
The Cell, Dir. Tarsem Singh, USA: 2000.
The Celluloid Closet, Dir. Rob Epstein and Jeffrey Friedman, UK: 1996.
Coronation Street, ITV, UK: 1960– .
The Cosby Show, NBC, USA: 1984–92.
Crash, Dir. David Cronenberg, Canada: 1996.
Crime Scene Investigation: Las Vegas, CBS, USA: 2000– .
Dallas, CBS, USA: 1978–91.
Debbie Does Dallas … Again, Dir. Paul Thomas, USA: 2007.
Desperate Housewives, ABC, USA: 2004– .
Desperately Seeking Susan, Dir. Susan Seidelman, USA: 1985.
Dreamworlds II: Sex and Power in Music Video, Dir. Sut Jhally, USA: 1997.
Dunlop: *Tested for the Unexpected*, Dir. Tony Kaye, Abbott, Mead Vickers BBDO, UK: 1993.
Dynasty, ABC, USA: 1981–89.
Ellen, ABC, USA: 1994–98.
Entourage, HBO, USA: 2004–11.
Family Guy, Fox, USA: 1999– .
Farscape, Nine Network, Australia: 1999–2003.
Fatal Attraction, Dir. Adrian Lyne, USA: 1987.
Frasier, Paramount, USA: 1993–2004.
Friends, Warner Bros, USA: 1994–2004.
The Full Monty, Dir. Peter Cattaneo, UK: 1997.
The Graduate, Dir. Mike Nichols, USA: 1967.
Heinz: *Deli Mayo*, Creative Steve Jones and Martin Loraine, Abbott, Mead Vickers BBDO, UK: 2008.
House, Fox, USA: 2004– .
How to Have Sex After Marriage, Channel 5, UK: 2007–08.
I Love You Man, Dir. John Hamburg, USA: 2009.
Interview with the Vampire, Dir. Neil Jordan, USA: 1994.
Is Oral Sex Bad for You?, BBC3, UK: 10 January 2011.
The Jeremy Kyle Show, ITV, UK: 2005– .

The Jerry Springer Show, NBC, USA: 1991– .
Jurassic Park, Dir. Steven Spielberg, USA: 1993.
Keep Britain Tidy: *Don't be a Gimp!*, Dir. Paul Morgans, Encam, UK: 2005.
The Killing of Sister George, Dir. Robert Aldrich, USA: 1968.
The L Word, Showtime, USA: 2004–09.
The League of Gentlemen, BBC, UK: 1999–2002.
Matador, Dir. Pedro Almodóvar, Spain: 1986.
Midnight Cowboy, Dir. John Schlesinger, USA: 1969.
Mini: *Dominates Winter*, Dir. Shin Sugino, John St Dennis Agency, Canada: 2006.
Misfits, E4, UK: 2009– .
Mistresses, BBC, UK: 2008–10.
My Best Friend's Wedding, Dir. P.J. Hogan, USA: 1997.
Once Were Warriors, Dir. Lee Tamahori, New Zealand: 1994.
Oranges are Not the Only Fruit, BBC, UK: 1990.
The Out of Towners, Dir. Arthur Hiller, USA: 1970.
The Out of Towners, Dir. Sam Weisman, USA: 1999.
The Outer Limits, Showtime, Canada: 1995–2002.
Panorama: Too Much Too Young?, BBC, UK: 15 January 2011.
Paris, Texas, Dir. Wim Wenders, USA: 1984.
Queer as Folk, Channel 4, UK: 1999–2000.
Quills, Dir. Philip Kaufman, USA: 2000.
Rambo, Dir. Ted Kotcheff, USA: 1982.
Requiem, Dir. k r buxey: 2002.
Romance, Dir. Catherine Breillat, France: 1999.
Roseanne, ABC, USA: 1988–97.
Scrubs, ABC, USA: 2001–10.
Secretary, Dir. Steven Shainberg, USA: 2002.
Sex and the City, HBO, USA: 1998–2004.
Sex and the City: The Movie, Dir. Michael Patrick King, USA: 2008.
The Sex Education vs Pornography Show, Channel 4, UK: 2009.
The Sex Inspectors, Channel 4, UK: 2004–06.
Skins, Channel 4, UK: 2007–11.
Snow White, Dir. David Hand, USA: 1937.
Some Like It Hot, Dir. Billy Wilder, USA: 1959.
Stargate Atlantis, Sci-Fi Channel, Canada/USA: 2004–09.
Star Trek, NBC, USA: 1966–69.
Sugar Rush, Channel 4, UK: 2005–09.
Thelma and Louise, Dir. Ridley Scott, USA: 1991.
There's Something About Mary, Dir. Bobby Farrelly and Peter Farrelly, USA: 1998.
There's Something About Miriam, Sky1, UK: 2004.
Tipping the Velvet, BBC, UK: 2002.
Vivid Valley, World of Wonder, USA: 2001.
The Wedding Crashers, Dir. David Dobkin, USA: 2005.
Will and Grace, NBC, UK: 1998–2006.

Fiction

Bushnell, C. (1996) *Sex and the City* (New York: Grand Central Publishing).
Cooney, C. (1992) *The Cheerleader* (New York: Scholastic Inc.).
Meyer, S. (2005) *Twilight* (New York: Little, Brown and Company).
Rice, A. (1976) *Interview with the Vampire* (New York: Alfred A. Knopf).
Stine, R.L. (1990) *The Boyfriend* (New York: Scholastic Inc.).
Stine, R.L. (1991) *The Girlfriend* (New York: Scholastic Inc.).